CAMBRIDGE PRIMARY
Mathematics

2

Teacher's Resource

Cherri Moseley and Janet Rees

CAMBRIDGE
UNIVERSITY PRESS

CAMBRIDGE
UNIVERSITY PRESS

University Printing House, Cambridge CB2 8BS, United Kingdom

One Liberty Plaza, 20th Floor, New York, NY 10006, USA

477 Williamstown Road, Port Melbourne, VIC 3207, Australia

4843/24, 2nd Floor, Ansari Road, Daryaganj, Delhi – 110002, India

79 Anson Road, #06–04/06, Singapore 079906

Cambridge University Press is part of the University of Cambridge.

It furthers the University's mission by disseminating knowledge in the pursuit of education, learning and research at the highest international levels of excellence.

Information on this title: education.cambridge.org

First published 2014

20 19 18 17 16 15 14 13 12 11 10 9 8 7

Printed in Great Britain by CPI Group (UK) Ltd, Croydon CR0 4YY

A catalogue record for this publication is available from the British Library

ISBN 978-1-107-64073-3 Paperback

Cover artwork: Bill Bolton

Contents

Term 1

Term 2

Term 3

The Ethos of the *Cambridge Primary Maths* project

Cambridge Primary Maths is an innovative combination of curriculum and resources designed to support teachers and learners to succeed in primary mathematics through best-practice international maths teaching and a problem-solving approach.

Cambridge Primary Maths brings together the world-class Cambridge Primary mathematics curriculum from **Cambridge International Examinations**, high-quality publishing from **Cambridge University Press** and expertise in engaging online eFment materials for the mathematics curriculum from **NRICH**.

Cambridge Primary Maths offers teachers an online tool that maps resources and links to materials offered through the primary mathematics curriculum, NRICH and Cambridge Primary Mathematics textbooks and e-books. These resources include engaging online activities, best-practice guidance and examples of *Cambridge Primary Maths* in action.

The Cambridge curriculum is dedicated to helping schools develop learners who are confident, responsible, reflective, innovative and engaged. It is designed to give learners the skills to problem solve effectively, apply mathematical knowledge and develop a holistic understanding of the subject.

The Cambridge University Press series of *Teacher's resources* printed books and CD-ROMs provide best-in-class support for this problem-solving approach, based on pedagogical practice found in successful schools across the world. The engaging NRICH online resources help develop mathematical thinking and problem-solving skills.

The benefits of being part of *Cambridge Primary Maths* are:
- the opportunity to explore a maths curriculum founded on the values of the University of Cambridge and best practice in schools
- access to an innovative package of online and print resources that can help bring the Cambridge Primary mathematics curriculum to life in the classroom.

To get involved visit www.cie.org.uk/cambridgeprimarymaths

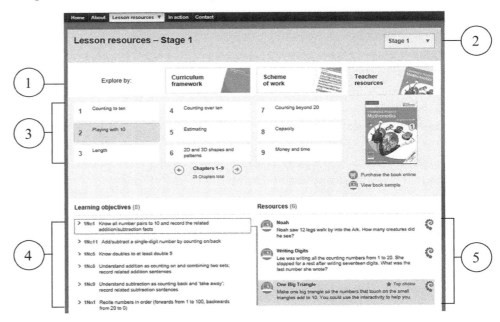

1　You can explore the available resources on the *Cambridge Primary Maths* website by curriculum framework, scheme of work, or teacher resources. In this example, the 'Teacher resources' tab has been selected.
2　The drop-down menu allows selection of resources by Stage.
3　Following selection of the 'Teacher resource' and 'Stage 1', the chapters in the Cambridge University Press textbook '*Teacher's resource 1*' are listed.
4　Clicking on a chapter ('2 Playing with 10' in this example) reveals the list of curriculum framework objectives covered in that chapter. Clicking on a given objective (1Nc1 in this example) highlights the most relevant NRICH activity for that objective.
5　A list of relevant NRICH activities for the selected chapter are revealed. Clicking on a given NRICH activity will highlight the objectives that it covers. You can launch the NRICH activity from here.

The *Cambridge Primary Maths* project provides a complete support package for teachers. The *Teacher's Resource* is a standalone teaching textbook that can be used independently or together with *Cambridge Primary Maths* website. The free to access website maps the activities and games in the *Teacher's Resource* to the Cambridge Primary curriculum. It also highlights relevant online activities designed by the NRICH project team based at the University of Cambridge.

The additional material that the *Cambridge Primary Maths* project provides can be accessed in the following ways:

As a Cambridge Centre:
If you are a registered Cambridge Centre, you get free access to all the available material by logging in using your existing Cambridge International Examinations log in details.

Register as a visitor:
If you are not a registered Cambridge Centre you can register to the site as a visitor, where you will be free to download a limited set of resources and online activities that can be searched by topic and learning objective.

As an unregistered visitor:
You are given free access an introductory video and some sample resources, and are able to read all about the scheme.

Introduction

The *Cambridge Primary Maths* series of resources covers the entire content of the Cambridge Primary Mathematics curriculum framework from Cambridge International Examinations. The resources have been written based on a suggested teaching year of three, ten week terms. This can be amended to suit the number of weeks available in your school year.

The Cambridge Primary Mathematics framework provides a comprehensive set of learning objectives for mathematics. These objectives deal with what learners should know and be able to do. The framework is presented in five strands: the four content strands of Number (including mental strategies), Geometry, Measures and Handling Data are all underpinned by the fifth strand, Problem Solving. Problem solving is integrated throughout the four content strands. Whilst it is important to be able to identify the progression of objectives through the curriculum, it is also essential to bring together the different strands into a logical whole.

This series of printed books and CD-ROMs published by Cambridge University Press is arranged to ensure that the curriculum is covered whilst allowing teachers flexibility in approach. The Scheme of Work for Stage 2 has been fully covered and follows in the same 'Unit' order as presented by Cambridge International Examinations (1A–C, 2A–C and then 3A–C) but the order of objective coverage may vary depending on a logical pedagogy and teaching approach.

The components of the printed series are as follows:
- *Teacher's Resource* (printed book and CD-ROM)
  This resource covers all the objectives of the Cambridge framework through lessons referred to as '*Core activities*'. As a 'lesson' is a subjective term (taking more or less time depending on the school and the learners) we prefer to use the terms '*Core activity*' and 'session' to reinforce that there is some flexibility. Each *Core activity* contains the instructions for you to lead the activity and cover the objectives, as well as providing expected outcomes, suggested dialogue for discussion, and likely areas

of misconception. A section called '*More activities*' provides you with suggestions for supplementary or extension activities.

The *Teacher's Resource* can be used on its own to **completely cover** the course. (The *Learner's Book* and *Games Book* should **not** be used without the associated teacher resource, as they are not sufficient on their own to cover all the objectives.)

The accompanying CD-ROM contains:
- a Word version of the entire printed book. This has been supplied so that you can copy and paste relevant chunks of the text into your own lesson plans if you do not want to use our book directly. You will be able to edit and print the Word files as required but different versions of Word used on different PCs and MACs will render the content slightly differently so you might have some formatting issues.
- *Questioning* – This document outlines some of the different types of question techniques for mathematics and how best to use them, providing support for teachers.
- *Letters for parents* – a template letter is supplied along with a mapping grid to help you to write a letter per Unit of material in order to inform parents what work their child is doing, and what they can do to support their child at home.
- *Photocopy masters* – resources are supplied as PDFs, and as Word files so that you can edit them as required.

- *Learner's Book* (printed book)
  This resource is **supplementary** to the course. As the ethos of the *Cambridge Maths Project* is to avoid rote learning and drill practice, there are no accompanying workbooks. The *Learner's Book* instead combines consolidation and support for the learner with investigations that allow freedom of thought, and questions that encourage the learner to apply their knowledge rather than just remembering a technique. The investigations and questions are written to assess the

learner's understanding of the learning outcomes of the *Core activity*. Learners can write down their answers to investigations and questions in an exercise book in order to inform assessment. The overall approach of the *Teacher's Resource* accompanied by the *Learner's Book* allows a simple way for you to assess how well a learner understands a topic, whilst also encouraging discussion, problem-solving and investigation skills.

At Stage 2, the *Learner's Book* acts as a useful support tool for the learners by providing visual reminders or points for discussion to develop problem-solving skills and support learning through discovery and discussion. Ideally, a session should be taught using the appropriate *Core activity* in the *Teacher's Resource*, with the *Learner's Book* open at the correct page in order to provide visual reminders and support; additional questions beyond the *Core activity* are provided in the *Learner's Book* to encourage discussion and independent thinking.

There is generally a single page in the *Learner's Book* for each associated *Core activity* in the *Teacher's Resource* for Stage 2. The *Teacher's Resource* will refer to the *Learner's Book* page by title and page number, and the title of the *Core activity* will be at the bottom of the *Learner's Book* page. **Please note** that the *Learner's Book* does not cover all of the Cambridge objectives on its own; it is for supplementary use only.

- *Games Book* (printed book and CD-ROM)
  This resource is complete in its own right as a source of engaging, informative maths games. It is also a **supplementary** resource to the series. It can be used alongside the *Teacher's Resource* as a source of additional activities to support learners that need extra reinforcement, or to give to advanced learners as extension. Each game comes with a '*Maths* focus' to highlight the intended learning/reinforcement outcome of the game, so that the book can be used independently of any other resource. For those who are using it as part of this series, relevant games are referred to by title and page number in the '*More activities*'

section of the *Teacher's Resource*. The accompanying CD-ROM contains nets to make required resources; it also contains a mapping document that maps the games to the other resources in the series for those who require it. **Please note** that the *Games Book* does not cover all of the Cambridge objectives on its own; it is for supplementary use only.

Each chapter in the Teacher's Resource includes

- A *Quick reference* section to list the title of each of the *Core activities* contained within the chapter. It provides an outline of the learning outcome(s) of each *Core activity*. (See page vii and later in this list, for a reminder of what is meant by a *Core activity*.)
- A list of the *Objectives* from the Cambridge Primary Mathematics curriculum framework that are covered across the chapter as a whole. **Please note** that this means that not all of the listed objectives will be covered in each of the chapter's *Core activities*; they are covered when the chapter is taken as a whole. The objectives are referenced using sub-headings from the framework, for example '**1A: Calculation** (*Mental strategies*)' and the code from the Scheme of Work, for example, '2Nc3'.

Please be aware that the content of an objective is often split across different *Core activities* and/or different chapters for a logical progression of learning and development. Please be assured that provided you eventually cover all of the *Core activities* across the whole *Teacher's Resource*, you will have covered all of the objectives in full. It should be clear from the nature of a *Core activity* when parts of an objective have not been fully covered. For example, a chapter on length will list 'Measure' objectives that also include weight, such as '1MI1' (Compare lengths and weights by direct comparison...) but the weight aspect of the objective will not be covered in a chapter on length(!); that part of the objective will be covered in a chapter on weight. Or a chapter focussing on understanding teen numbers as 'ten and some more' might cover the action 'recite numbers in order' but only up to 20 and therefore only partially cover objective '1Nn1' (Recite numbers in order … from 1 to 100…)). But please be reassured that, by the end of the *Teacher's Resource*, all of objectives 1MI1 and 1Nn1 will have been covered in full; as will all objectives. The *Summary* bulleted list at the end of each *Core activity* lists the learning outcome of the activity and can add some clarity of coverage, if required.

- A list of key *Prior learning* topics is provided to ensure learners are ready to move on to the chapter, and to remind teachers of the need to build on previous learning.
- Important and/or new *Vocabulary* for the chapter as a whole is listed. Within the *Core activity* itself, relevant vocabulary will be repeated along with a helpful description to support teaching of new words.

The *Core activities* (within each chapter) collectively provide a comprehensive teaching programme for the whole stage. Each *Core activity* includes:

- A list of required *Resources* to carry out the activity. This list includes resources provided as photocopy masters within the *Teacher's Resource* printed book (indicated by '(pxx)'), and photocopy masters provided on the CD-ROM (indicated by '(CD-ROM)'), as well as resources found in the classroom or at home. '(Optional)' resources are those that are required for the activities listed in the '*More activities*' section and thus are optional.
- A main narrative that is split into two columns. The left-hand (wider) column provides instructions for how to deliver the activity, suggestions for dialogue to instigate discussions, possible responses and outcomes, as well as general support for teaching the objective. Differences in formatting in this section identify different types of interactivity:
  ○ Teacher-led whole class activity
    The main narrative represents work to be done as a whole class.
  ○ Teacher-Learner discussion
    "Text that is set in italics within double-quotation marks represents suggested teacher dialogue to instigate Teacher-Learner disccusion."
  ○ Learner-Learner interaction

  Group and pair work between learners is encouraged throughout and is indicated using a grey panel behind the text and a change in font.

The right-hand (narrow) column provides,
  ○ the vocabulary panel
  ○ side-notes and examples
  ○ a *Look out for!* panel that offers practical suggestions for identifying and addressing common difficulties and misconceptions, as well as how to spot advanced learners and ideas for extension tasks to give them
  ○ an *Opportunity for display* panel to provide ideas for displays.
- A *Summary* at the end of each *Core activity* to list the learning outcomes/expectations following the activity. This is accompanied by a *Check up!* section that provides quick-fire probing questions useful for formative assessment; and a *Notes on the Learner's Book* section that references the title and page number of the associated *Learner's Book* page, as well as a brief summary of what the page involves.
- A *More activities* section that provides suggestions for further activities; these are not required to cover the objectives and therefore are optional activities that can be used for reinforcement and differentiation. The additional activities might include a reference to a game in the *Games Book*. You are encouraged to also look on the *Cambridge Maths Project* website to find NRICH activities linked to the Cambridge objectives. Together, these activities provide a wealth of material from which teachers can select those most appropriate to their circumstances both in class and for use of homework if this is set.

We would recommend that you work through the chapters in the order they appear in this book as you might find that later chapters build on knowledge from earlier in the book. If possible, work with colleagues and share ideas and over time you will feel confident in modifying and adapting your plans.

Teaching approaches

Learners have different learning styles and teachers need to appeal to all these styles. You will find references to group work, working in pairs and working individually within these materials.

The grouping depends on the activity and the point reached within a series of sessions. It may be appropriate to teach the whole class, for example, at the beginning of a series of sessions when explaining, demonstrating or asking questions. After this initial stage, learners often benefit from opportunities to discuss and explain their thoughts to a partner or in a group. Such activities where learners are working collaboratively are highlighted in the main narrative as detailed in the previous section. High quality teaching is oral, interactive and lively and is a two-way process between teacher and learners. Learners play an active part by asking and answering questions, contributing to discussions and explaining and demonstrating their methods to the rest of the class or group. Teachers need to listen and use learner ideas to show that these are valued. Learners will make errors if they take risks but these are an important part of the learning process.

Talking mathematics

We need to encourage learners to speak during a maths session in order to:
• communicate
• explain and try out ideas
• develop correct use of mathematical vocabulary
• develop mathematical thinking.

It is important that learners develop mathematical language and communication in order to (using Bloom's taxonomy):

Explain mathematical thinking (I think that... because...)
Develop understanding (I understand that...)
Solve problems (I know that... so...)
Explain solutions (This is how I found out that...)
Ask and answer questions (What, why, how, when, if ...)
Justify answers (I think this because...)

There is advice on the CD-ROM about the types of questioning you can use to get your students talking maths (*Questioning*).

Resources, including games

Resources can support, assist and extend learning. The use of resources such as *Ten frames, 100 squares, number lines, digit cards* and *arrow cards* is promoted in the *Teacher's Resource*. Games provide a useful way of reinforcing skills and practising and consolidating ideas. Learners gain confidence and are able to explore and discuss mathematical ideas whilst developing their mathematical language.

Calculators should be used to help learners understand numbers and the number system including place value and properties of numbers. However, the calculator is not promoted as a calculation tool before Stage 5.

NRICH have created an abundance of engaging and well-thought-out mathematical resources, which have been mapped to the Cambridge Primary scheme of work, and are available from the *Cambridge Primary Maths* website. Their interactive and downloadable activities can provide an alternative learning style or enrichment for some of the core concepts.

The Ten Frame

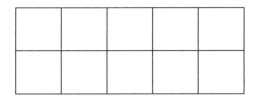

The Ten Frame is used throughout Stage 1 and into Stage 2 as a simple, consistent image of the number ten. Ten is a key part of our number system and it is essential to help learners develop a clear picture of ten that they can use and manipulate.

The Ten Frame can be used in so many ways to illustrate number and is not restricted to numbers to ten. It provides a strong image of ten that helps learners to develop an awareness of the size of numbers, leading to the understanding of place value. Such an understanding is vital for mental calculations and a deep understanding of our number system.

As a counting frame

The Ten Frame can be introduced as a simple counting frame. Learners count objects onto the frame by placing one in each space, using the Ten Frame as a mat to work on. Doing this with a variety of objects helps learners to understand that numbers can be transferred from one object to another. This solid grounding is essential. They are not simply counting but are building an image of ten and numbers to ten that will support their understanding of our number system.

Eventually, the Ten Frame becomes an image of ten in its own right and learners no longer need to place an object in each space. They can use it to support counting in tens, and can instantly recognise the arrangement of numbers below ten. This recognition means that you can also cut the Ten frame to show each single digit number, supporting learners to develop understanding of place value.

To develop understanding of number relationships

Once learners are confident that the frame will always hold ten objects, no matter what those objects are, the frame can be used to help develop a learner's understanding of number relationships.

Addition

Placing nine objects of one colour and one object of a different colour helps learners to clearly see that nine and one more makes ten. All the number pairs (or additions) to ten can be explored in this way. Learners can be shown the shorthand that we use to write these relationships down ($9 + 1 = 10$) and they can begin to record what they see.

Subtraction

Later, subtraction can be explored in the same way as addition. With ten objects on the Ten Frame, removing one but keeping it within sight clearly shows that ten take away one leaves nine ($10 - 1 = 9$).

Doubles

With the Ten Frame orientated horizontally across the page or desk, placing a counter of one colour on the bottom row and one of a different colour on the top row allows learners to explore double 1, then double 2, 3, 4 and 5.

Numbers beyond ten

As learners begin to extend their understanding from ten to 20, a second Ten frame helps them to see these numbers as 'ten and some more', again laying firm foundations for understanding the number system.

Even and odd

By consistently using the pattern of twos, odd numbers always have an unmatched space, while even numbers are rectangles.

Blank page

Quick reference

Core activity 1.1: Making a 100 square (Learner's Book p4–5)

Learners gain a good understanding of the 100 square by recognising and using the repeating number patterns it contains, and by writing numbers between each pair of multiples of 10.

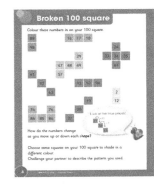

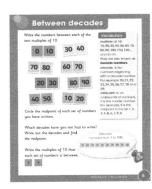

Prior learning	Objectives* – please note that listed objectives might only be partially covered within any given chapter but are covered fully across the book when taken as a whole
Some experience of exploring numbers to 100.	**1A: Number** (*Numbers and the number system*) 2Nn1 – Count, read and write numbers to at least 100 and back again. 2Nn9 – Say a number between any given neighbouring pairs of multiples of 10 e.g. 40 and 50. **1A: Problem solving** (*Using techniques and skills in solving mathematical problems*) 2Pt2 – Explain methods and reasoning orally. 2Pt3 – Explore number problems and puzzles.

*for NRICH activities mapped to the Cambridge Primary objectives, please visit www.cie.org.uk/cambridgeprimarymaths

Vocabulary

decade number • decade • multiple of 10 • midpoint

> **Resources:** *100 square* photocopy master (p4); one per learner. *Make a 100 square* photocopy master (CD-ROM); one per learner. One sheet of A4 paper for each learner (ideally in different colours). Scissors. Glue. (Optional: *100 square jigsaw* photocopy masters (CD-ROM); coloured paper; scissors; glue and bead string/bars.)

Begin with the *100 square* photocopy master. Invite learners to talk about what they see. *"Tell me about a pattern you can see on the 100 square. How do the numbers change in each row (or column)?"* Finish by focusing on the 1 to 9 pattern in each row and column.

Tell the learners that they are going to make their own 100 square. Give each learner a copy of the *Make a 100 square* photocopy master. Ask them to count how many 1 to 9 rows they have. Ask questions such as, *"Do you need all those? How could you use the 1 to 9 strips to make a 100 square? Why have you only got one row of tens numbers? Where do they appear on the 100 square?"* If necessary, explain that they need to cut out each of the 1 to 9 strips and keep one strip as it is, turn one strip into teen numbers, another into the 20 numbers, and so on.

Once learners have a strip for each row of the 100 square, they can stick the strips in order on paper. They should then cut the decade number strip into squares and place each decade number at the right-hand end of the correct row.

Explain that the tens numbers are multiples of 10; they are the numbers we say when we are counting in tens from zero. They are also called decade numbers. 'Dec-' means 10, so a decade is the ten numbers starting with the decade number. For example, the numbers 20, 21, 22, 23, 24, 25, 26, 27, 28 and 29 are a decade.

When everyone has completed a 100 square, call out numbers one at a time, asking learners to put a finger on that number on their 100 square. Occasionally ask a learner to describe where that number is. For example, 21 is near the top of the square on the left-hand side, below number 11 and above 31. You may need to continue this activity, and the rest of the activities, in a second session.

Ask learners to put a finger on a decade number (a multiple of 10) such as 30 and another finger on the next decade number, 40. Ask learners to tell you a number between those two numbers. Ask someone else to tell you another, and another. Ask questions such as,

Vocabulary

decade number: 10, 20, 30, 40, 50, 60, 70, 80, 90.

decade: ten numbers beginning with a decade number, for example 20, 21, 22, 23, 24, 25, 26, 27, 28 and 29. A period of 10 years is called a decade, so the 10 years from 2010 to 2019 are a decade.

multiple of 10: 10, 20, 30, 40, 50, 60, 70, 80, 90, 100, 110, 120…and so on.

midpoint: the middle number in a list of ordered numbers. For example, 5 is the midpoint of the list, 1, 2, 3, 4, **5**, 6, 7, 8, 9.

"Which is the midpoint? How many different answers are there? What if you had your fingers on 50 and 60? Or 80 and 90? Or 20 and 30?" Draw out that there are always nine numbers between each multiple of ten. The pattern is always something-one, something-two up to something-nine, so there will always be nine numbers between. For example, the numbers 21–29 are the numbers between the two decade numbers 20 and 30. As a class, get learners to call out the numbers between other two decade numbers.

Look out for!

Learners who want to include the multiples of 10 (or decade numbers) when giving numbers **between** two decade numbers. *Explain that the classroom floor is between the walls; the walls are not between, they mark the beginning and the end.*

Summary

Learners have a good understanding of the layout of the 100 square and can talk about the patterns they see.

Notes on the Learner's Book

Broken 100 square (p4): after learners have explored how the numbers change, as they move up or down the blue shapes, challenge them by asking if this will always happen with any set of numbers in this shape on a 100 square.

Between decades (p5): challenge learners to fill in the numbers between the decade numbers. Encourage them to see that '50–60' is missing from the set of decades. They should fill in the numbers and find the midpoint.

Check up!

- *"What is the next multiple of 10 after 30?"*
- *"Which numbers come between 40 and 50?"*
- *"Tell me about a pattern you have noticed on the 100 square."*

More activities

100-square jigsaws (class, group or individual)

> You will need the *100 square jigsaw* photocopy masters (CD-ROM).

Reproduce each of the four jigsaws onto different coloured paper. Learners write in the missing numbers and then cut out the pieces. They then swap jigsaws with a partner and complete each other's. The jigsaws become more difficult, with fewer numbers already completed on each piece. Cutting out the pieces before completing the numbers on the 100 square makes this a more difficult challenge, particularly for jigsaws three and four. Numbers could be completed on each piece or after the jigsaw has been completed.

Bead bar counting (class, group or individual)

> You will need a bead bar.

Count the beads together from one. Stop occasionally and invite a learner to write that number where everyone can see it. Check that the number is written correctly and that everyone agrees it is correct before moving on. Count together from before the beads start (zero) in tens to 100 and back again, moving the beads as you say each number.

Games Book (ISBN 9781107623491)

100 Square Muddle (p1) is a game for two or three players. Learners use their understanding of the patterns in the 100 square to find the correct number.

100 square

1	2	3	4	5	6	7	8	9	10
11	12	13	14	15	16	17	18	19	20
21	22	23	24	25	26	27	28	29	30
31	32	33	34	35	36	37	38	39	40
41	42	43	44	45	46	47	48	49	50
51	52	53	54	55	56	57	58	59	60
61	62	63	64	65	66	67	68	69	70
71	72	73	74	75	76	77	78	79	80
81	82	83	84	85	86	87	88	89	90
91	92	93	94	95	96	97	98	99	100

Quick reference

Core activity 2.1: Counting in twos, fives and tens (Learner's Book p6–7)

Learners explore the patterns made when counting in twos, fives and tens. They use counting in tens to count larger quantities. Learners count amounts of up to 100 objects accurately by arranging them in tens and ones.

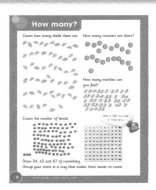

Prior learning	Objectives* –	please note that listed objectives might only be partially covered within any given chapter but are covered fully across the book when taken as a whole
Some experience of exploring numbers to 100.	**1A: Number** (*Numbers and the number system*)	
	2Nn1 – Count, read and write numbers to at least 100 and back again.	
	2Nn2 – Count up to 100 objects, e.g. beads on a bead bar.	
	2Nn3 – Count on in ones and tens from single and two digit numbers and back again.	
	2Nn4 – Count in twos, fives and tens, and use grouping in twos, fives or tens to count larger groups of objects.	
	2Nn7 – Find 1 or 10 more/less than any two-digit number.	
	2Nn9 – Say a number between any given neighbouring pairs of multiples of 10, e.g. 40 and 50.	
	2Nn14 – Understand odd and even numbers and recognise these up to at least 20.	
	1A: Problem solving (*Using techniques and skills in solving mathematical problems*)	
	2Pt2 – Explain methods and reasoning orally.	

*for NRICH activities mapped to the Cambridge Primary objectives, please visit www.cie.org.uk/cambridgeprimarymaths

> **Vocabulary**
>
> total • count • twos • fives • tens

Resources: *100 square* photocopy master (chapter 1, p4). A beadstring/bar photocopy master (CD-ROM). *100 square patterns* photocopy master (p10). Prepare 20 bags (each with a large write-on label) each containing between 50 and 100 of a small item such as pebbles, beans, peas, feathers, dice, red counters, blue counters and so on. *Blank 10 by 10 grid* (CD-ROM). (Optional: *1–100 number cards* use cards 1 to 20; four separate cards with +1, –1, +10, –10 for each pair of learners made using *Blank cards* (CD-ROM).)

Display the *100 square* photocopy master for the whole class to see. Ask a learner to choose a number for everyone to find on the 100 square, then count on in ones or tens from that number. If you have a beadstring, carry out the same activity on the string, first finding the correct number of beads by counting in tens and ones, and then count on. Repeat with three or four different learners choosing a different number. Ask the learners to talk about the patterns they notice in the numbers they say.

"It can be hard to see the patterns when we just say the numbers, so it is better if we colour them in."

Give each learner a copy of the *100 square patterns* photocopy master and explain that they need to count in twos and colour in each number they say on the first 100 square. Challenge them to continue the pattern all the way up to 100. Explain that they need to do the same for the other two 100 squares, counting in fives on the second one and in tens on the last one.

When the learners have completed their patterns, talk about the patterns together. Ask questions such as, *"What do you notice about the fives and tens patterns? Which numbers are coloured in on every 100 square? Why is that? Which numbers are not coloured in on any of the 100 squares? Why is that? Does the pattern on the first 100 square remind you of a pattern we have looked at before?"* **(odd and even)**

Show the learners the bags of small items and explain that you do not know how many of each item is in each bag and it would be useful to know before you tidied up all the items, so you need some help.

Vocabulary

total: how many altogether.

Look out for!

- Learners who find it hard to continue one or more of the patterns at first. *Count along on the 100 square with them to support counting on the correct amount.*
- Learners who find this very straightforward. *Ask them to predict how the patterns would continue on a 101 to 200 square. Give them blank 10 by 10 grids for them to make their own number square and explore continuing the patterns. Ask questions such as, "How will this be different to the 100 square? How will you need to change the decade numbers strip (or multiples of 10 strip)?" Once the learners are comfortable with the layout of the 101 to 200 square, challenge them to make their own jigsaws or muddle game.*

Ask each pair of learners to count how many there are in a bag and write the number on the label, even if they get a different total from the learners who counted it before. Explain that you would like each bag to be counted two or three times in case anyone makes a mistake. Allow the learners to begin without any more discussion.

Look at how the learners arrange the objects to count them. If some learners are arranging the items in twos, fives or tens stop the session and explain that it seems to be taking a long time and some learners are getting in a muddle. Say that some learners seem to have got organised and are getting on faster, so you would like everyone to explain how they are counting.

If no one is counting in twos, fives or tens, stop the session after a while and explain that it seems to be taking a long time and some learners are getting in a muddle. Then ask for ideas to speed things up and count correctly. Talk through the learners' ideas. If necessary, remind the learners that they have been counting in tens, so perhaps that could help them. Draw out that it would be useful to put the items in rows of tens and then count them in tens and ones.

After the contents of the bags have been counted at least twice, ask the learners to finish off the bag they are counting and not start a new one. Choose a bag and look at the numbers on the label. If all the numbers are the same, comment that, *"That must be right because you all got the same total"*.

When you find a bag with different numbers on it, comment that, *"We need to count this one together as there are two (or three) different numbers written on the label"*. Carefully count out the items, putting them in rows of ten. Then count in tens and ones to find the total. Explain that what you have done is used an imaginary 100 square to help you. Put a 100 square next to the arrangement to show the children how your arrangement is the same as the 100 square. Point out the number on the 100 square and how it is made up of the same number of rows of ten as your arrangement. If there is time, count out a second bag, this time counting up in twos or fives.

Explain that you could count small items by putting one on each little square in the hundred square, but that would not work for bigger items. Tell the learners that it is very useful to keep a picture of the 100 square in their heads and arrange things in rows of 10, like on the 100 square, when counting them.

Look out for!

- Learners who are finding it difficult to get organised. *Put their items into rows of ten and encourage them to take over. Count the rows in tens each time another row is added.*
- Learners who find it hard to switch from counting in tens to counting in ones. *Model indicating along the row for tens and touching each single one as you count. If necessary, count the total together.*
- Learners who find this straightforward. *Ask them to tell you how many more of a particular item would be needed to make 100, or to find two bags which total 100 or near 100. You could also ask them how many counters altogether, if you have two bags of counters, or some other combination of two or even three bags. They could use their 101 to 200 square to help them find the total.*

Opportunity for display

Display the bags with their labels on a table or other surface. Add a large label inviting learners and adults to check if the labels are correct. Alternatively, take the labels off the bags and add a large label inviting learners and adults to find the correct label for each bag.

Summary

- Learners recognised and continued the patterns made when counting in twos, fives and tens.
- Learners are able to count amounts of up to 100 objects accurately by arranging them in tens and ones.

Notes on the Learner's Book

How many? (p6): Ask learners to count the number of each object in twos, fives or tens. Challenge the learners to draw an arrangement for a particular number that would make it easier to count the number in twos/fives/tens.

Bags (p7): ask learners to write a number of items that could be in each bag. Compare results.

Check up!

- Start counting and invite a learner, or groups of learners, to take over and continue the count. For example, 2, 4, 6, 8… or 10, 20, 30… or 5, 10, 15, 20… Ask the learners to explain how they knew what came next.
- Ask learners to picture a 100 square in their heads, then imagine a counter on 23. Ask, "*Where do you need to look to find the number that is ten more (or ten less or one more or one less)?*" Repeat with a different start number.

More activities

Counting (pairs or group)

> You will need *1–100 number cards* photocopy master (CD-ROM); use cards 1 to 20, and four separate cards with +1, –1, +10, –10 made using *Blank cards* (CD-ROM).

Both sets of cards need to be shuffled and placed face down in front of the learners. A card from the 1 to 20 set is turned over to tell the learners where to start their count. A card from the set of four cards is turned over to tell the learners how to count. +1 means count on in ones, –1 means count back in ones, +10 means count on in tens and –10 means count back in tens. Each pair continues their count until they reach 100 or 0 if they can. They then turn over the next card in each pile and start a new count. Some learners will find it useful to have a 100 square in front of them for support. Learners could count together or take it in turns.

Bead bar counting (group)

> You will need a beadstring/bar.

Part the beads into two groups. Ask the learners to tell you how many beads are in the first group. Support them to count in tens then ones to find out how many. Ask learners how many are in the second group. Remind them that they are 100 altogether and challenge the second group together to check.

Counting rhymes (class)

Practise counting in twos, fives and tens using counting rhymes, clapping rhythms or other actions. Here are some suggestions, but make up your own too.

Counting in twos – clap on each number. 2, 4, 6, 8, 10, "*You're doing great, let's do it again*".

Counting in fives – show alternate fists opening for each five. 5, 10, 15, 20 clap twice. 25, 30, 35, 40 clap twice. 45, 50, 55, 60, clap twice. Continue in the same way to 100.

Counting in tens – show both fists opening then closing as you say each ten. 10, 20, 30, 40, 50, *"Counting is so nifty!"* 60, 70, 80, 90, 100, *"Counting to 100 is easy!"*

Play Clap Click (class)

Each clap means ten, each click of the fingers means one. So clap, clap, clap, click is 31. After demonstrating a few times, choose a learner to Clap Click a number. The learner who says the correct number first can then make the next number. As they get better at the game, sometimes do the Clicks before the Claps to make the game more challenging.

Games Book (ISBN 9781107623491)

100 square games (p3) *Game 1* is a game for two or three players. Learners practise adding ten using the 100 square.
100 square games (p3) *Game 2* is a game for two or three players. Learners practise taking away ten using the 100 square.

100 square patterns

Count in 2s, 5s or 10s. Colour in the numbers on the 100 square as you say them.

Carry on the patterns to the end of each 100 square.

What do you notice about each pattern?

count in twos

1	2	3	4	5	6	7	8	9	10
11	12	13	14	15	16	17	18	19	20
21	22	23	24	25	26	27	28	29	30
31	32	33	34	35	36	37	38	39	40
41	42	43	44	45	46	47	48	49	50
51	52	53	54	55	56	57	58	59	60
61	62	63	64	65	66	67	68	69	70
71	72	73	74	75	76	77	78	79	80
81	82	83	84	85	86	87	88	89	90
91	92	93	94	95	96	97	98	99	100

count in fives

1	2	3	4	5	6	7	8	9	10
11	12	13	14	15	16	17	18	19	20
21	22	23	24	25	26	27	28	29	30
31	32	33	34	35	36	37	38	39	40
41	42	43	44	45	46	47	48	49	50
51	52	53	54	55	56	57	58	59	60
61	62	63	64	65	66	67	68	69	70
71	72	73	74	75	76	77	78	79	80
81	82	83	84	85	86	87	88	89	90
91	92	93	94	95	96	97	98	99	100

count in tens

1	2	3	4	5	6	7	8	9	10
11	12	13	14	15	16	17	18	19	20
21	22	23	24	25	26	27	28	29	30
31	32	33	34	35	36	37	38	39	40
41	42	43	44	45	46	47	48	49	50
51	52	53	54	55	56	57	58	59	60
61	62	63	64	65	66	67	68	69	70
71	72	73	74	75	76	77	78	79	80
81	82	83	84	85	86	87	88	89	90
91	92	93	94	95	96	97	98	99	100

Quick reference

Core activity 3.1: Number pairs to 100 (Learner's Book p8)
Learners will find all pairs of multiples of ten with a total of 100, recording them as **addition facts** and linking them to the number pairs for ten.

Core activity 3.2: Adding and subtracting number pairs to 100 (Learner's Book p9)
Learners will generate and record the related **subtraction facts** for all pairs of multiples of ten with a total of 100.

Prior learning	Objectives* – please note that listed objectives might only be partially covered within any given chapter but are covered fully across the book when taken as a whole
• Explored number pairs for 10. • Count in tens from zero to 100.	**1A: Calculation** (*Mental strategies*) 2Nc3 – Find all pairs of multiples of 10 with a total of 100 and record the related addition and subtraction facts. 2Nc1 – Find and learn by heart all numbers pairs to 10 and pairs with a total of 20. **1A: Calculation** (*Addition and subtraction*) 2Nc14 – Understand that addition can be done in any order, but subtraction cannot. **1A: Number** (*Numbers and the number system*) 2Nn11 – Recognise and use ordinal numbers up to at least the 10th number and beyond. **1A: Problem solving** (*Using techniques and skills in solving mathematical problems*) 2Pt2 – Explain methods and reasoning orally. 2Pt3 – Explore number problems and puzzles.

*for NRICH activities mapped to the Cambridge Primary objectives, please visit www.cie.org.uk/cambridgeprimarymaths

Vocabulary

number pair • sum • total • plus • minus • less • take away • difference between • fact family • addition facts • subtraction facts

Resources: Prepare a large 100 square, a large 0 to 100 Number line (with the tens numbers enlarged or emphasised in some way). *0–100 Number line* photocopy master (p18); per pair of learners. *Multiples of 10* photocopy master (CD-ROM); per pair of learners. Scissors for the class.

Begin by revising number pairs for ten with the learners by drawing up a list of addition facts for the whole class to see. Accept the learners' ideas and if necessary reorder into an ordered list. Remind the learners that there is no need to continue beyond $5 + 5$ as all the other number pairs beyond this are repeats of earlier pairs just written in a different order (Stage 1, chapter 7).

$0 + 10 = 10$ ⟶	$10 + 0 = 10$
$1 + 9 = 10$ ⟶	$9 + 1 = 10$
$2 + 8 = 10$ ⟶	$8 + 2 = 10$
$3 + 7 = 10$ ⟶	$7 + 3 = 10$
$4 + 6 = 10$ ⟶	$6 + 4 = 10$
$5 + 5 = 10$	

Vocabulary

number pair: two numbers that add together to make the target number, for example $7 + 3 = 10$.

addition facts: when you add two numbers together you find how many you have in total. For example, an addition fact for $3 + 1 = 4$.

subtraction facts: subtraction is removing objects from a group, for example, $5 - 3 = 2$. Three objects are taken away from a group of five and two remain. So the subtraction fact is $5 - 3 = 2$.

Move on to counting forward and back in tens to 100 with the learners, starting from zero. Show the learners how the numbers in the tens column of the 100 square repeat themselves, with 100 in front. Explain that the tens pattern is repeated over and over again as we count further and further.

Show the learners a large 0 to 100 number line. Count along in tens from 0 to 100. Either draw a ring around each tens number, or clip a peg below each of the numbers if the number line is hanging. Explain that, "*We have been counting in tens from zero. The numbers that we have been calling out are called multiples of ten. So 10, 20, 30 and so on are all multiples of ten.*" Ask questions such as, "*Which number is the first multiple of ten? Which is the third?*" Extend all the way to the tenth multiple. Finish by pointing to the numbers 10 to 100, but saying, "*first, second, third . . . . tenth*". Repeat, inviting the learners to join in.

Remind the learners that they started the session by revising number pairs to ten and now you would like to move on to number pairs to 100. Give each pair of learners a copy of the *Multiples of 10 cards* from the photocopy master. They will also need a number line from the *0–100 Number line* photocopy master. Ask the learners to look at the numbers they have, then ask questions such as, "*What do you notice about the numbers? Are any the same?*" Make sure the learners are aware that the numbers are the multiples of ten and that they have two 50 cards.

Explain, "*I would like you to organise your numbers into pairs that make 100, and you can use your 0–100 Number line to help you. If you take a card and put a finger on that number on the number line, your partner can then count in tens from your finger to 100 to see how many more you need to make 100.*" Model the activity by putting a finger on 40, then count on in tens (10, 20, 30, 40, 50, 60) moving along the number line to 100. "*So, 40 and 60 make 100. 40 and 60 are a number pair for 100. See if you can find all the pairs of multiples of 10 with a total of 100.*"

Give the learners about ten minutes to explore and ask them if they have noticed anything about their number pairs. If necessary, write one or more of the number pairs to 100 next to the matching number pair for ten and read the two number sentences. For example, 9 add 1 makes 10, 9 tens add 1 ten makes 10 tens. Challenge the learners to write a list of number pairs to 100 just like the list of number pairs to ten.

With the help of the learners, complete your list of pairs of multiples of ten with a total of 100 as addition facts.

Look out for!

- Learners who make an extended list of pairs of multiples of ten with a total of 100 by including the swapped pairs as well as the original pairs. *Remind them that they only need to write the pairs they made with the number cards because we know we can swap the numbers around, just as we did with our number pairs to ten.*
- Learners who find this very straightforward. *Challenge them to explore making pairs of multiples of ten with a total of 200. Either provide a set of number cards of the multiples of ten from 110 to 200, or give them some blank cards to make their own.*

Example: pairs of multiples of 10 with a total of 100.

   0 tens + 10 tens = 10 tens
   1 ten + 9 tens = 10 tens
   (10) + (90) = (100)

$0 + 100 = 100 \longrightarrow 100 + 0 = 100$
$10 + 90 = 100 \longrightarrow 90 + 10 = 100$
$20 + 80 = 100 \longrightarrow 80 + 20 = 100$
$30 + 70 = 100 \longrightarrow 70 + 30 = 100$
$40 + 60 = 100 \longrightarrow 60 + 40 = 100$
$50 + 50 = 100$

Summary

Learners are able to work out, all the pairs of multiples of ten with a total of 100 and record them as **addition facts**.

Notes on the Learner's Book

100 grams (p8): learners are given a list of weights that are multiples of ten, and asked which weights could be in the pan of a set of scales reading 100g. Learners should recognise that they are being asked to list the multiples of ten number pairs to 100 and the associated addition facts. For example, 20g + 80g = 100g. Do not worry if they forget the units as that is not the purpose of the activity. Challenge more able learners by asking them, *"What if three weights were in the pan? What could they be?"*

Check up!

- *"Which number goes with 30 to make 100?"*
- *"20 and what makes 100?"*
- *"50 and what makes 100?"*
- *"Which number goes with 80 to make 100?"*
- *"List three multiple of ten number pairs to 100."*

More activities

Multiples of 10 game (pairs)

You will need the *Multiples of 10* photocopy master (CD-ROM).

Learners play in pairs. They shuffle the cards and lay them face down in a 3 by 4 grid. The learners take it in turns to turn two cards face up. If the two cards are a number pair to 100, the learner who turned the cards over keeps them and play moves on to the next player. If not, the cards must be turned face down again in the same position and it is the next player's turn. The winner is the player who collects the most cards once all the pairs have been made.

	10	
	90	

The learner who turned the cards over gets to keep them as they are a pair to 100.

30		
	50	

The learner who turned the cards over must turn them face down again as they do not make a pair.

100 Snap (pairs)

You will need three sets of cards from the *Multiples of 10* photocopy master (CD-ROM); per pair of learners.

Shuffle three sets of *Multiples of 10* cards together and share between two learners so that each learner has a pile of cards, face down. Learners take it in turns to turn over a card and place it face up on the table. Each learner makes a pile, so that the two piles are side by side. If two cards make 100, the first learner to say 'Snap!' collects both piles. Play continues until one learner has collected all the cards and is declared the winer.

Games Book (ISBN 9781107623491)

100 Target – Game 1, Addition (p5) is a game for two players. Recall of addition facts for the pairs of multiples of ten with a total of 100.

Resources: A beadstring/bar. *0–100 Number lines* photocopy master (p18); two copies per pair of learners. Scissors. (Optional: *Triangle fact families* photocopy master (CD-ROM).)

Begin by counting forward and back from zero to 100 in tens with the learners; you could use a beadstring if you have one. You could challenge the more able learners to start at 100 and count to and from 200 in tens. Ask the learners to remind you of the pairs of multiples of 10 with a total of 100 from the previous session. As you draw up a list of the number pairs together, ask questions such as, "*Which tens number goes with the first multiple of 10, to make 100? Which is the third multiple of 10? Is that the fifth multiple of 10?*" and so on.

Tell the learners that they have written all the addition facts for these numbers but now you would like them to find all the subtraction facts too. Give each pair of learners two copies of the *0–100 Number line* photocopy master and a pair of scissors. Tell them to cut out each number line. Demonstrate the upcoming task using one of the number lines: cut across it at the 40 mark, as you do this, explain to the learners, "*I am starting with 100 and cutting off 40, so what have I got left?*" Ask the learners to do the same cut, so they can see that the two pieces are 40 and 60.

Ask, "*Does that remind you of one of our pairs of multiples of ten with a total of 100?*" If the learners do not make the link, help them by writing the subtraction pair next to 60 + 40 = 100. Ask if they can use their two pieces in another way to make another subtraction fact. If the learners do not tell you that 100 − 60 = 40, swap around the two pieces of your number line to show them.

> Challenge the learners to use their number lines to help them find the rest of the subtraction facts for multiples of 10 to 100. Remind them that they are starting with 100 each time, and they need to cut each number line only once to find two matching subtraction facts.

Give the learners some time to work together and produce all the subtraction facts, then complete the list of addition and subtraction facts for the whole class to see. Tell the learners that there is a quicker way to remember the number facts. Draw a triangle and complete it as per the example to the right to display a number fact family. Read it to the learners, pointing to

Vocabulary

total: how many altogether.

sum: the answer to an addition calculation.

minus: another word for take away and subtraction.

fact family: the set of four addition and subtraction facts that can be found from one set of numbers. For example, the fact family for 3, 4 and 7 is

$$3+4=7 \qquad 4+3=7$$
$$7-4=3 \qquad 7-3=4$$

Example:
$$40+60=100 \qquad 60+40=100$$
$$100-60=40 \qquad 100-40=60$$

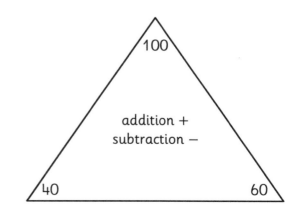

each number as you read the four facts contained in the triangle ($40+60=100$, $60+40=100$, $100-40=60$ and $100-60=40$).

Explain that the number at the top of the triangle is the always the biggest number and is the total.

Remind the learners that the triangle shows them that they can add the numbers in any order. But they must always start with the biggest number, at the top of the triangle, when they are doing subtraction because they will be taking some of that total away.

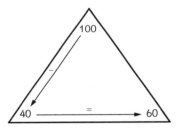 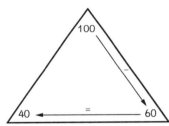 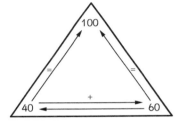

Challenge the learners to draw a triangle for each set of four addition and subtraction facts.

Look out for!

- Learners who find it hard to relate the addition and subtraction facts to the triangle. *Draw a triangle and show how each fact can be found.*
- Learners who find this idea straightforward. *Challenge them to draw a triangle for a number fact they know, such as $7+8=15$ and then find the other three facts in the fact family.*

Opportunity for display

Display large triangles of each of the addition and subtraction families with a label such as, *"Can you read our triangles? There are four addition and subtraction facts in each triangle."*

Summary

Learners are able to work out all the subtraction facts for pairs of multiples of 10 with a total of 100, linking them with the matching addition facts.

Notes on the Learner's Book
Triangle fact families (p9): challenge learners to make triangles for any number fact, then read all four facts in the triangle.

Check up!

- *"What do I need to take away from 100 to leave 20?"*
- *"100 less ten leaves what?"*
- *"What do I need to subtract from 100 to leave 50?"*

More activities

__Triangle fact families__ (individual)

You will need the *Triangle fact families* photocopy master (CD-ROM).

Write the numbers for one of the number fact families in the triangle, then complete the word sentences correctly.

Games Book (ISBN 9781107623491)

100 Target – Game 2, Subtraction (p5) is a game for two players. Recall of subtraction facts for the pairs of multiples of 10 with a total of 100.

0–100 Number line

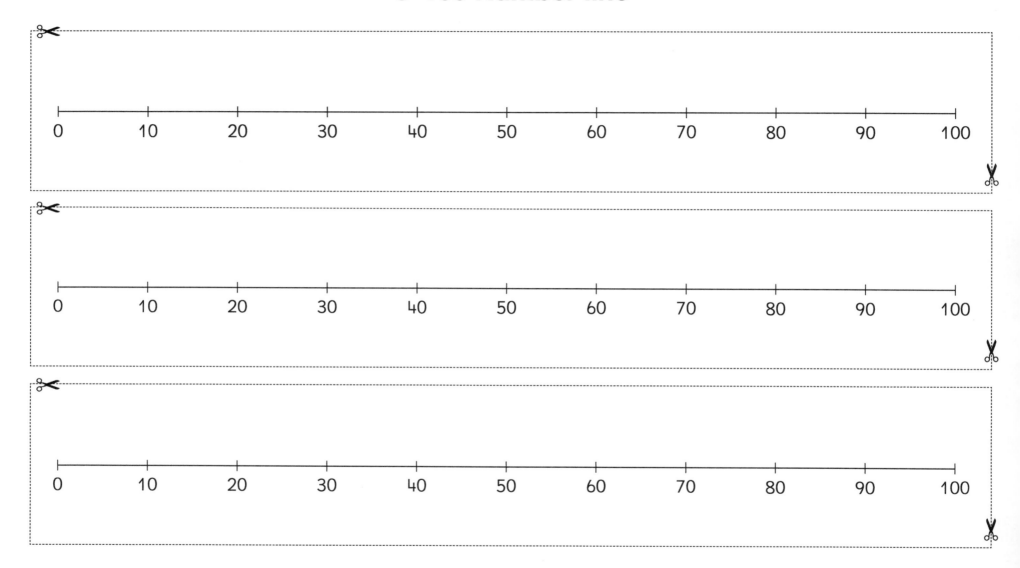

Quick reference

Core activity 4.1: Using a number line (Learner's Book p10)

Learners use a beadstring to help them place a two-digit number on a 0 to 100 number line marked in tens.

Core activity 4.2: Rounding using a number line (Learner's Book p11)

Learners use a number line to round two-digit numbers to the nearest 10.

Prior learning	Objectives* – please note that listed objectives might only be partially covered within any given chapter but are covered fully across the book when taken as a whole
Explored numbers to 100.	**1A: Numbers** (*Numbers and the number system*)
	2Nn8 – Round two-digit numbers to the nearest multiple of 10.
	2Nn10 – Place a two-digit number on a number line marked off in multiples of ten.

*for NRICH activities mapped to the Cambridge Primary objectives, please visit www.cie.org.uk/cambridgeprimarymaths

Vocabulary

number line • rounding

Core activity 4.1: Using a number line

Resources: Prepare a large 0 to 100 number line marked in tens; you can use the *1–100 number line* photocopy master (chapter 3, p18). 1 to 100 beadstrings/bars(s), if available. *Beadstrings and number lines* photocopy master (p24); per learner. A selection of two-digit number cards or cloakroom tickets for each learner; if not available, use the photocopy master *1–100 number cards* but remove cards 1–9. *Blank 0–100 number line* photocopy master (CD-ROM). (Optional: *What's my number?* photocopy master (CD-ROM); a metre rule or stick.)

Begin by counting forward and back in tens from 0 to 100 with the learners. Show the learners the number line marked in tens. Explain that it is easy to see where the tens numbers are but what about all the other numbers?

If you have a beadstring available, ask some learners to show you where the beads numbered 10, 20, 30 and so on are. Give each learner a copy of the *Beadstrings and number lines* photocopy master. Count along the beadstring in tens together. Ask, *"Find bead number 11. How can you explain where it is?"* The learners will tell you that it is right next to or just after, bead 10. Ask, *"What about 21? 31? 41?"* The learners will tell you that each of these numbers comes after a tens or decade number.

Repeat for 9, 19, 29 and so on, with the learners explaining that each of these numbers is just before the tens or decade number. Continue to ask questions such as, *"How could you work out where 32 would be on the number line? How about 48?"*

Ask questions about numbers which are further from each tens number until you can ask, *"What is special about 5, 15, 25, and 35? Where will they be on the beadstring and number line?"* The learners will explain that these numbers come in the middle, between each tens number.

Remind learners that all the numbers from 10 to 99 are two-digit numbers. The first digit tells us how many tens there are and the second digit tells us how many ones there are.

Write a selection of two-digit numbers where all the learners can see them, or give each learner a selection of two-digit number cards or cloakroom tickets; do **not** include 10, 20, 30, 40, 50, 60, 70, 80, 90 and 100. Challenge them to mark four different numbers one on each number line on the *Beadstrings and number lines* photocopy master, using the beadstring to help them. Encourage the learners to fold back the top part of the sheet and complete the last number line without the support of the beadstring.

Look out for!

- Learners who find it difficult to estimate where to mark a number on number line. *Use a beadstring or row of cubes to show how to mark the numbers on an enlarged number line.*

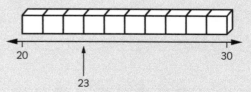

- Learners who find this straightforward. *Get these learners to use a number line without the tens marked on.* (you can use the *Blank 0–100 number line* photocopy master.)

Finish the session by discussing how the learners know where to mark 37, 64 and 82 on the number line. Mark the numbers on the large 0 to 100 number line if they are not already shown.

Summary

Learners are able to place a two-digit number on a number line marked in multiples of ten.

Notes on the Learner's Book

Number line muddle (p10): give learners a copy of the *0–100 number line* photocopy master; learners mark the numbers from the page onto their number line in the correct places. Challenge the more able learners to extend their number line beyond 100 before marking their own numbers on the number line.

Check up!

Ask learners to describe where a number would be on a number line.

- *"Would it be to the left or right of the 10?"*
- *"Would it be close to the 10 or further away?"*
- *"Which two numbers would be next to 27 on a number line?"*
- *"What about 40?"*

More activities

What's my number? (pair)

You will need *What's my number?* photocopy master (CD-ROM) and a metre rule/stick.

Learners work in pairs to estimate the numbers marked on the top number line. Explain that the bottom line represents a metre rule/stick, and that each small line is 1cm. Ask the learners to write the correct numbers in the boxes. Show them a metre rule/stick if you have one.

Core activity 4.2: Rounding using a number line

Resources: *100 square* photocopy master (chapter 1, p4). A large 0 to 100 Number line. Beadstring/bar(s) (1 to 100), if available. *0–100 number cards* photocopy master (CD-ROM). *Rounding* photocopy master (p25). (Optional: *5UP* photocopy master (CD-ROM); colouring pencils.)

Begin by counting in tens to 100 starting at 7, forward and back. Use the column starting with 7 on the 100 square for support. You can ask the more able learners to predict the pattern if the number square continued to 200. Learners try counting from 7 to 97.

Remind learners of the activity when they marked numbers on a number line and how useful it was to have the tens numbers on the line. Remind them that in two-digit numbers the first digit tells us how many tens there are, the second digit how many ones. Explain that we sometimes only need to know a number 'to the nearest 10' and we call this 'rounding' the number.

Look at part of a number line or a beadstring, between 20 and 30. Talk through whether each number is nearer to 20 or 30 by counting how many spaces there are between the number and the tens number. Look at 25 and say that it is 5 away from both tens numbers. Explain that mathematicians have agreed that 1 to 4 are rounded down to the previous 10 and 5 to 9 are rounded up to the next 10, to make sure that everyone always does the same thing. Tens numbers do not need rounding to the nearest ten as they are already tens! Look at some of the numbers on the number line to be sure that the learners understand.

Lay out the tens cards from the photocopy master *0–100 number cards* in order so that the learners can see them. Shuffle the rest of the cards and turn over the top card. Show the number to the learners and ask them to call out the nearest ten. Repeat several times, placing the numbers next to the appropriate tens number card.

Show the learners the *Rounding* photocopy master and explain that they need to mark each number on its number line, then round it to the nearest ten. They should then write that tens number in the last box of the row.

After the learners have completed the activity, check they all agree.

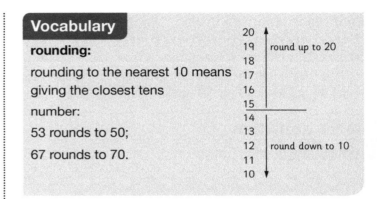

Vocabulary

rounding:

rounding to the nearest 10 means giving the closest tens number:

53 rounds to 50;

67 rounds to 70.

20
19 round up to 20
18
17
16
15
14
13
12 round down to 10
11
10

Look out for!

- Learners who find it hard to know what to do with numbers that contain a zero in the 'ones' column, for example 20, 50, 90 and often round them to the next ten. *Remind them that these are already a tens number, so they do not need to be rounded up or down.*
- Learners who find rounding to the nearest 10 straightforward. *Challenge them to explore how you could round to the nearest 100, asking which numbers would you round up and which numbers would you round down.*

Summary

Learners are able to round a two-digit number to the nearest ten.

Notes on the Learner's Book

Number drop (p11): provides opportunity for learners to practise rounding numbers to the nearest 10, and asks learners to think about why numbers ending in 5 or more are rounded up. Note: rounding to the nearest 100 is beyond the scope of the Stage 2 framework, but if you want to challenge some more able learners, you could extend the activity by asking "What if the numbers were rounded to the nearest 100? Which numbers would be rounded to 100? What number would the other numbers be rounded to?"

Check up!

- Ask learners to describe where a number would be on a number line, as per the Check up in Core activity 4.1 (p21), but this time also ask:
- *"What number would you round it to?"*

More activities

5UP

You will need the *5UP* photocopy master (CD-ROM).

Design a can of drink called 5UP, showing that numbers 5 to 9 are rounded up to the next 10, while 1 to 4 are rounded down to the previous ten.

Games Book (ISBN 9781107623491)

100 Target – Game 3, Rounding (p5) is a game for two players. Players practise rounding numbers to the nearest ten.

Beadstrings and number lines

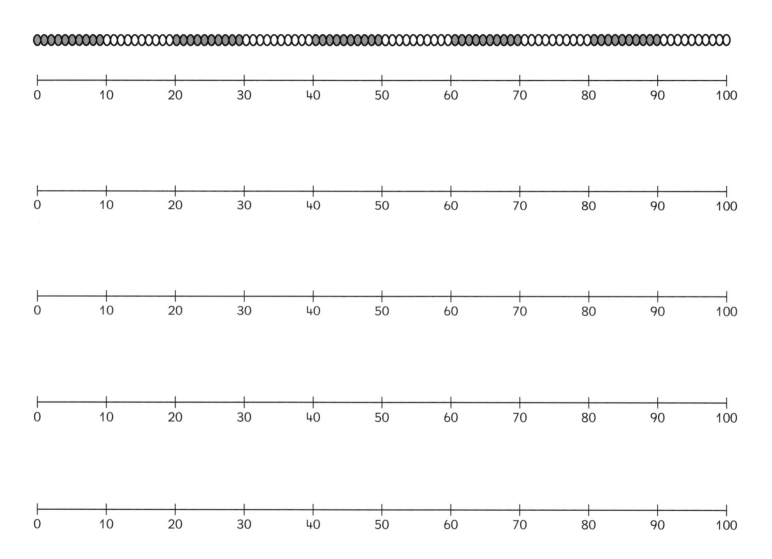

Rounding

Mark each number in a box on the number line next to it.

Then round the number to the nearest 10.

Blank page

Quick reference

<u>**Core activity 5.1: Number pairs to 20**</u> (Learner's Book p12)
Learners use ten frames to explore pairs with a total of 20 and record the related addition and subtraction facts.

<u>**Core activity 5.2: Number pairs between 10 and 20**</u> (Learner's Book p13)
Learners use ten frames to explore pairs with a total between 10 and 20 and record the related addition and subtraction facts.

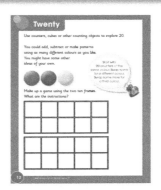

Prior learning	Objectives* – please note that listed objectives might only be partially covered within any given chapter but are covered fully across the book when taken as a whole
• Count to 20, forwards and back. • Count in multiples of ten, forward and back. • Add and subtract numbers to ten and beyond.	**1A: Calculation** (*Mental strategies*) 2Nc1 – Find and learn by heart all numbers pairs to 10 and pairs with a total of 20. 2Nc2 – Partition all numbers to 20 into pairs and record the related addition and subtraction facts. **1A: Calculation** (*Addition and subtraction*) 2Nc14 – Understand that addition can be done in any order, but subtraction cannot. **1A: Problem solving** (*Using techniques and skills in solving mathematical problems*) 2Pt3 – Explore number problems and puzzles. 2Pt4 – Make sense of simple word problems (single and easy two-step), decide what operations (addition or subtraction, simple multiplication or division) are needed to solve them and, with help, represent them, with objects or drawings or on a number line.

*for NRICH activities mapped to the Cambridge Primary objectives, please visit www.cie.org.uk/cambridgeprimarymaths

Vocabulary

number pairs • fact family

Resources: *Number pair cards* photocopy master (CD-ROM) per learner. *Ten frames* photocopy master (CD-ROM). 40 counters (20 in one colour, 20 in another colour). *Fact family triangles* photocopy master (p32). (Optional: *20 Board* photocopy master (CD-ROM).)

Begin by revising number pairs to ten with the learners, drawing up a list where everyone can see it.

Prepare the six cards from the *Number pair cards* photocopy master and explain that each number on the card is part of a number pair to 10 and that when you show them a card, you would like them to tell you what number is on the back i.e. the other number in the pair to 10. Practise by going through the cards three or four times, remembering to shuffle and turn them around.

Explain that, *"In Stage 1 you did lots of 'playing with 10' activities. We are going to do some 'playing with 20' activities."*

Learners should work in pairs. Each learner will need two ten frames and 40 counters, 20 of one colour and 20 of another. Tell the learners to place their two ten frames in a line to make 20. Then ask them to choose a colour and put one counter of that colour in each square of both ten frames. Explain that what the learners can see is the number pair $20 + 0 = 20$ and $0 + 20 = 20$ since they have 20 counters of one colour and none of the other colour. Ask the learners to swap one counter at the end for the other colour and check that what they now see is $19 + 1 = 20$ and $1 + 19 = 20$.

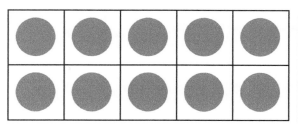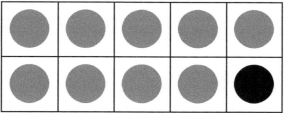

Explain that if they carry on swapping one counter for the other colour, what they will see on the ten frames are the addition pairs for 20. Remind them that a quick way of recording this is by using a triangle to create a fact family.

Example: number pairs to 10.

$0 + 10 = 10 \longrightarrow 10 + 0 = 10$
$1 + 9 = 10 \longrightarrow 9 + 1 = 10$
$2 + 8 = 10 \longrightarrow 8 + 2 = 10$
$3 + 7 = 10 \longrightarrow 7 + 3 = 10$
$4 + 6 = 10 \longrightarrow 6 + 4 = 10$
$5 + 5 = 10$

Look out for!

- Learners who forget about one of the ten frames and record number pairs for ten instead. *Make sure the two ten frames are next to each other and model counting 10, 11, 12 and so on, pointing to the first ten frame then the same coloured counters on the second ten frame.*
- Learners who notice the patterns in the numbers and do not need to use the counters after the first few times. *Ask them to check that they have all the number pairs and no duplicates. This will be easier if they have worked systematically. They could go on to explore sets of three numbers to make 20, using three different colours of counters, or number pairs to 30.*

Give each learner a copy of the *Fact family triangles* photocopy master, tell them to write '20' in the box at the top of the page. Explain that they are going to use one triangle for each number pair to 20. Help them to complete the first triangle for 20 and 0. Ask them to read the triangle back to you. The learners might realise that they have recorded four number facts, two addition and two subtraction. If not, point this out to them and check that they can also 'see' the subtraction facts.

Ask the learners to work through the photocopy master in pairs, using their ten frames and counters to help them, changing one counter at a time and recording the additions and subtractions in the *Fact family triangles* photocopy master.

End the session by checking that everyone has completed eleven different triangles. Draw one of the triangles where everyone can see and invite a learner to come and write the four number facts from the triangle. Repeat with another triangle. Remind the learners that the triangle shows them that they can add the numbers in any order, but they must always start with the biggest number, at the top of the triangle, when they are doing subtraction because they will be taking some of that total away.

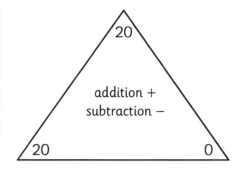

Opportunity for display

Display a large *Fact family triangles* photocopy master for the number 20 to help the children remember each of the number pairs. Add questions such as "*Can you read the four number facts in each triangle?*"

Summary

Learners are able to recall or work out the pairs of numbers with a total of 20 and write the related addition and subtraction facts.

Notes on the Learner's Book
Twenty (p12): learners explore 20 with counters, cubes or other counting objects on two ten frames. They could make some addition calculations and record the number sentences, and do something similar for subtraction from 20, or even invent a game.

More activities

__20 board__ (individual)

You will need *20 board* (CD-ROM).

Learners complete each piece by writing in the number pair to 20.

Games Book (ISBN 9781107623491)

Playing with 10. Use this game from Stage 1 to revise number pairs to 10.
Playing with 20 (p7) is a game for two players. Learners explore and record addition pairs for 20. Game 3, 11 to 19 take away is a game for two players. Learners explore and record subtraction pairs for 20.

Check up!

Point to one of the triangles on the wall and ask a learner to read it to you. Can they find all four facts? Ask questions such as '*Which number goes with 3 to make 20? What about 16?*'

Resources: *Number pair cards* photocopy master (CD-ROM) as per *Core activity 5.1*, for each learner. 2 *Ten frames* (CD-ROM). Counters in two colours a copy of *Fact family triangles* (p32). (Optional: *19 Board, 18 Board,... 11 Board* photocopy master (CD-ROM).)

Begin by working through the *Number pair cards* photocopy master three or four times. Ask the learners, "*What if the total on each card, front and back, was 20 instead of 10? What number would be on the back then? How do you know?*" Make sure the learners understand that the number on the reverse would be 10 more, so when they see 3, they need to say 17 (rather than seven). Work through the cards three or four times again, but this time with the total 20.

List the number pairs for 20 where everyone can see them. Choose a fact and draw the fact family triangle for it. Ask the learners to read the four facts in the triangle to you. Repeat for another triangle.

Remind the learners of how they used two ten frames to help them work out all the number pairs for 20. Ask them to suggest how they might do the same for any number **between** 10 or 20. Learners could decide to colour in some of the squares on one of the ten frames, or cut off the correct number of squares from one of the ten frames.

Challenge the learners to choose a number between 10 and 20 to work with. They will need two ten frames, counters in two different colours and a *Fact family triangle* photocopy master to record on.

Number	Number of triangles
20	11
19	10
18	10
17	9
16	9
15	8
14	8
13	7
12	7
11	6
10	6

Towards the end of the session, draw one of the triangles where everyone can see it and invite a learner to come and write the four number facts from the triangle. Repeat with another triangle.

End the session by asking the learners how many triangles they needed to use for their number. Draw up a chart where everyone can see it. Look at the pattern together and explore what is happening. Can the learners explain why the number of triangles does not increase every time the number the goes up?

Look out for!
- Learners who read the subtraction facts from the triangle incorrectly. *For a triangle with 18, 12 and 6 in it, they might read this as 12−6=18. Remind them that when they are subtracting, they must always start with the biggest number.*
- Challenge learners who find this straightforward to predict how many triangles they will need to record all the number pairs for their chosen number. *Will it be more or less than it was for 20? How many more or less?*

Opportunity for display
As suggested before, large triangles of these fact families could also be displayed.

Summary

Learners will be able to recall or work out the pairs of numbers with a total number between 10 and 20 and write the related **addition** and **subtraction facts**.

Notes on the Learner's Book

Clock pairs (p13): encourage learners to complete the number pairs, before drawing a fact family triangle for two of the number pairs to 20, and then writing out the four number facts for each number pair.

Check up!

Ask questions such as:
- *"Which number goes with 7 to make 11?"*
- *"Which number goes with 9 to make 16?"*
- *"Give me a number pair for 13."*

More activities

19 Board (individual)

You will need *19 board* photocopy master (CD-ROM).

Learners complete each piece by writing in the number pair to 19. There are also boards for each of the numbers from 11 to 18 on the CD-ROM.

Games Book (ISBN 9781107623491)

Playing with 20 (p7) Game 2: playing with 11 to 19 is a game for two players. As Game 1 but for a number between 10 and 20.

Game 4: 11 to 19 take away, is a game for two players. As Game 3 but for a number between ten and 20.

Fact family triangles

for [ ]

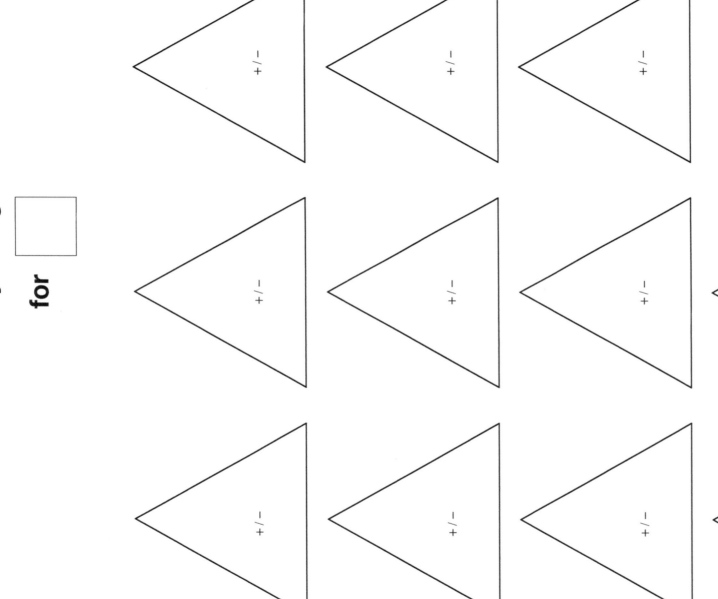

Instructions on page 29

Quick reference

Core activity 6.1: Adding using number pairs (Learner's Book p14)

Learners use number pairs to ten to add four or five numbers together.

Core activity 6.2: Checking your solutions (Learner's Book p15)

Learners explore a range of ways of checking the solution to an addition or subtraction calculation.

Learners begin to explore number pairs to 30.

Core activity 6.3: Equal and equivalent (Learner's Book p16)

Learners explore using the equals sign to show the equality of two calculations.

Prior learning	Objectives* – please note that listed objectives might only be partially covered within any given chapter but are covered fully across the book when taken as a whole
• Explored numbers to 100. • Explored number pairs for numbers to 20.	**1A: Calculation** (*Addition and subtraction*) 2Nc8 – Add four or five small numbers together. 2Nc11 – Add and subtract a single digit to and from a two-digit number. 2Nc14 – Understand that addition can be done in any order, but subtraction cannot. 2Nc7 – Use the = sign to represent equality, e.g. $16+4=17+3$. **1A: Problem solving** (*Using techniques and skills in solving mathematical problems*) 2Pt1 – Choose appropriate mental strategies to carry out calculations and explain how they worked out the answer. 2Pt4 – Make sense of simple word problems (single and easy two-step), decide what operations (addition or subtraction, simple multiplication or division) are needed to solve them and, with help, represent them, with objects or drawings or on a number line. 2Pt6 – Check the answer to an addition by adding the numbers in a different order or by using a different strategy, e.g. 35+19 by adding 20 to 35 and subtracting 1, and by adding 30+10 and 5+9. 2Pt7 – Check a subtraction by adding the answer to the smaller number in the original subtraction.

*for NRICH activities mapped to the Cambridge Primary objectives, please visit www.cie.org.uk/cambridgeprimarymaths

Vocabulary

value

Core activity 6.1: Adding using number pairs

> **Resources:** *Number pair cards* (from *Core activity 5.1*). *1–9 spinner* photocopy master (p40) and a split pin, or 1–9 digit cards (CD-ROM); per pair of learners. (Optional: *Elephant adds* photocopy master (CD-ROM).)

Begin by revising number pairs to ten. Work through the number pairs to ten, repeating three or four times. Remind the learners that we spend time learning our number pairs for ten because they are so useful. Explain, "*They are especially useful when we are adding, so we will be using them a lot today.*"

Write four small numbers where everyone can see them, for example 7, 9, 2 and 8. Ask the learners if they notice anything about the numbers. If necessary, ask if they can see a number pair to ten. They should notice $2 + 8 = 10$, but be aware that there are no other pairs for ten. Explain that, "*9 is nearly a 10, so if I took one from the 7, that would make another 10 and leave me with 6 left over. So now it is easy to add the 4 numbers together.*"

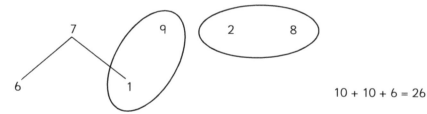

$10 + 10 + 6 = 26$

Say, "*Let's try another set of numbers.*" Write up 4, 5, 6 and 8.
This time the learners should notice that $4 + 6 = 10$. Ask for ideas on how to make it easier to add the 5 and the 8. The 5 could be split into 3 and 2, adding the 2 to 8 to make 10. Or the 8 could be split into 5 and 3, adding 5 to 5 to make 10.

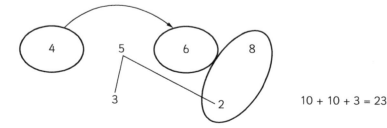

$10 + 10 + 3 = 23$

Vocabulary

value: number given to something to show its size.

Make sure that the learners realise there is often more than one way to combine the numbers, because we can add numbers in any order we choose and will always get the same total.

Pairs of learners will need a 1–9 spinner or a set of 1–9 digit cards (without zero). They need to spin the spinner four times; or shuffle the cards and turn over four cards. After recording the four numbers in a line, they should draw a ring around pairs of numbers which make 10 and decide how to split the rest of the numbers. Sometimes there will not be any immediate number pairs for 10 and they will have to split two or even three of the numbers. Challenge each learner to find a different way of using the numbers from their partner. Once they are confident, suggest they try five numbers.

Finish the session by showing how some learners worked with a particular combination of numbers and asking if anyone can see a different way. You could also work through a set of numbers such as 3, 5, 4, 8 where there are no immediate pairs to make 10.

Look out for!

- Learners who find it hard to recall the number pairs for ten. *Either provide them with a Ten Ant from Stage 1 or help them to list the number pairs for ten at the top of the paper they are working on. These learners may find it easier to work with digit cards rather than a spinner as they can move the numbers around to help them notice the pairs for ten or match with one of the written number pairs.*
- Learners who spot the number pairs easily. *Challenge them to add together five then six numbers or to focus on one set of numbers and find three or four different ways of adding them.*

Summary

Learners are able to add four or five small numbers together by noticing or creating pairs of numbers that make ten.

Notes on the Learner's Book
How many ways? (p14): challenge learners to find a different way to add each set of numbers in order to check their answer.

Check up!

- *"How would you add 5, 6 and 7 together?"*
- *"Tell me a number pair for ten. And another pair."*

More activities

Elephant adds (individual)

You will need the *Elephant adds* photocopy master (CD-ROM).

Learners add the value of each letter to find the total value of a word.

Games Book (ISBN 9781107623491)

Adding Game (p10) is a game for two players. Learners generate numbers to practise different addition strategies.

Resources: *Number pair cards* (from *Core activity 5.1*). *0–100 number cards* photocopy master (CD-ROM). (Optional: *Adding* photocopy master (CD-ROM); *Subtracting* photocopy master (CD-ROM) *1–9 digit cards* photocopy master (CD-ROM).)

Begin by revising number pairs to 20. You could start by revising number pairs to 10 using the *Number pair cards* photocopy master to remind the learners of the patterns after telling the learners that they should be thinking of number pairs to 20 this time; or make a new set of cards for 20.

Use the cards 1 to 9 and 11 to 19 from the *0–100 number cards* photocopy master. Shuffle each set separately. Turn over the top card from each set. Ask the learners how you could add the two numbers together. List the suggestions where everyone can see them. Your list should include:
- Look for number pairs for 10 or 20.
- Look for doubles.
- Use a number line to count on.
- Count on in your head.

Discuss how learners can use one method to do the calculation and then a different one to check their solution for the first calculation.

Ask the learners how you could subtract the smaller number from the larger number and list the suggestions. Look at how the two lists are almost the same.

Write two numbers where everyone can see them, then add them together **incorrectly**. For example $17 + 6 = 24$.

Ask the learners to talk to a partner about how they would check the answer.
Invite some learners to share their ideas.

These might include:
- double 6 is 12 and 1 more makes 13 and 10 more makes 23
- Or double 7 is 14, take away 1 is 13 and another 10 is 23

Look out for!
- Learners who find it hard to choose which method to use. *Work through the same calculation with them, using different methods to see which one they find easiest.*
- Learners who find adding a single digit to a teen number straightforward. *Challenge them by suggesting that they explore using either higher two-digit numbers or two two-digit numbers.*

- Or 17 + 3 makes 20 and another 3 makes 23
- Or 7 and 3 is 10, add 3 makes 13, add 10 makes 23
- Or 6 and 4 is 10, add 3 makes 13, add 10 makes 23.

Turn over two more numbers and this time subtract them incorrectly.

For example 13 − 8 = 4. Explain, "*We can check the answer by adding the smaller number in the original calculation to our answer … But 8 + 4 = 12 so where have I gone wrong?*"

Again, ask the learners to talk to a partner about how they would work it out and how they would check the answer. Invite some learners to share their ideas.

Summary

Learners recognise and use a range of different methods for adding and subtracting, and for checking a calculation.

Notes on the Learner's Book
Hearts and stars (p15): the learners investigate number pairs to 20 and number pairs to 30, and try to spot similarities and differences between the sets.

Check up!
- "*How would you add 14 and 8?*"
- "*What if you were taking away 8 from 14?*"

More activities

Adding (individual or pair)

You will need the *Adding* photocopy master (CD-ROM) and *1–9 digit cards* photocopy master.

Learners generate a series of additions using digit cards in the frame provided.

Subtracting (individual/or pair)

You will need the *Subtracting* photocopy master (CD-ROM) and *1–9 digit cards* photocopy master.

Learners generate a series of subtractions using digit cards in the frame provided.

Resources: *Equal (1)* photocopy master (CD-ROM). *Equal (2)* photocopy master (CD-ROM). *0–100 Number cards* photocopy master (CD-ROM). (Optional: *Happy L* photocopy master (CD-ROM).)

Begin the activity by choosing a number such as 17 and ask the learners to tell you two numbers that make 17. Record these as a string, for example, $17 = 12 + 5 = 14 + 3 = 9 + 8 = \ldots$

Ask the learners for some subtractions where the answer is 17 and continue to write them in the same way. Explain that many people forget what the equals (=) sign really means; that both sides have the same value or total. Even though the two calculations might not look the same, they are actually equivalent.

Pick out two of the calculations and write them with the equals sign in the middle. For example, $13 + 4 = 19 - 2$. Show the learners the *Equal (1)* and *(2)* photocopy masters and talk about how they are different.

Ask them to work with a partner, choosing which sheet they would like to explore. Explain that they cannot write just any numbers in the spaces, instead they are going to work with a set of digit cards. Each space must have a digit card in it. Explain that this will make them think more carefully about the numbers they are using. As they only have one of each digit, they cannot make $13 + 4 = 19 - 2$ for example, as they cannot use the '1' twice. Talk through how a similar calculation could be done, such as $13 + 4 = 25 - 8$. Give each pair of learners their chosen sheet and a set of digit cards. Allow some time for the learners to explore, making suggestions for other numbers to try if they are stuck. Allow learners to change from *Equal (1)* to *Equal (2)* if necessary.

At the end of the session, show some solutions where the learners have clearly explored changing part of the calculation rather than starting again.

Look out for!

- Learners who find it hard to accept that $12 + 5$ and $14 + 3$ are equivalent. *Although they might recognise that both equal 17, they will claim that they are not the same. Explain that to be equivalent they must have the same total, not be identical. Explain that if a balance scale had an eraser in one pan and two building blocks in the other pan, and the scale balanced, it would show that the eraser and the two blocks have the same weight; they are equivalent, even though they look different.*
- Learners who find the *Equal (1)* photocopy master easy to use. *Challenge them by giving them the Equal (2) photocopy master. To make both sides equal, they will need to realise that the two-digit number must have either one or two tens.*

Summary

Learners develop a wider understanding of equality through using the equals sign to show that calculations are equivalent.

Notes on the Learner's Book
Equal machine (p16): encourage learners to study different calculation pairs to investigate which are equal/equivalent.

Check up!
- *"Tell me two numbers with the same total as 11 + 3."*
- *"Can you think of another equivalent pair of numbers?"*

More activities

Happy L (individual or group)

> You will need the *Happy L* photocopy master (CD-ROM).

Learners place digit cards in the spaces to make both arms of the L add up to the same total. They see how many different ways they can do it.

1 to 9 spinner

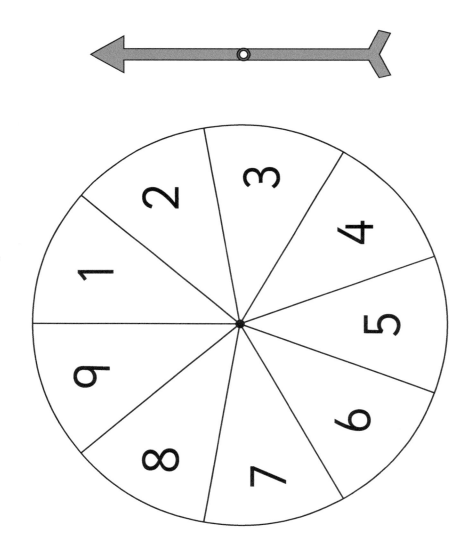

Insert split pin as shown through hole in pointer and spinner.

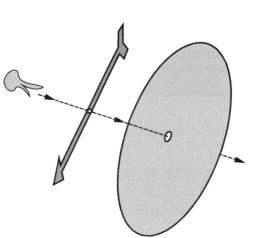

Instructions on page 35

Quick reference

Core activity 7.1: Introducing Arrays (Learner's Book p17)
Learners explore representing repeated addition in an array.

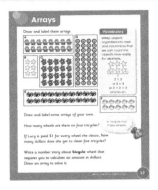

Prior learning	Objectives* – please note that listed objectives might only be partially covered within any given chapter but are covered fully across the book when taken as a whole
• Counting in 2s, 5s and 10s. • Explored patterns of 2, 5, and 10 on a 100 square.	**1A: Number** (*Numbers and the number system*) 2Nn14 – Understand odd and even numbers and recognise these up to at least 20. **1A: Calculation** (*Mental strategies*) 2Nc4 – Learn and recognise multiples of 2, 5 and 10 and derive the related division facts. **1A: Calculation** (*Multiplication and division*) 2Nc16 – Understand multiplication as repeated addition and use the × sign. 2Nc17 – Understand multiplication as describing an array. **1A: Problem solving** (*Using techniques and skills in solving mathematical problems*) 2Pt5 – Make up a story to go with a calculation, including in the context of money.

*for NRICH activities mapped to the Cambridge Primary objectives, please visit www.cie.org.uk/cambridgeprimarymaths

Vocabulary

array • multiply • multiplication

Resources: *100 square* photocopy master (chapter 1, p4). *Array cards* photocopy master (CD-ROM). Counters, cubes or other counting items. Strips of paper for labels.

Begin by counting in twos, fives and tens from zero, forward and back to 100. Remind the learners of the 100 square pattern sheet they completed (Core activity 2.1). They looked at the pattern of numbers when they counted in twos, fives and tens.

Ask the learners to describe the pattern of numbers for each count. You may need to count through the 100 square together to revise the patterns. The learners should notice that all the numbers have zero ones when they count in tens. When they count in fives, there are five ones then zero ones. When they count in twos, they are saying the even numbers.

Say a number such as 34 and ask the learners, "*Would you say 34 if you were counting in twos? What about if you were counting in fives? Or tens?*" Repeat for other numbers such as 15, 30 and 26.

Show the learners the 2 by 5 array card from the *Array cards* photocopy master and ask them what they see. Some learners will see five lots of two, others will see two lots of five.

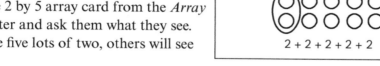

$2 + 2 + 2 + 2 + 2$

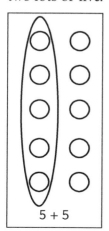

$5 + 5$

Show the learners the twos first. Draw a loop around each two and write 2 underneath. Then write '+' between each 2. Explain, "*2 + 2 + 2 + 2 + 2 = 10. That's a lot of twos. There is an easier way to write it, five lots of two, 2 × 5 (two, five times), 2 multiplied by 5.*"

Turn the card the other way round. This time, draw a loop around the fives and write 5 underneath. Explain, "*5 + 5 = 10. There is an easier way to write it, two lots of five, 5 × 2 (five, two times).*"

Tell the learners, "*When we organise our objects like this, we call the arrangement an array. Use your counters to make an array for 2 × 10, that's two ten times.*" Once the learners have made the array, ask them how may twos they have. Ask them to label their array, write 2 + 2 + 2 . . . to show

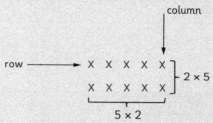

what they did. Then ask the learners to think how they might write that the short way, 'ten lots of two' or 'two, ten times'. 2×10, 2 multiplied by 10.

Make some more arrays together, labelling them as repeated addition and as multiplications.

Show the learners some array cards from the *Array cards* photocopy master and ask them to write the labels for them.

Finish the session by reminding the learners that a bicycle has two wheels. Ask the learners to make an array to show how to solve the following number story:

Lucy gets paid $1 for every bicycle wheel she cleans for her next door neighbour. So far this week she has cleaned three bicycles, which means she has cleaned 3 lots of 2 or 2×3 wheels, so she has made $6. How many more dollars would she make if she cleaned a further 7 bicycles? Ask learners to suggest a different bicycle number story/problem.

Summary

Learners will begin to relate repeated addition and arrays to multiplication.

Notes on the Learner's Book
Arrays (p17): encourage learners to label the arrays in different ways, both as repeated addition and as multiplication.

Check up!

Ask learners to draw you an array for three lots of two (2×3) or other multiples of two, five or ten.

More activities

Array Us (pairs)

You will need the *Array cards* photocopy master (CD-ROM).

Ask the learners to get into pairs and tell them to form arrays that match what you call out. Then call out multiplications such as, "2×5 or two, five times; 2×2, two, two times; 2×3, two, three times." Say it in different ways but remind the learners that they must stay in their pairs. Repeat for groups of five learners.

Games Book (ISBN 978110762349)

Multiplication grid (p12) is a game for two players. Learners practise multiplying two dice numbers together.

44 Blank page

Quick reference

Core activity 8.1: 2D shapes (Learner's Book p18)

Learners sort, name, describe, visualise and draw 2D shapes, referring to their properties. They can identify simple relationships between shapes and recognise common 2D shapes in different orientations.

Core activity 8.2: 3D shapes (Learner's Book p19)

Learners sort, name, describe and make 3D shapes, referring to their properties. They will also be able to recognise 2D drawings of 3D shapes.

Core activity 8.3: Symmetry (Learner's Book p20 and p21)

Learners identify reflective symmetry in patterns and 2D shapes.

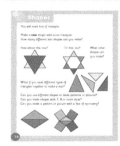

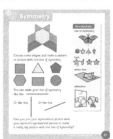

Prior learning	Objectives* – please note that listed objectives might only be partially covered within any given chapter but are covered fully across the book when taken as a whole
• Knowledge of different 2D shapes and some initial ideas of their properties. • Knowledge of different 3D shapes and initial ideas of their properties. • The beginnings of understanding simple relationships between shapes.	**1B: Geometry** (*Shapes and geometric reasoning*) 2Gs1 – Sort, name, describe, visualise and draw 2D shapes (e.g. squares, rectangles, circles, regular and irregular pentagons and hexagons) referring to their properties; recognise common 2D shapes in different positions and orientations. 2Gs2 – Sort, name, describe and make 3D shapes (e.g. cubes, cuboids, cones, cylinders, spheres and pyramids) referring to their properties, recognise 2D drawings of 3D shapes. 2Gs3 – Identify reflective symmetry in patterns and 2D shapes; draw lines of symmetry. 2Gs4 – Find examples of 2D and 3D shapes and symmetry in the environment. **1B: Problem solving** (*Using techniques and skills in solving mathematical problems*) 2Pt9 – Identify simple relationships between numbers and shapes, e.g. this number is double . . .; these shapes all have . . . sides.

*for NRICH activities mapped to the Cambridge Primary objectives, please visit www.cie.org.uk/cambridgeprimarymaths

Vocabulary

base • circular • cone • cube • cuboid • cylinder • hexagon • irregular • line of symmetry • octagon • pentagon • polygon • prism • pyramid • rectangular • reflective symmetry • regular • sphere • triangular

Core activity 8.1: 2D shapes

Resources: *2D shapes* photocopy master (p57); large version for class display. Examples of a regular pentagon, hexagon and octagon: prepare illustrations for class display. Six paper squares and a pair of scissors; per learner. *3, 4, 5, 6, 8 dice net* photocopy master (p59). Paper triangles. (Optional: Geoboards (also known as pinboards); elastic bands; Geostrips; straws or strips of paper; *Shape bingo grid* photocopy master (CD-ROM); *Shape bingo cards* photocopy master (CD-ROM) counters; *Shape snap* photocopy master (CD-ROM).)

Before the start of the session, prepare a regular pentagon, hexagon and octagon by cutting the same paper squares as used for the first activity (see below), and make sure you (and each learner) have six paper squares. Make the 3–8 dice and colour the blank face green.

Introducing pentagons, hexagons and octagons

Display both sides of the *2D shapes* photocopy master for the whole class to see.

Ask learners to identify triangles, circles, squares, rectangles and stars: "*How many circles can you see? Who can tell me the name of a shape that has three sides? What about four sides? Tell me something that is the same between a square and a rectangle. Tell me something that is different.*" Choose pairs of different shapes to compare and contrast.

Say, "*We're going to look at some different shapes today. What shape is this?*" Show one of the paper squares. "*Look carefully at what I'm going to do. I'm going to change this shape into a different one by cutting off one corner.*" Cut one corner off the square.

"*Let's count how many sides this new shape has: 1, 2, 3, 4, 5. It's now a five-sided shape. Does anyone know what that shape is called?*" If no one knows, say, "*This shape has five sides and five corners. It's called a pentagon. Any shape with five sides and five corners is a pentagon.*" Display the shape with its name written so that all of the class can see.

Start with another square. Cut one corner from the square and check that learners recognise it as a pentagon. Then cut the opposite corner from the square. "*How many sides does the shape have now? Count with me: 1, 2, 3, 4, 5, 6. It has six sides and six corners. Do you know what this shape is called?*" If no one knows say, "*This shape is called a hexagon. A hexagon has six sides and six corners.*"

Vocabulary

pentagon: a five-sided polygon.

hexagon: a six-sided polygon.

octagon: an eight-sided polygon.

regular: a shape that has all sides the same length and all angles the same size.

irregular: a shape that is not regular, i.e. lengths of sides are not all the same.

Display the hexagon with its name next to the pentagon.

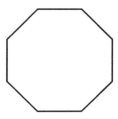

Ask, "*What do you think will happen if I cut off all four corners? How many sides do you think the shape will have? Tell the person next to you how many sides and corners the new shape will have.*" Collect some ideas from the class. Cut the corners from the square.

Say, "*Let's count the sides together: 1, 2, 3, 4, 5, 6, 7, 8. The shape has eight sides. Does anyone know what this shape is called?*" If no one knows, say, "*It's called an octagon. Any shape with eight sides and eight corners is an octagon.*"

Display the shape and its name with the other two shapes.

Say, "On your tables you have a set of squares and a pair of scissors each. I want you to start with a square and cut some corners so that you can show me a triangle, a square, a pentagon, a hexagon and an octagon; five different shapes. Your shapes can look different from others in your group but they must have the right number of sides and corners. You will need to think carefully before you make the cuts." Allow time for learners to make the shapes.

Review what they have learned by sharing the work done by the class and talking about similarities and differences between their cut shapes.

Introducing regular and irregular shapes

Return to the pentagon, hexagon and octagon that you made from cutting the squares, and make sure the *2D shapes* photocopy master is still on display. Hold up the shapes you made one at a time and introduce the idea of **regular** and **irregular** shapes. First, hold up one of the uncut squares and explain that a square is a regular shape because it has all four sides the same length and all four angles the same size. Then show the pentagon you made from cutting off a corner of the square and explain that **this** pentagon is an irregular pentagon because it has sides of different lengths and angles of different sizes. Compare it to the regular pentagon on the *2D shapes* photocopy master. Compare the irregular and regular versions of the hexagon and octagon.

Finish the session by playing a game with the 3, 4, 5, 6, 8 dice and the shapes from the session. Show the dice and explain that the green face means 'have another go'. Choose a learner to come and throw the dice and say the number thrown (e.g. 5). Then say, "*Who can tell me the name of a five-sided shape? How do you know? What else can you tell me about that shape?*" Repeat using different learners.

Look out for!

- Learners who cannot count accurately when counting the sides of a shape. *If they are finding it difficult suggest some strategies, such as colouring a corner, so that they know when they are back at the beginning.*
- Learners who can quickly and correctly finish the task. *Give these learners more experience of finding 2D shapes in context (e.g. in the classroom, in the playground) which they can share with the others. Ask them to find shapes that fit together (tessellate) and shapes that don't. Can they explain reasons for this? Use both regular and irregular shapes.*

Opportunity for display

Display the 2D shapes with their names and properties.

Summary

- Learners are able to sort, name, describe, visualise and draw 2D shapes, referring to their number of sides and angles, and identify simple relationships between shapes.
- They will also be able to recognise common 2D shapes in different positions and orientations and find examples of 2D shapes in the environment.

Notes on the Learner's Book

Shapes (p18): learners investigate how many new shapes can be made with a 2D shape. The activities require learners to develop reasoning and problem-solving skills, as well as apply what they know to find something they don't know. Give each learner some paper triangles for the activity.

Check up!

Hold up a series of squares, pentagons, hexagons and octagons of different proportions and shape (so that not all pentagons, for example, look the same). Then ask:
- *"What is this shape? How do you know?"*
- *"How can I make a pentagon from a square?"*
- *"How can I make a hexagon from a square?"*

Provide each group with a 3, 4, 5, 6, 8 dice, paper and pencils. Learners take turns to roll the dice and draw the 2D shape with the thrown number of sides. Some learners can also write the name of the shape.

More activities

Look see and say shapes (individual or groups)

> You will need Geoboards and elastic bands.

Geoboard

Use Geoboards and elastic bands to make shapes; name them and say something about them.

Make and share (group)

> You will need Geostrips, straws or paper strips.

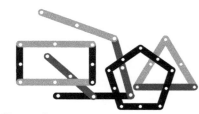

Give each group a different shape to work with. As a group, they work together to make a set of regular and irregular shapes.

Geostrips

Go on a 2D shape hunt (class)

Go on a shape hunt around your classroom, school or town. Look at road signs, square window panes, triangular roofs, round door knobs! Before you go, familiarise learners with the shapes you'll be looking for (e.g. circle, square, triangle, rectangle, pentagon and hexagon). You may want to take a camera, paper and pencil with you.

Shape bingo (individual)

> You will need the *Shape bingo grid* and *Shape bingo cards* photocopy master (CD-ROM).

A caller turns over the cards one a time, saying what is on the card and showing it to the players. Any player who has a matching picture covers it with a counter. The first to cover all their pictures calls out 'Bingo!' or 'House!' and wins the game.

Shape Snap (pairs)

You will need *Shape snap* photocopy master (CD-ROM).

Two players take it in turns to lay a card on the table, making a pile. If two cards match, the first player to say 'Snap!' collects the pile. Play continues until one player has collected all the cards, and is declared the winner.

Games Book (ISBN 9781107623491)

Shape match (p70) is a game for two to three players. This game looks at recognition of shape and uses memory and thinking.

Resources: *2D shapes* photocopy master (p57); large version for class display. Assemble a collection of packaging containers including a cylinder, cube, cuboid, cone, pyramid and sphere. *2D nets* photocopy master (page 60) and a pair of scissors for each learner. A roll of sticky tape for each group. *3D shapes* photocopy master (CD-ROM); prepare a large version for class display. (Optional: six sorting hoops; *1–9 digit cards* photocopy master (CD-ROM); a selection of 3D solids or building blocks (including two cubes, cones, cuboids, cylinders, pyramids and one sphere). 1–6 dice; a screen (e.g. a book); a box or bag to hold a selection of 3D solids.)

Before the start of the session, make name cards for the shape of each container you have. Use the *2D nets* photocopy master to make examples of the 3D shapes for each group and put a copy of the *2D nets* photocopy master on learners' table so that each learner has one. This session is designed to develop learners' spatial imagination through the construction of three-dimensional (3D) containers from two-dimensonal (2D) nets.

Show learners the containers. Say, *"I have lots of different packets, containers and boxes for you to look at. Who can tell me something about this one?"* Choose one of the containers and hold it so that the learners can see. Give time for discussion then ask, *"Do you know what we call the 'sides' in a 3D shape?"* (**Answer: edges**). *"How many edges can you see? How many corners? Do you know another word for corners?"* (**Answer: vertices**) *"Do you know another name for these flat parts?"* If no one knows, say, *"They are called faces."* (A face is a flat surface of a three-dimensional figure.) *"How many faces does this shape have? Does anyone know the name of this shape?"* Once the container has been named, place it on a table with a name card next to it.

Choose another container and repeat. Give learners opportunities to touch, feel and lift the containers. Can they tell you anything about them? Ask, *"Are they all the same? Are they all different? What is the same and what is different?"* Now relate the 3D containers/shapes to their 2D counterparts using the *2D shapes* photocopy master.

Say, *"On your table are some nets for you to cut out and make your own 3D shapes. You will need to cut on the solid lines and fold along the dotted lines very carefully."* Allow time for the class to make the nets of the solids (learners can look at your previously made examples to help them). Challenge more able learners to design their own net for a square, cylinder, cone or a sphere.

Vocabulary

circular: in the shape of a circle.

triangular: in the shape of a triangle.

rectangular: in the shape of a rectangle.

cuboid: a 3D shape with rectangular faces.

cube: a 3D shape with square faces; all six faces are the same-sized square.

polygon: any 2D shape with three or more straight sides.

base: bottom face of a 3D shape.

pyramid: a 3D shape with a polygon base and all other faces triangles, meeting at a corner (vertex).

sphere: a circular shape with one curved face, no edges and no corners (vertices).

cone: a 3D shape with a circular base and one corner (vertex).

prism: a 3D shape with two identical polygon bases, and the other faces are all rectangles.

cylinder: a prism with two circular bases.

Share what they did and what they found out. Ask, "*What was the most difficult shape to make? Why? What did you do to make it easier?*" If anyone made a cylinder, cone, or other nets of a cube, ask, "*What did you find out? Tell us what you did. How many different nets of a cube do you think there are?*" Then ask, "*Has anyone managed to make a sphere? Do you think it is possible? What could we use to show a sphere? A sphere is a three-dimensional object shaped like a ball. Every point on the surface is the same distance from the centre. Does that give you a clue?*"

Make a display of the solids made by the class as well as those brought into the classroom. Group them and label them according to their properties.

Display the *3D shapes* photocopy master and label the drawings of the 3D shapes as a class. Make sure learners are able to recognise 2D drawings of 3D shapes.

Summary

- Learners will be able to sort, name, describe and make 3D shapes, and be able to refer to their properties.
- They will also be able to recognise 2D drawings of 3D shapes.
- By using everyday opportunities in and out of the classroom, and within different lessons, they will be able to find examples of 3D shapes in the environment.

Notes on the Learner's Book
Look for faces (p19): uses knowledge and understanding of a basic 3D shape (the cube) and extends it to cover problem-solving within that shape. Each learner will need three cubes and a selection of other 3D shapes.

Opportunity for display

Create a display with common 3D shapes labelled; 2D drawings of 3D shapes and include models made by the class.

Check up!

Provide each group with a set of 3D shapes or building blocks and six sorting hoops labelled 1 to 6 using cards from the *1–9 digit cards* photocopy master, and a dice. Learners take turns to roll the dice and sort the shapes into the correct hoops according to their number of faces. For example, if they throw a 6, they find a shape with six faces and place it in the hoop numbered 6.

The game continues until all the shapes are sorted.

More activities

Block and build (pairs)

> You will need two cubes, cones, cuboids, cylinders, pyramids and a screen (e.g. a book).

Divide learners into pairs. Learner A builds a simple model behind a screen. Learner B then tries to create a copy of the model by following instructions from their partner. For example, *"Put a cube on the table. Put a cylinder on top of the cube. Put a cone on top of the cylinder."* When the model is complete, remove the screen and the learners can compare the models. Learner B then builds a model behind a screen and the activity is repeated.

See and say (class)

> You will need 3D solids in a bag or box.

Select the cone and display its flat, circular face to the class and ask if they can identify the shape. *"Can you be sure what this shape is? How do you know? Could it be anything else?"* More information may be needed. Show part of the curved side. *"How do you know that this is a cone and not a cylinder?"* Show the whole solid to confirm that it is a cone. Repeat for other 3D solids.

Grab and guess (group or class)

> You will need a pyramid, cube, cuboid, sphere, cone and cylinder in a bag or box.

Ask a learner to secretly choose a solid from the bag without showing or telling what it is. The rest of the group asks questions about the solid and its properties that need 'yes' or 'no' answers. (*"Is it round? Does it have corners?"*) The learner who correctly identifies the solid gets a turn to secretly choose a different one. Keep playing until all of the solids have been chosen.

Go on a 3D shape hunt (group or class)

A good way to teach learners about shapes is to go on a shape hunt around your classroom, school, neighbourhood or town. There are lots of shapes to be found, shapes are everywhere! Before going on your shape hunt, help familiarise the learners with the 3D shapes you'll be looking for. You may want to take a camera and paper and pencil with you.

Design and make nets for 3D shapes (individual, pairs, group, class)

How many different nets can be made for the different shapes?

Games Book (ISBN 9781107623491)

Shape match (p70) is a game for two or three players. This game looks at recognition of shape and uses memory and thinking.

Name that shape (p74) is a game for two players. This game involves travelling along a track, collecting and naming shapes.

Resources: Paper for folding – a large sheet for demonstration, and another sheet per learner. Three different colours of thick paint and six paint brushes (two per colour). Collect pictures of natural and man-made objects (or the objects themselves) – with and without a line of symmetry. A mirror, a pair of scissors, large squares of coloured paper, rulers and pencils; per learner. *2D shapes* photocopy master (p57). (Optional: *Make a robot helmet* photocopy master (CD-ROM); scissors; glue or sticky tape; crayons/colouring pencils/felt tips; *Make a wand* photocopy master (CD-ROM); a thin stick (e.g. ice lolly stick, pipe cleaner); 2 cm² paper; counters or tiles.)

Show the learners a large sheet of paper and whilst folding it in half say, "*I have an empty sheet of paper. I am going to fold this edge over to meet the opposite edge and then press down hard along the fold I have made.*" Open the paper out and ask, "*Can you see this folded line across the middle of the paper?*" Make sure that all the learners can see it. Say, "*Now I am going to put some paint on this side of the paper, fold it over again and carefully squash it flat.*" Open the paper again. "*Look at what has happened to the paint. What do you notice?*" Give time for the learners to share their ideas. Ask, "*What do you notice about the picture and the folded line?*"

Take another sheet of paper and ask a learner to come to the front of the class and fold it in half. Whilst the learner is folding, talk through the action to reinforce the new vocabulary. "*Take this edge and fold it over to meet the opposite edge. Press down hard along the fold. Now open the paper and what can you see?*" Choose a different learner to put some paint on one side of the paper. "*Fold the paper in half and press gently. Open the paper.*"
Ask, "*Who can tell me what they think **reflective symmetry** is?*"

Ask the learners to look at the picture and talk to the person next to them. Give time for discussion and take feedback.

Use the positive points from the feedback from several learners to make the definition of symmetry. "***Something has reflective symmetry if it has a mirror image on each side of the line of symmetry. We say that something with reflective symmetry is 'symmetrical'.***" Then explain that, "*The line of symmetry is a straight line that splits a pattern/object/shape into two patterns/objects/shapes that are the mirror image of each other.*" Explain how the fold in the sheet of paper is the line of symmetry for the patterns they have been making. If necessary, explain what is meant by **mirror image**.

Vocabulary

reflective symmetry: when one half of a pattern/object/shape is a mirror image of the other half.

line of symmetry: a straight line that splits a pattern/object/shape into two halves that are mirror images of each other.

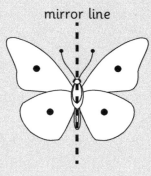

mirror line

Say, "*On your tables are some paints and sheets of paper. Make your own symmetrical paint patterns. See how many different ones you can make. You can change the colours or change where you put the paint. Remember to fold the paper carefully and rub it gently before you open it out.*" Give time for two or three patterns to be completed per learner.

Ask, "*What did you think about your symmetrical patterns? Were you surprised by how they turned out? Were you able to predict what they would look like?*"

Now say, "*Let's look at some other symmetrical things and see if we can find the line of symmetry.*" Show the learners your collection of pictures of natural and man-made symmetrical objects (or the objects themselves), and ask the learners to tell or show you where the line of symmetry is.

Then show the pictures (or objects) that have no line of symmetry. Ask, "*How do we know they are not symmetrical?*" Divide the pictures or objects into two sets or groups, one for those that show symmetry and one for those that do not. Label them 'symmetrical' and 'not symmetrical'.

Return to the *2D shapes* photocopy master from Core activity 8.1. Ask learners to identify the lines of symmetry in these shapes.

Look for symmetry in the classroom (e.g. door handles) and outside (e.g. leaves).

Summary

Learners are able to identify reflective symmetry in patterns and 2D shapes and draw lines of symmetry in their own patterns or pictures.

Notes on the Learner's Book

Paper flowers (p20): is a practical activity to make a symmetrical flower.
Symmetry (p21): is a practical activity that gives learners the opportunity to design their own symmetrical patterns using common 2D shapes. Learners will require paper, pencils, small round plates, scissors and a selection of 2D shapes.

Look out for!

- Learners who have difficulty recognising a line of symmetry. *Give more practice in folding, marking in the line of symmetry (fold line) with a pencil. Use a mirror along that line to show the complete paint pattern.*
- Learners who easily spot a single line of symmetry. *Use the lines in different orientations (vertical, horizontal, diagonal) and use squares to make a pattern along that line, or use two lines of symmetry.*

Opportunity for display

Use the paint pictures the class made.

Check up!

Give each learner a large square of coloured paper, scissors and a mirror. Each learner halves their square (in any direction) and, beginning on the fold line, cuts a random shape through both layers of paper. They then open the paper and draw the line of symmetry.

More activities

Make a robot helmet (individual)

> You will need the *Make a robot helmet* photocopy master (CD-ROM), scissors, crayons/colouring pencils/felt tips and paper.

Learners decorate their helmets then cut out the shaded rectangles to make eye holes. They should cut an extra strip of paper and stick this to the tabs by the ears to make the helmet the right size for each learner's head. Some learners may be able to work in pairs and fit the helmet for their partner. Talk about the shapes that can be seen and discuss things that they notice (same one side as the other, symmetrical, line of symmetry.)

Make a wand (individual)

> You will need the *Make a wand* photocopy master (CD-ROM), scissors, crayons/colouring pencils/felt tips and paper.

Learners use crayons to decorate the star, then use glue or tape to attach the star to one end of a thin stick. Discuss the pattern on the star. What do they notice? Is each part the same or are they different? What is the same? What is different? Discuss the shapes on the star. Some may notice that the pattern is the same on each star but one is upside down. What happens when you fold it along the line of symmetry? Do the patterns match now? You can use a mirror to show reflection. Some learners may like to make their own design for a symmetrical star.

What will it be? (individual)

> You will need a square sheet of paper and a pair of scissors.

Fold a square in half and cut a random shape through both layers Open the square and place a mirror along the line of symmetry so that the whole symmetrical shape can be seen.

Matching the shapes (individual or pair)

> You will need 2 cm² paper and counters or tiles.

Learners make their own symmetrical patterns.

Plant a garden (class)

Make a grid to represent a garden. Draw pairs of pictures of plants/flowers to be placed in the garden. Draw a line of symmetry down or across the grid. For more able learners, use two lines of symmetry so that they are working in all four quadrants. Choose a learner to pick the first thing for the garden and place it in one section of the grid. Choose another learner to place an identical picture in its symmetrical place in the garden. For less confident learners, do this as group work so that each group can discuss the position before it is placed. Keep filling the garden until all of the pictures have gone. Ask the learners for other ideas for symmetrical places.

Games Book (ISBN 9781107623491)

Collect and build shapes (p76) is a game for two to four players. This game gives practice in, and development of, understanding of reflective symmetry in patterns. *The symmetry game* (p78) is a game for two players. This game focuses on developing patterns with reflective symmetry with one or two lines of symmetry.

2D shapes

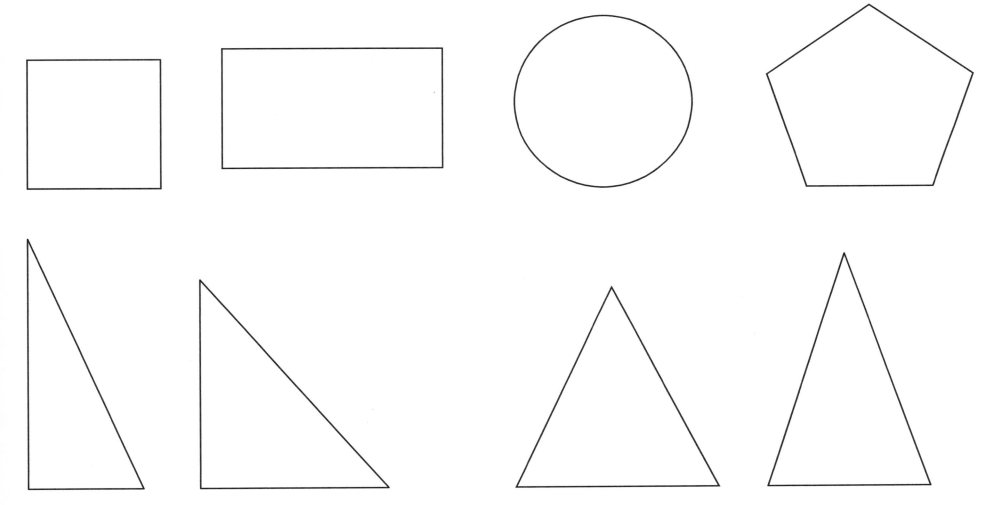

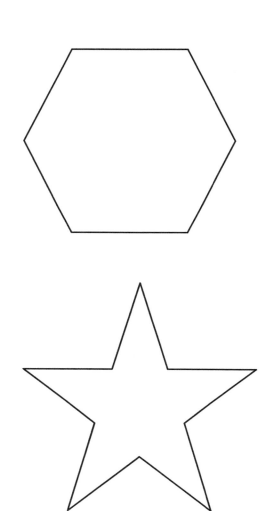
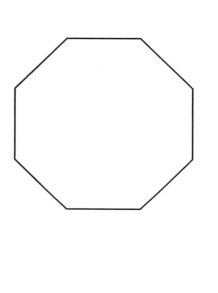

3, 4, 5, 6, 8 dice net

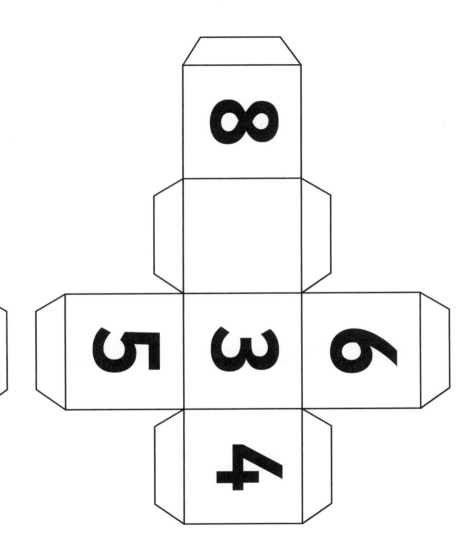

2D nets

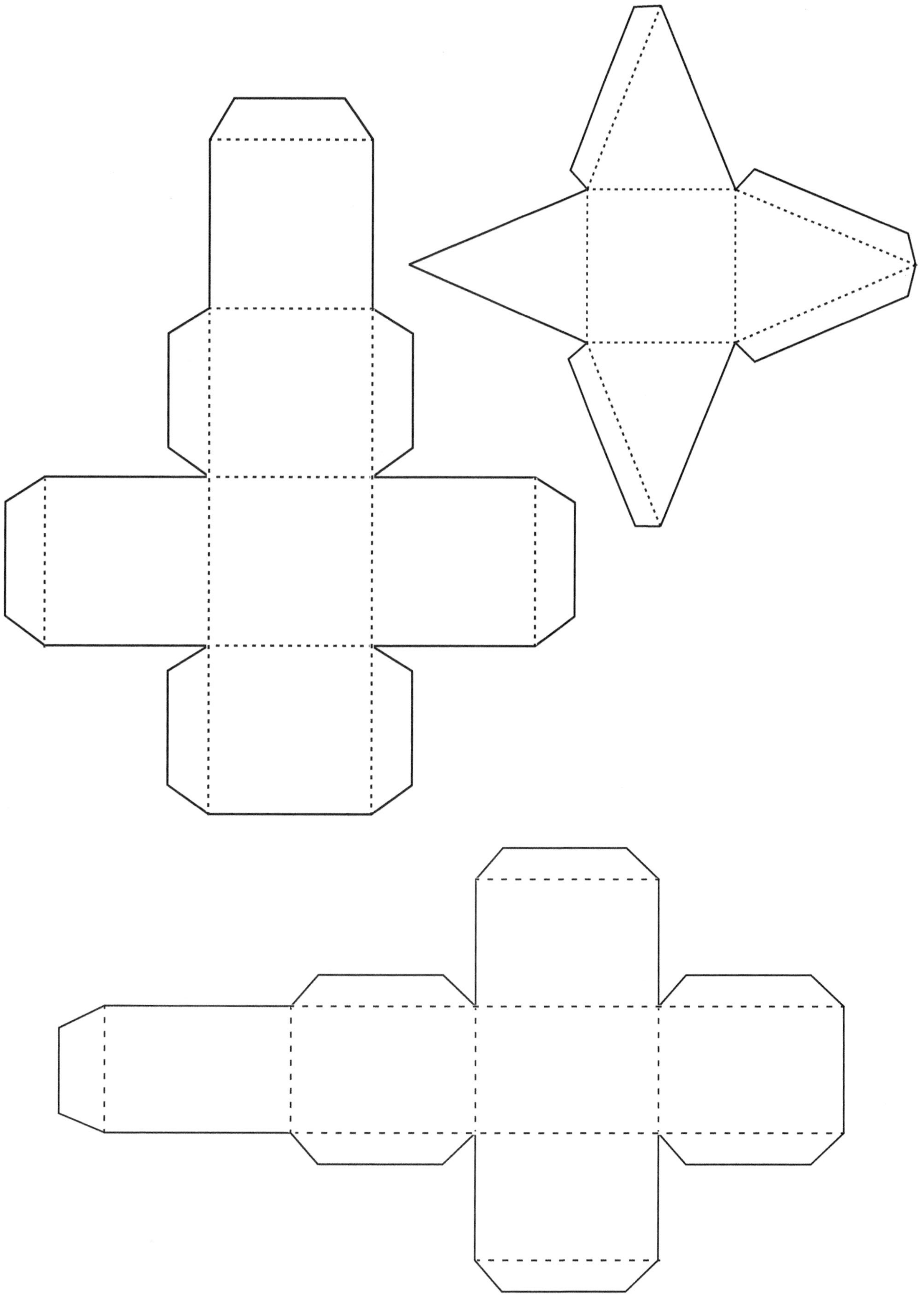

Instructions on page 50

Quick reference

Core activity 9.1: Making a box (Learner's Book p22)
Learners investigate standard and non-standard units of measurement, they then practise by making a box to fit a cuddly toy using metric units.

Core activity 9. 2: Measuring distance (Learner's Book p23)
Learners investigate standard and non-standard units in the measurment of distance. They then practise this by measuring the distance cars reach after rolling down a slope.

Core activity 9. 3: Making mobiles (Learner's Book p24)
Learners investigate lengths and balance. They practise this by making mobiles.

Prior learning	Objectives* – please note that listed objectives might only be partially covered within any given chapter but are covered fully across the book when taken as a whole
• Knowledge of previous associated vocabulary. • Knowledge and understanding of comparison of length.	**1A: Number** (*Numbers and the number system*) 2Nn1 – Count, read and write numbers to at least 100 and back again. 2Nn9 – Say a number between any given neighbouring pairs of multiples of 10 e.g. 40 and 50. **1A: Problem solving** (*Using techniques and skills in solving mathematical problems*) 2Pt2 – Explain methods and reasoning orally. 2Pt3 – Explore number problems and puzzles.

*for NRICH activities mapped to the Cambridge Primary objectives, please visit www.cie.org.uk/cambridgeprimarymaths

Vocabulary
about • balance • centimetre • further • furthest • mobile • tape measure

Resources: One soft/cuddly toy per pair of learners. Five or six boxes for storing single toys. Per pair of learners: large sheets paper, scissors, sticky tape, cubes, pencils, rulers (15 or 30 cm with mm markings) and tape measures. (Optional: range of containers; cubes; paper/card; sticky tape.)

Show learners the soft toys and the empty boxes that they will fit into.

Say, "*All of the toys have fallen out of their box. We need to fit them back in.*" Hold up one of the toys and choose a learner to come to the front of the class. Ask, "*Which box do you think this toy will fit into? Try it and see.*" Wait for the learner to fit the toy into a box. "*What do the rest of you think? Is the box about the right size? Is it long enough. Is it wide enough?*" Allow a short amount of time for discussion. Then say, "*We'll leave it in this box for now, but we can change it to a different box later if we need to.*"

Repeat with the other toys. Then say, "*Now all of the toys are in their boxes. Do you want to change any of them to a different box? Why? Which would you like to change?*" Allow time for any changes, always asking about the reasons for the change. Encourage use of vocabulary such as 'longer than', 'shorter than', 'wider than', 'taller than' 'about the same as', 'just over', 'just under', etc. that they will have learned in Stage 1.

Each pair of learners is given a soft toy, a large sheet of paper, a pair of scissors and some sticky tape. Explain the next task. "*Work with a partner to make a box that your soft toy will fit into.*" Learners should start to understand that in order to make a box to fit their toy, they need to measure their toy (width and height) and use this information to inform their box-making.

Explain, "*You have only one piece of paper for you and your partner. You don't have to use it all, but you can't have any more. You will need to think about how you are going to measure the toy and the paper. You can use cubes, pencils, rulers, a tape measure or anything else that you think might help you measure. Talk to your partner while you are working and help each other to measure and make decisions.*" While the pairs are working, walk round the room and ask, "*How are you going to tackle this? What equipment do you think you will need?*" As work progresses change the questions to, "*Can you explain what you have done so far? Could there be a quicker way to do this?*"

Vocabulary

about: a rough guess, e.g. there are about 50 marbles in the jar.

tape measure: a device for measuring long distances.

centimetre: a metric unit of measurement.

As this is a very individual activity, and learners work at their own level, there may be wide differences in the understanding of the word 'box' plus the ability to make one. All 'boxes' should be accepted, as each pair were given the task to make their own decisions, and the similarities, differences and discussion following the activity will help those who may have had misconceptions.

Each pair must check the size of their box and compare it against their soft toy. Ask, "*What do you think about the size of your box? Is it the right length/width/height for your toy?*"

Give time for the pairs to share what they have done and what they found out with another pair.

Ask, "*Can you tell us what you did? What did you use to measure? Did anyone use a metre stick? Why not?*"(**Answer: too big against the boxes so inappropriate**). "*If you were doing it again would you do it the same or would you do it differently? Why?*"

Use the finished models to make a display and talk about the similarities and differences. Below are some examples of how varied the boxes can be:

Explain that so far they have used uniform non-standard units to measure length and that these are things such as: cubes, pencils, hand span, etc. that are useful but are not very accurate.

Explain that sometimes it is important to measure length more accurately. Say that, in order to compare the lengths of objects worldwide, we need a standard way of measuring that is the same everywhere. Ask, "*Why might we need a standard unit of measurement?*" Explain that if an object is made in one country but sold for use in other countries we need to make sure that measurements are the same in both countries, otherwise the object might not fit in the ship transporting it, or in the warehouse storing it in the destination country. Therefore, we have standard units of measurements that are used worldwide, that everyone can understand.

Ask, "*Can you think of other examples where accurate measurements are important?*" Take answers from the class and discuss. Possible suggestions might include: making sure clothes fit properly; making sure car parking spots are big enough; making sure seats on buses are wide enough to seat one/two people. Say, "*The standard units of measurement that we are going to use are called 'metric units' and include the centimetre.*"

Give pairs of learners a 15 or 30 cm ruler with centimetre and millimetre markings. Spend some time explaining the markings, what they mean and what the distance between them is. Now ask them to measure their box and their toy again, this time using a ruler. Ask again, "*What do you think about the size of your box? Is it the right length/width/height for your toy?*" If any learners change their opinion about their box, discuss the reasons why and reinforce the importance of accurate measuring.

Summary

- Learners have estimated, measured and compared lengths using suitable uniform non-standard and standard units and appropriate measuring instruments.
- They are able to compare lengths, using standard units (blocks, cubes) and centimetres, and can explain methods and reasoning orally.

Notes on the Learner's Book
Best box? (p22): gives opportunities to develop the idea of length and width by investigating ways of packing cubes; finding the best way to hold cubes using packing in a random as well as a measured way. Learners will need cubes and boxes (e.g. ice cream box, shoe box etc.) Boxes per learner or pair of learners must be the same size.

Check up!
Ask:
- "*Is this the right length for this toy?*"
- "*Is it too long or too short?*"
- "*Is it wide enough or too narrow?*"
- "*Is it just about right?*"

More activities

Which container? (pairs, group or class)
Using containers and classroom equipment, ask the learners to put an object, or a number of objects, into a suitable box or container.

Find a box for 20 cubes (pairs, group or class)

> You will need 20 cubes, suitable containers.

Allow the learners to arrange 20 cubes in any way they like. Investigate different ways, e.g. 10×2, 4×5. Find or make different boxes to hold each different array. Ask, "*Is this the right length? Is it too long/too short? Is it wide enough or too narrow? Is it just about right?*"

Make a box to hold 17 cubes (pairs, group or class)

> You will need 17 cubes, suitable containers/material to make containers.

Which will use the least amount of paper/card? As this is a prime number, there will only be one regular array (1 × 17) but a learner may decide to make a cylinder or a pyramid. Allow discussion both before and after the construction and ask questions such as, "*Was this easy or difficult? What made it difficult? What did you do about any problems you had? If I asked you to do it again would you change anything? Why?*"

Games Book (ISBN 9781107623491)

Snakes and ladders (p47) is a game for two to four players. This game looks at length as part of measures. Players collect card and make their own snakes. But watch out for the snakes on the board!

Resources: Toy vehicles (learners can bring in their own); there should be a good mix of size and weight in order to demonstrate different distances travelled. Material to make a slope such as wood or heavy card; bricks, blocks or piles of books to support the slopes. Standard measures (metre rules/ sticks and 15 or 30cm rulers with mm markings). Non-standard measures (tape measures, string, wool, strips of paper). Timers (stopwatches, sand timers etc.). (Optional: construction or modelling materials; range of materials for covering slopes – wood, plastic, carpet; selection of other toys – balls, tins, beads, marbles; paper.)

The learners need to see, feel and pick up the toy vehicles in order to have a clear impression that they are of different sizes and weights. Say, "*Look at the collection of vehicles. Let me put one of them on the floor. Will it go along the floor on its own? Why not?*" Encourage discussion about the need for some force (pushing) in order to make the vehicle move.

Choose two learners to come to the front of the class. Say, "*Choose one vehicle each and put it on the floor. When I say, 'go', I want you to gently push your vehicle and then let go.*" Demonstrate if necessary. Ask, "*Which vehicle went the furthest? How can you check this?* **(Answer: learners should suggest checking by sight, or if they are close together then by measuring the distance that each car moved).**

Ask a couple of learners, one at a time, to measure the distance using a measure of their choice. If none of the learners use a standard measure, ask another learner to make the same measurement using a ruler. Once you have confirmed that one vehicle did go a longer distance, ask, "*Why do you think that happened?*" (Was it pushed harder by one learner? Does one 'feel' heavier than the other?)

"*Do you think this is a fair test for looking at the distance the vehicles move? Why not?*" Discussion should bring out the fact that the strongest push went the longest distance so in order to compare vehicles you need the same force to be acting on them; that it is difficult to measure the difference exactly as each learner might have let go of the car at a slightly different starting point.

"*We need to find a way to make it fair. Let's see if this helps.*" Using a learner to help you, construct a gentle slope where the vehicles can be placed at the top, with the back wheels flush with the start of the slope, and then released. Choose two learners to demonstrate to

Vocabulary

further: the biggest distance, e.g. 'My car has gone further than yours.'

furthest: the most far away, 'My car has gone the furthest.'

weight: how much matter there is in an object, i.e. how heavy or light it is.

estimate: a sensible guess of something, e.g. distance, length etc.

Look out for!

- Learners who are not able to compare distances, measure accurately using standard measures or use correct mathematical vocabulary. *Use other resources to measure and compare distances such as string, wool, strips of paper, hand spans. Use them against centimetres to make the connection.*

- Learners who are able to effectively and efficiently use the measures asked of them. *Introduce a different type of measure such as time. Which car was the fastest/slowest to reach a certain point? Supply stopwatches or sand timers as accurate measures, or counting rhythmically as a non-standard measure. Look for standard ways of recording the results.*

the rest of the class. "*What do you think about this? Is it a fair way to test the distance that the cars will travel?*" Ensure learners understand that this is a more fair way, provided that the slope used is always the same, and that the car is released (not pushed) from the same point at the top of the slope each time.

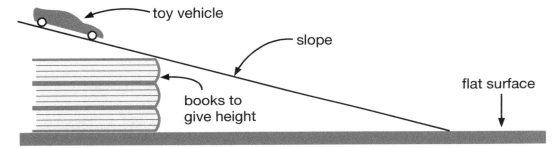

Explain that each group is to build their own slope and test their cars. "*Each group will need a slope, and each person in the group will need a vehicle. First estimate which vehicle will travel the longest distance and explain your reasons. Then find out which of your vehicles goes furthest. You need to choose what you want to use to measure the distance. You will need to find a way to record what you have found out so that you can share it at the end of the session.*" Make sure that all the groups understand the task and have found a way to record their results. At a suitable point in the lesson ask, "*I wonder what would happen if you made the slope steeper by adding more [books/ bricks etc]. Do you think the vehicle would go further or not? Try it and see. Keep a record of what happens as well as the height of the top of the slope.*"

Before the session ends, gather the learners together with their findings. Choose some of the groups to tell the others what they did and what they found out. Use the records of the learners findings as part of a display with the vehicles. "*What did you use to measure the distance? Did you all use the same thing? Were your estimates correct? Why?*"

Now say, "*In your group, take it in turns to hold the vehicle that went the furthest in one hand and the vehicle that went the shortest distance in the other hand. What do you notice?*" Learners should spot that the vehicles that 'feel' the heaviest (by comparison) were the ones that went furthest; some more capable learners might even be able to explain why (**Answer: gravity is a force acting on weight**). Ask learners to put their vehicle next to either a 'Heavy' or 'Light' label in a display area. They can also be re-sorted into 'went the furthest', 'went the shortest'.

Opportunity for display

Learners' vehicles with their recording.

Follow with a discussion about the vehicles that were heaviest/travelled the longest distance. Did it always happen that the heavy vehicles went the furthest?

You can extend the activity by asking the learners to measure the weight of each vehicle.

Summary

- Learners are able to estimate, measure and compare lengths using suitable uniform non-standard and standard units and appropriate measuring instruments.
- They will also be able to compare lengths, using the standard units: centimetres, metres, and are increasingly able to explain their methods orally.

Check up!

Ask:
- *"How far has this car travelled?"*
- *"Which car travelled the furthest?"*
- *"Would you use a metre stick, 30 cm ruler or 15 cm ruler to measure the distance this car travelled? Why?"*

Notes on the Learner's Book
How long? How high? (p23): gives opportunities to develop the ideas by investigating how we move – both inside and outside the classroom – first using estimation, and then more accurate measurements. This gives practice with using estimates of length and deciding whether the estimated answer was reasonable.

More activities

Testing, testing (individual or pairs)

> You will need construction or junk modelling materials.

Learners make their own vehicles and test them for stopping distance using a slope. The finished models can then be placed in the display area.

Slip or slide? (individual, pairs or group)

> You will need a toy car and ramps made of different materials.

What happens on a ramp made or covered with wood, plastic, water, carpet, snow, ice, sand … ? Which surface allows the car to go the furthest? What's the difference in length between the car that goes the furthest and the car that goes the least distance?

And the winner is … ? (individual, pairs or group)

> You will need toys: balls, tins, beads and marbles and slopes.

Vary the angle of the slope and the length of the slope.

Guess and go (individual, pairs or group)
Learners stand next to each other (in a PE lesson or in the playground) and put a piece of paper in front of them as an estimate of how far they can jump. 1 – 2 – 3 go! All jump at the same time! Who was closest to their estimate? Who jumped the furthest? How far did each person jump?

Games Book (ISBN 9781107623491)

Rally track (p51) is a game for two to four players. In order to finish, this game gives players opportunities to make decisions and to reason, using the language of measures.

Core activity 9.3: Making mobiles

Resources: To make a mobile you will need: rulers, pencils or other straight, rigid items (one per pair), light items to hang on mobiles (two per pair), scissors (per pair); string or thread, sticky tape (per pair) and balance scales.

Begin the session by discussing what a mobile is and the learners' understanding of a mobile. Show a mobile that you have. Ask, *"Does anyone know what this is called? Does anyone have anything like this at home?"* Collect learners' ideas. Ask, *"What is special about a mobile? Look at what is on this end and look at what is on the other end, then look carefully at the arm that they are hanging on."*

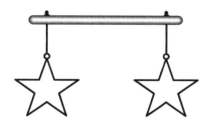

Say, *"The arm across is very straight and we can see that the two things that are hanging will* **balance**. *What does balance mean? What do we know about the two objects if they balance?*

Draw out that 'balance' is where there is the same weight on each side so that the arm is flat/horizontal. Ask several learners to hold the two objects on either side of the mobile, so that there is one in each hand, and using 'comparison' confirm that they seem to be the same weight.

Now ask, *"What do you notice about the distance from the top of each string holding the object and the centre of the arm?"* Allow time for discussion with a partner and then class feedback. Learners should say that it looks as though the tops of the strings holding the objects are about the same distance (horizontally) from the centre of the arm. Invite learners to measure the distance using a suitable method, to confirm that they are the same distance from the centre of the arm.

Vocabulary

mobile: mobiles are free-moving, hanging sculptures.

balance: an even distribution of weight.

Move the string from one end closer to the centre. Say, "*If I move this string closer to the middle, look and see what happens. What did you notice?*"

Moving the first string closer towards the middle should mean that one object hangs lower than the other, so that they are no longer balanced.

"*What do you think will happen if I move the other string to the same distance away from the middle but on the other side?*" Move the other string closer to the middle until the arm is flat/level again. Learners should see that they balance again. Ask a learner to check.

Say that the two objects balance because: they are the same weight; the top of the string is the same (horizontal) distance from the centre of the arm.

Ask, "*What do you think would happen if I replaced one of the hanging objects with a heavier object?*" Learners should agree that the arm would no longer be balanced and would tip downwards with the heavier object. Ask, "*How could I make them balance again without changing the objects?*" Allow time for learners to pose suggestions and try them out together. Either through trial and improvement, or your direction, demonstrate that you can make a heavier object balance with a lighter object by moving the top of the string holding the heavier object closer to the middle of the arm. Encourage estimation, then trial and improvement to reduce the distance from the top of the string to the centre of the arm until the arm balances again.

Explain that learners are going to make their own mobiles. "*You are going to work in pairs to make your own mobile. You will need to think about what you are going to use as the balance arm. You could use a ruler, or a pencil or anything else that is straight and won't bend. You will also need to think about what you want to hang and where to fix the top of the string. How will you check this? What will you do if it doesn't balance?*" Learners work in pairs to make a simple mobile. There may be some problems making them balance but 'trial and improvement' methods should be encouraged rather than giving the answer.

Gather the class together to end the session. Choose several pairs of learners to stand at the front of the class to show the mobiles they made. Choose one from each pair to share what

Look out for!

- Learners who could not make their mobile balance, and learners who did not make accurate measurements. *Reinforce the meaning of balance by using balance scales.*
- Learners able to make a mobile that balanced and also understand the effect of moving the string closer to or further away from the point of balance? *Encourage them to make a mobile with more than one level.*

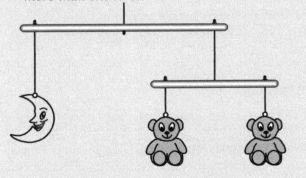

Opportunity for display

Find a space where the mobiles can be hung

they did and what they found out. "*Can you tell us what you did? Can you explain why it works? What could you try next? Would it work with different weights? How did you check the distance of the top of the string from the middle of the arm? What have you learned or found out today? If you were doing it again, what would you do differently? Why?*"

Summary

- Learners compare lengths, using the standard units, direct comparison or centimetres.
- Learners are able to explain methods and reasoning orally.

Notes on the Learner's Book
Mobiles (p24): can be used to guide and reinforce the activity.

Check up!
"*If one end of your mobile is lower than the other end, how can you make it balance? How can you measure the distance of the top of the string from the middle of the arm?*"

More activities

Grow and grow (individual, pairs or group)

> You will need rulers, pencils, items to hang on mobiles, string, sticky tape and balance scales.

Make a new hanging mobile toy. Make it balance then add one more piece to it. See what happens. Adjust it so that it balances.
Write or draw instructions for someone else to make your mobile. What would you use to make a mobile for a baby, a mobile for an adult?

Challenge! (pairs)

> You will need rulers, pencils, items to hang on mobiles, string, sticky tape and balance scales.

What's the largest number of hanging pictures/objects you can put on your mobile so that it still balances. Work with a partner.
Draw or write how you made your mobile so that others can follow your instructions. Include some helpful hints. What did you find difficult and what did you do about it?

Quick reference

Core activity 10.1: Measuring time (Learner's Book p25)
Learners get more experience of measuring the passage of time in the context of a race; they also touch on linear measurement and handling data (recording).

Core activity 10. 2 Measuring distance (Learner's Book p26)
Learners measure distance in the context of throwing a bean bag; they also record and organise data.

Core activity 10. 3 Measuring height (Learner's Book p27)
Learners investigate how high they can jump. They make sense of the problem, discuss ways of solving it, collect and analyse data and measure height.

Prior learning	Objectives* – please note that listed objectives might only be partially covered within any given chapter but are covered fully across the book when taken as a whole
<ul><li>Knowledge and understanding of data collection and representation. This means making a recording in the learner's own way, using a method that makes sense to that learner/ group.</li><li>Some experience of measuring length, height and time.</li><li>Knowledge of basic vocabulary linked to measures and data handling.</li></ul>	**1C: Measure** (*Time*) 2Mt1 – Know the units of time (seconds, minutes, hours, days, weeks, months and years). 2Mt2 – Know the relationships between consecutive units of time. 2Mt4 – Measure activities using seconds and minutes. **2B: Organising, categorising and representing data** 2Dh1 – Answer a question by collecting and recording data in lists and tables, and representing it as block graphs and pictograms to show results. **1C: Problem solving** (*Using techniques and skills in solving mathematical problems*) 2Pt2 – Explain methods and reasoning orally. 2Pt5 – Make up a number story to go with a calculation, including in the context of money.

*for NRICH activities mapped to the Cambridge Primary objectives, please visit www.cie.org.uk/cambridgeprimarymaths

Vocabulary
clock/watch • close • distance • far • faster • fastest • height • high • higher • metre (*m*) • metre stick • minute • near • quick • quicker • quickest • quickly • fast • ruler • second • shortest • slow • slower • slowest • slowly • tall • timer • longest

Core activity 10.1: Measuring time

LB: p25

> **Resources:** Small (sports) bean bag; one per group. Stopwatch and alternative instruments to measure time such as a cooking timer, sand timer, an analogue clock with a minute hand. (Optional: *Time* photocopy master (CD-ROM) obstacles for an obstacle course.)

Allocate a different time-measuring instrument to each group. In a suitable space, measure three metres and mark the start and end for learners to walk along. The main aim of this session is to get more experience of measuring the passage of time, but it will also include handling data (recording).

Ask learners if they remember the one minute challenge from Stage 1 (Unit 2C, chapter 18). Remind them that one minute is a unit of time, and is equal to 60 seconds. It can be recorded using sand timers, an analogue clock with a minute hand; an analogue stopwatch; a digital stopwatch and so on. Show the learners the various time-measuring instruments you have and make sure they understand how they all work. Explain that they will be doing an activity that requires them to record time in minutes and seconds.

Introduce the idea of a Sports Day. "*Who has taken part in an egg and spoon race? Who has taken part in a three-legged race? These are some typical examples of silly races in a sports day.*" Then say, "*We're going to do a 'bean bag balance' race.*" Ask learners about their understanding and knowledge of the word 'balance'; this should be fresh from the session in chapter 9 on mobiles (p70).

Choose a learner to come to the front of the class and balance a bean bag on their head. "*You need to keep very still while it balances on your head. Is it easy? What if I asked you to walk with it on your head? Try that.*" Make sure there is some space for the learner to walk safely. "*Was it easy to keep it on your head when you were walking? Did you walk fast or slowly? Why?*" Choose some other learners to do the same. Learners should establish that the faster they walk the more likely the bean bag is to lose balance and fall off their head.

Introduce the group activity. "*I want you to take turns walking with the bean bag on your head. While you are doing that, someone else in the group will time how long it takes for you to get from the start to the finish. You will all walk a set distance marked out on the floor. If the bean bag falls off you must stand still while you put it back on your head, then carry on walking. You will need to keep a record of each person's time. In your groups you must decide how you will do that and how you will record it.*"

If required, you might find it useful to revise time using the *Time* photocopy master.

Look out for!

Learners who need support with measuring length and measuring time. *Make sure another learner can work alongside them for support.*

Opportunity for display

Develop a 'Sports day' display. Put on a table the stopwatches or timers and other resources that measure time, such as sand timers and clocks. Take photos of the learners as they are doing the challenge.

As the groups are working move around the room answering any questions the learners may have. Check that they understand the task and that they have found a way of recording the time.

When each member of the group has finished, gather the class together with their recordings. Choose a group to share what they did and what they found out. Ask, "*What instrument did you use to measure the time? Did anyone walk very quickly? Did anyone take a very long time? What was the time difference between the slowest and fastest? Was it easy to measure?*" Choose other groups to share.

Discuss the different ways of recording the time taken. Then ask, "*Who was the fastest in the class? Who was the slowest?*" Ask each learner, "*How did your group measure the time it took to walk the distance?*" Find out if the methods used were the same (making the measures fair to compare) or if they used vastly different methods (making it less fair to compare). "*Which method was more accurate? Why?*" **(Answer: learners should understand that a stopwatch measures time precisely in minutes, and seconds and therefore is more accurate than say a sand timer, where the user has to estimate if half a minute has passed, or a third of a minute etc.)**

Summary

- Learners use their knowledge and understanding of units of time to measure activities using seconds and minutes.
- Learners answer questions by collecting and recording data, explaining their methods and reasoning orally.

Notes on the Learner's Book

Measuring time (p25): provides examples of recording time using a sand timer, analogue stopwatch and digital stopwatch. Learners are asked to read the time in minutes and seconds from the various time-measuring instruments. The first section introduces the idea of using tallies to record the number of minutes using timers such as sand timers and analogue stopwatches that only measure to one minute.

Check up!

Give each learner a different instrument to measure time, making sure that there is a variety of different types across the classroom. Then ask learners to time you as you do various activities such as clapping, jumping, hopping, holding a single song note. Ask learners what time they recorded and discuss any discrepancies between learners' results and why they might have occurred.

More activities

More sports (pairs or group)

You will need a stopwatch, obstacles for obstacle course.

How long can you stand on one leg? How many hops on one leg can you do in 30 seconds/one minute?
Learners work in pairs or small groups to set up specific time and distance challenges for the class (Olympic type activities). Use league tables to sort the results.
Set up a simple obstacle course; time and record the completion times.
How far can you run round the playground/field in 30 seconds/one minute?

Core activity 10.2: Measuring distance

> **Resources:** Rulers and tape measures. Each group should have a set of different coloured bean bags and a metre stick. (Optional: various balls for throwing.)

This session is best done in a hall or outside.

Remind learners of the standard units for measuring distance and length they used in an earlier session (chapter 9). Explain that another metric unit of measurement is a metre, and this contains 100 centimetres. 50 centimetres is half a metre. Metres can be measured using metre sticks/rules or tape measures. They could also be measured by using a 15/30 cm ruler but this would not be as accurate.

Say, "*During our last session, we balanced a bean bag on our head. This time we're going to look at how far we can throw a bean bag. How many* [strides or table lengths or other non-uniform measure] *do you think you could throw the bean bag? How many metres and centimetres do you think this is? Talk to the person next to you and tell them what you think.*"

Divide the learners into groups and explain the task. "*You will each have a bean bag to throw as far as you can. You must all start at the same place. You will need to measure how far you threw the bean bag. How could you do that? Talk to the person next to you and find a way to measure that distance.*" Leave a few minutes for discussion. Then take feedback and address any issues that might cause problems when measuring. Some ideas may be: using strides/paces, using a ruler, using a metre stick, using a tape measure; measuring from the tip of the person's toes whilst they stand there; putting a marker in place of the end of their toes etc.

Say, "*Estimate how far you think you can throw the bean bag using the units of your chosen measuring instrument. You will have to keep a record of the distances that the bean bags have been thrown. In your groups you will need to decide how that is going to be done and who is going to do it.*" Encourage learners to use their own methods of recording rather than a single standard method. The methods might include: drawings, written lists, diagrams or graphs that they have met during previous teaching.

While the learners are working, walk around and answer any questions they may have. Check that they understand the task and that they have found a way of recording distance.

Look out for!

- Learners who may need extra help to measure and read measurements accurately. *Place these learners in groups where there are others who can support them. As the recording is done at the learner's own level of understanding and knowledge this should not present a problem.*
- Learners who find the task easy and can measure and record accurately. *Ask them to collate all the results for the class and design a league table to show the results.*

Opportunity for display

Add to the 'Sports day' display using photos and linear measurement resources. Use the learners' recordings as part of the display These can be put in a folder or a book if there is limited wall space. Use data from previous Olympic events to compare and contrast achievements in different events

When each group has finished, gather the learners together with their recordings. Choose a group to share what they did and what they found out.

Ask, "*Were there any surprises in your group? Did anyone throw the bean bag a long way? What was the longest throw? What was the shortest throw? What was the difference between them?*" Choose other groups to share and discuss the different ways of recording the distances thrown.

Choose two learners to throw a bean bag in front of the class. Choose two other learners to measure the distance **each** learner threw the bean bag. One learner should measure using a metre stick/rule or a tape measure (standard uniform) and the other learners should use a uniform non-standard measure of their choice. Compare the two measurements and discuss which is more accurate.

If there is time at the end of the session, group together all the learners who threw the furthest and ask them to do it again as a group. All start at the same point. Choose a learner to measure and record the distances thrown. Ask, "*Did you throw a further or shorter distance this time? Why do you think that was?*" (**Answers: might include different method of recording, distance was more/less accurate than used before**)

Do the same for the learners who did the shortest throws, as well as those who threw the second shortest, third shortest and so on.

Keep a record of the class performance to refer to.

Summary

- Learners are able to estimate, measure and compare lengths, choosing and using suitable uniform non-standard and standard units and appropriate measuring instruments.
- They will also be able to compare lengths, using the standard units, centimetres and metres.
- Learners will be able to answer a question by collecting and recording data and to explain their methods using oral reasoning.

Notes on Learner's Book

Who's the winner? (p26): this page is designed to examine different ways of winning, where the highest score is not always the winner (for example the longest time in a 100m race would not be the winner). There will be opportunities to discuss the results which, in turn, will lead to a deeper understanding of measures.

Check up!
- "*Look out of the window and tell me something you can see that is far away/near.*"
- "*What's the furthest/nearest thing you can see?*" *Estimate how far away it is in metres*".
- "*Tell me something in this room that is about one metre away from you.*"
- "*Estimate how long your pencil is!*"
- "*Can you find me three things that are about 10 cm long?*"

More activities

Balls (individual, pairs or group)

> You will need a ball and a measuring device, e.g. tape measure.

Use a ball and see how far it can be thrown, waiting for it to stop. Compare the distances that can be thrown with a variety of balls. Compare the distances that different learners can throw the ball.

Other length challenges (pairs, group or class)

> You will need a tape measure or metre stick.

How far can you jump? How far can you throw a paper aeroplane? How far can you hop? Make the measurements more precise using standard units of measure. Ask questions such as, *"How much further would you need to jump to get to exactly a metre/two metres/three metres? How many centimetres would that be?"*

Resources: Rulers and tape measures. Each group should have a small dish of flour and a metre stick.

This activity involves learners investigating how high they can jump. It involves making sense of the problem, discussing ways of solving it, collecting and analysing data and measuring height.

Tell learners, "*Our sport today is finding how high you can jump. How do you think we could do that? Talk to the person next to you and share your ideas.*" Give several minutes for the discussion to take place and then take feedback by choosing different learners to share their ideas. Then choose some learners to model some of the ideas. Ask, "*What do you think about that idea? Was it easy or hard to measure how high you jumped? Why? What made it easy/ hard?*"

Depending on the ideas given, you may want to make a suggestion. For example, "*Do you think it is important to know how tall you are? Why? How would that help you to find out how high you jumped?*" or, "*When you jump, are you going to measure how much higher your head is or your feet? Or is there another way you could measure?*" Allow time for feedback and discussion.

Then choose a learner to come to the front of the class and tell them to, "*Stand up straight and put your hands in the air as far as you can reach up.*" Stand the learner on a stable surface above the ground (a large table or chair) and ask them to do the same thing again. Say, "*Let's pretend that the height of this chair is the height of the jump. We could measure the top of the hands when you are standing on the floor, and again where they are now. Do you think that would work to find the difference in height?*"

Say, "*There is a problem. You may not jump as high as the chair or you may jump higher than the chair, so we need to think of a way of getting the height right for you. Any ideas?*" Discuss any ideas that might arise.

Opportunity for display

Add to the 'Sports day' display using photos and linear measurement resources. Use the learners' recording as part of the display. These can be put in a folder or a book if there is limited wall space.

Then explain the following method. *"Let's try this way. You need to work in pairs (or small groups) and each of you take turns to dip your fingers in the flour, stand against the wall and stretch up to leave a mark of flour at the highest possible point. Keep your feet flat on the floor. Keeping your feet flat on the floor, crouch down and spring up (jump) to touch the wall as high as you can. Use a measuring tool to measure the distance between the top of the bottom mark and the top of the mark you left when you jumped. That is the height of your jump."* If necessary choose a learner to demonstrate. *"You will need to keep a record of all of your jumps. As a group you must decide how you will do that before you start jumping."*

While the learners are working, move amongst them answering any questions they may have. Check that they understand the task and that they have found a way of recording height. When each group has finished, gather the class together with their recordings. Choose different groups to share what they did and what they found out.

Finish the session by asking the class to reflect on the activity. Ask questions such as, *"Who jumped the highest? What's the difference in height between the highest and the lowest jump? How many learners jumped the same height? Why do you think this is? What have you learned or found out today? If you were doing it again, what would you do differently? Why?"*

Summary

- Learners estimate, measure and compare heights choosing and using suitable uniform non-standard and standard units and appropriate measuring instruments, and compare heights using the standard units of centimetres and metres.
- Learners are able to answer a question by collecting and recording data, explaining methods and reasoning orally.

Notes on the Learner's Book

How high can you jump? (p27): this page is designed to develop the *Core activity* by examining different ways of beginning a jump to see its effect on the height of the jump.

Look out for!

- Learners who need extra help in measuring and reading measurements accurately. *Place these learners in groups where there are learners who can support them. As the recording is done at the learner's own level of understanding and knowledge this should not present a problem.*
- Learners who find the task easy and can measure and record accurately. *Ask them to collate all of the results for the class and design a league table to show the results.*

Check up!

Use classroom resources to check on vocabulary and understanding:

- *"Look around the classroom and tell me two things that are higher than your table."*
- *"Find the clock, the window and the door. Which is the highest?"*

More activities

Questions, questions (individual, pairs, group or class)

Start an investigation with a question, *"Can boys jump higher than girls? Can a taller learner jump higher? How do you know? How can we find out?"*

Animals (individual, pairs, group or class)

Collect data on the height of jumps of animals. Make a leaflet or book about interesting facts found out about animals. Are there any animals that can't jump? Why is this?

Games Book (ISBN 9781107623491)

Sports day (p54) is a game for two to four players. Learners use knowledge of the units of length, height and time and comparing total measurements.

11 Measuring weight, time and cost

Quick reference

Core activity 11.1: Measuring ingredients (Learner's Book p28)
Learners investigate how to measure weight using standard units. They use a flow chart to practise sequencing by making biscuits.

Core activity 11.2: Cooking time (Learner's Book p29)
Learners investigate using suitable units to measure weights.

Core activity 11.3: Pricey biscuits (Learner's Book p30)
Learners investigate timings in hours and minutes and practise costing numbers of biscuits.

Prior learning	Objectives* – please note that listed objectives might only be partially covered within any given chapter but are covered fully across the book when taken as a whole
• Basic knowledge of local currency. • Understanding of capacity and weight and the difference between them. • Knowledge and understanding of time. • Experience of solving problems. • Understand the sequencing of events (flow diagram).	**1C: Measure** (*Length, mass and capacity*) 2Ml1 – Estimate, measure and compare weights and capacities choosing and using suitable uniform non-standard and standard units and appropriate measuring instruments. 2Ml2 – Compare lengths, weights and capacities using the standard units: centimetres, metres, 100 g, and litre. **1C: Measure** (*Time*) 2Mt1 – Know the units of time (seconds, minutes, hours, days, weeks, months and years). **1C: Money** 2Mm1 – Recognise all coins and some notes. 2Mm2 – Use money notation. 2Mm3 – Find totals; the coins and notes to pay a given amount; work out change. **1C: Problem solving** (*Using techniques and skills in solving mathematical problems*) 2Pt3 – Explore number problems and puzzles. 2Pt4 – Make sense of simple word problems (single and easy two-step), decide what operations (addition or subtraction, simple multiplication or division) are needed to solve them and with help, represent them with objects or drawings or on a number line. 2Pt6 – Check the answer to an addition by adding the numbers in a different order or by using a different strategy, e.g. 35 + 19 by adding 20 to 35 and subtracting 1, and by adding 30 + 10 and 5 + 9. 2Pt7 – Check the answer to a subtraction by adding the answer to the smaller number in the original subtraction.

*for NRICH activities mapped to the Cambridge Primary objectives, please visit www.cie.org.uk/cambridgeprimarymaths

Vocabulary
analogue scales • digital scales • weight • estimate • capacity • gram

Core activity 11.1: Measuring ingredients

Resources: *Measuring mass (1)* photocopy master (p93) and *Measuring mass (2)* photocopy master (p94); large versions for class display. *Baking biscuits flow diagram* photocopy master (CD-ROM); large version for class display and one per learner. Analogue and digital kitchen scales. Ingredients to make biscuits: 100 g soft margarine, 200 g flour, 100 g sugar, kitchen scales, child-friendly biscuit/cookie cutters, saucepan, stopwatch, large mixing bowl, a wooden spoon. Access to cooking facilities. Pastry board, rolling pin, biscuit cutters, baking tray; one per group. Paper and pencils. (Optional: printouts of simple recipes.)

Explain that the next three sessions will be about baking and making biscuits for the class to share. If cooking facilities are not available, this session can be done as a class demonstration with volunteers for measuring, without the final cooking.

Remind learners of the work they did in Stage 1 on weight (Unit 1C, chapter 10; Unit 2C, chapter 16 and Unit 3C, chapter 25): using balance scales and different number of cubes, learners directly compared the weights of different objects identifying them as 'heavier', 'lighter' or 'the same as'.

Explain that cubes are uniform non-standard units of measuring weight and that, like measuring length, there is also a standard measure for weight that is used across the world. The metric units of weight are **grams** and **kilograms**.

Display the *Measuring mass (1)* photocopy master. Explain that there are other types of scales to the balance scales they have seen so far. Analogue and digital scales will measure the weight of ingredients in grams. Show the class an example of an analogue kitchen scale and a digital kitchen scale or display the *Measuring mass (2)* photocopy master.

Make sure that all learners have washed their hands. Show them the *Baking biscuits* photocopy master for making biscuits. Display the basic biscuit recipe (below), or a suitable one of your own.

Vocabulary

analogue scales: measure the weight of an object; they display the weight using a dial and marked scales.

digital scales: measure the weight of an object; they display the weight using digital digits.

weight: is how heavy or light an object is; it is measured in grams.

gram: a metric unit of mass (weight); 1000 grams = 1 kilogram.

capacity: the amount that something can contain.

estimate: a sensible guess of something e.g. the weight of an object.

Ingredients	Instructions
100g margarine	Melt the margarine in a saucepan.
200g flour	Pour the melted margarine into a
100g sugar	mixing bowl containing the flour and
A mixing bowl	sugar. Mix the ingredients together
Wooden spoon	with a spoon.

Knead the dough to make it smooth, then roll it out.

Cut out biscuit shapes and place them on a baking tray. Bake on a very low heat until they are hard.

Ask, "*Who has done baking at home? Has anyone made biscuits?*" Allow some time for learners to share their experiences. Explain that you need flour, sugar and margarine, then refer to the flow chart. "*Look at the picture and tell me what is the first thing we need to do.*" Establish that you need to put some margarine in the saucepan to melt. Ask, "*Shall I put all of this margarine in? Would that be the right amount? Let's look at our recipe.*" Refer to the recipe to check the amount of margarine. "*We need 100 grams of margarine.*" Choose a learner to weigh 100 grams of margarine. "*Is that 100 grams? How do you know?*" Choose two or three learners to check that the scales read 100 g.

"*Now what do we need to do? Look at the flow chart. We need to put it in the saucepan to melt. I wonder how long that will take.*" If possible ask another adult to melt the margarine, and say, "*I'm going to set the stopwatch to see how long it takes.*" Ask, "*While the margarine is melting, what is the next thing we need to do?*" Allow time for learners to find the information from the diagram (weigh the flour and sugar and put them in the bowl). Choose two learners to weigh the sugar and two to weigh the flour. Choose two others to check the weight of the flour and two to check the weight of the sugar. "*Now we can put them both into the large mixing bowl. We'll use the spoon to gently mix them together.*"

When the margarine has melted, stop the stopwatch. Show learners the stopwatch and ask, "*How long did it take for the margarine to melt?*" Keep a record of the time. Carefully pour the melted margarine into the flour and sugar and ask a learner to stir it until all of the ingredients are mixed well.

Tell learners that on their tables each group has some dough mixture, a rolling pin, a pastry board, some biscuit cutters, and a baking tray. Tell them, "*You need to roll out the biscuit mix on the board and cut some biscuits to put on your tray so that we can bake them. You will need to think about how thick you want them to be. Do you think they will take longer to cook if they are thick than if they were thin? How long do you think it will take to bake the biscuits? We can set the stopwatch or we can use timers or we can look at our clock. In your group decide how you want to time the length of cooking time and write down your estimate.*"

If the biscuits are going to be cooked away from the class, the adult needs to keep a record of the cooking time for each group to check against their estimates.

Look out for!

- Learners who found it difficult to interpret the flow diagram. *Give them a familiar activity for ordering, such as a set of cards that show a morning or bedtime routine.*
- Learners who could interpret the flow diagram. *Encourage them to make a flow diagram of a recipe of their choosing brought in from home. Give other opportunities to make and use flow diagrams such as daily routines or planning a day out. Make flow diagrams for others to follow.*
- Learners who found it difficult to measure ingredients carefully. *Encourage them to find the weights of objects around them.*

Opportunity for display

Flow charts made by the learners.

While the biscuits are cooking, ask the learners to make their own diagrams to show the process of mixing and baking biscuits, including the timings (melting the margarine, cooking time).

When the biscuits are baked, allow them to cool and share them amongst the groups. Be aware of any food allergies or medical conditions of the learners. Review the quantities used. Ask, "*What if we double the ingredients? What if two groups joined together? How much flour/ margarine/sugar would we need?*"

Summary

- Learners are able to measure weight using standard units and appropriate measuring instruments.
- They are able to understand, use and develop the idea of sequencing through a flow diagram.

Notes on the Learner's Book
Baking biscuits (p28): can be used during class discussion or as a reminder while the learners produce their own flow charts.

Check up!
Ask:
- "*What is weight measured in?*"
- "*Why is it important to have standard units of weight?*"
- "*Why do we need to know how to measure weight when we are cooking?*"
- "*Why do we need to measure length of time when we are cooking?*"

More activities

Making food (group)

You will need printouts of simple recipes, pens and paper.

Working in groups, encourage the learners to talk about a simple recipe that they have used at home or that a family member has used. Discuss each of the stages to make sure that they understand the process. Ask each learner to draw a picture of one of the ingredients for the recipe. When this has been done, place the pictures face up on the table and rearrange them in the order in which they are used in the recipe.

Discuss what has to happen to each of the ingredients (weighing, mixing, and cutting). Each learner draws a picture of one of the operations and places it in the correct place to make a flow diagram. Each group can stick their flow chart on to a large piece of paper and use it as a display as they share their recipe with the rest of the class.

Design a flow chart for using numbers (group or class)

You will need paper and pens.

Start with a number in the first box and end with a different number in the last box. Follow the arrows through the boxes, adding or subtracting as you go, so that you end with the last number. These can be three boxes or up to five or six for the more able. Ask learners to make their own.

Resources: *Making dough* photocopy master (CD-ROM); one per group of learners. Ingredients to make dough: flour, salt, cooking oil; for each group of learners. Two cups (one for dry ingredients, one for wet); per group of learners. Water. Tools such as tablespoon, jug, mixing bowl, wooden spoon, pastry board, rolling pin, biscuit cutters; one per group. Baking tray. (Optional: range of different shaped biscuit cutters; card and paper.)

Explain to learners that you are going to make some biscuits but not eat them; again, if this is not possible to do as a class it can be done as a demonstration with volunteers for measuring. If you have done Core activity 11.1, ask, *"Do you remember doing something like this last time? What did we make?"* Allow some discussion about the previous activity of making biscuits. Then say, *"I have another flow diagram for us to look at for today's activity."* Display the *Making dough* photocopy master and discuss the sequence of events.

Then say, *"You have all the things that you need on your tables. Work as a group to make your own dough mixture which you can roll out and cut to make biscuits. Place your biscuits on the baking tray."* As the groups are working, walk around to check that they all understand the task and are able to use the flow diagram to keep to the sequence needed.

When all of the groups have filled their trays with their biscuits gather them together and ask, *"How did you like making the dough? Was there anything that was difficult? What did you do about it? Was there anything that didn't work well? What did you do about it? What worked best? What did you like the most?"*

Discuss how this time they used cups to measure the ingredients. This is a uniform non-standard measure of weight that is often used in baking. Ask for feedback on which was easier to use, the cup or the weighing scales. Is one more accurate than the other? **(Answer: yes, the weighing scales are more precise)** Does the accuracy matter? **(Answer: as long as the same cup is used for each measurement, and filled to the same point, then it doesn't matter that it's not as precise as the weighing scales)**

Ask, *"How many biscuits did you make?"* Note that the number made will depend on the size of the biscuit cutter, how thinly each learner rolled their dough, and how well they used up the available dough. Explain that if all the dough was used up, and rolled accurately into the

Look out for!

- Learners who could not follow the flow diagram instructions. *Use a flow diagram with fewer instructions.*
- Learners who were unable to count the biscuits accurately. *Arrange the biscuits in a regular array so that they can use their understanding of pattern to aid counting.*
- Learners who are confident with measuring. *The 'cup' measures can be converted into grams and litres.*

Opportunity for display

Plates of baked biscuits for use in a shop or role play area.

half a centimetre depth, then the number of biscuits made could be increased or decreased by using different amounts of each ingredient. In order to make sure the mixture is correct, you need to increase/decrease each ingredient by the same amount.

Then explain that you need to bake the dough for a very long time to make sure that it goes hard. *"How long do you think a very long time would be?"* Gather some ideas and record them as class, so that all the class can see and to use in the next session. **(Possible suggestions might include: 1 hour, 2 hours, 30 minutes, 20 minutes etc)**

The dough biscuits need to be baked and baking time noted before the next session.

Summary

- Learners are able to measure weights using suitable units and appropriate measuring instruments.
- They can use knowledge of time in a practical context and can interpret a flow diagram.

Notes on the Learner's Book
Gingerbread (p29): looks at the problem of increasing the ingredients in order to make more dough.

Check up!
Ask:
- *"Why do we need to measure the ingredients accurately?"*
- *"Does it matter if we fill the cup to a different level each time? Why/why not?"* **(Yes, in order to make sure the same amount is measured each time)**
- *"How can we make sure that the dough is rolled out to the correct thickness?"* **(Use a ruler to measure accurately)**
- *"If the dough was thinner could we make more biscuits?"*
- *"If the dough was thicker would we have fewer biscuits?"*
- *"Can you predict how to make more biscuits?"*

More activities

What shape is best? (individual, pairs, group or class)

> You will need dough and discuit cutters.

Using dough that has been made by the learners, ask them to try different biscuit cutters. Which cutter makes the most biscuits? Is there a way that you could get more biscuits? (e.g. Size of the cutter, thickness of the dough, the way they fit the shapes together when cutting.)

What box is best? (individual, pairs, group or class)

> You will need card and paper.

Design and make a box to hold the biscuits of different shapes. Which was the easiest to make? Which was the hardest? Why? Make a box that uses the least amount of card/paper. Use what they know about nets of shapes.

LB: p30

> **Resources:** *US dollars* photocopy master (CD-ROM); large version for class display. List of learners' baking time estimates from the last session. Coins and notes of low denomination of local currency and/or US dollars; if not available you can create equivalent play money using the *Blank coins and notes* photocopy master. Create a price list of dough ingredients using local currency (or US dollars of preferred), listing the cost of two cups of flour, one cup of salt, two cups of water and one tablespoon of oil, using words and pictures. (Optional: card/paper; ruler.)

Start by revising the previous session. Ask, "*What did we use to make our dough biscuits? How much of each ingredient did we use? The dough biscuits had to be baked. Let's look at the estimated times we thought they would take to bake.*"

Refer to the timings of the previous session. Ask, "*Would any one like to change their mind? Do you think it took more time than you said or less?*" Allow for discussion about time and for learners to change their minds. Then tell learners how long the biscuits actually took to bake. "*What do you think about that? Are you surprised? Did you expect it to take more or less time?*"

Then ask, "*So, if we put the biscuits in at 10 o'clock this morning, what time would they be ready to take out of the oven?*" Some learners may need a clock in order to find the answer. Depending on the actual time this can involve hours, half hours and minutes.

Now say, "*We used flour, salt, water and cooking oil to make our dough biscuits. If each lot of dough made ten biscuits, how many biscuits would two lots of dough make? What about three lots?*"

Ask, "*How many cups of flour would we need to make 15 biscuits? Talk to the person sitting next to you and see if you can find out.*" Allow time for discussion. **(Possible answers could include: three cups of flour, or two cups of flour and make the biscuits thinner, or four cups of flour and make the biscuits thicker)**

As learners give their answers ask them how they worked it out. As this is a question that can have different answers, allow all answers, as long the learner can explain why.

Explain that the list of ingredients and recipe from the previous session is meant to make ten biscuits. Show the prepared price list of all the ingredients as words and pictures. If required, spend some time discussing the value of each coin and note of the local currency (and/or US dollars) to ensure the learners understand their value. (If looking at US dollars, display the

Look out for!

Learners experiencing difficulty in their understanding of time and money. *Give practical resources for those who need support.*

Please note that learners do not need to recognise US currency until the Stage 3 Progression Test. Therefore, at this Stage, they might find it easier to grasp adding and subtracting money amounts if they use currency they are already familiar with, i.e., the local currency.

US dollars photocopy master to help you). Include notation and different denominations. Ask the learners to add up the total cost of making the ten biscuits. Now ask, "*How much does ten biscuits cost to make?*" Encourage learners to use the addition strategies from earlier sessions and to check their answers by adding the cost of each ingredient in a different order.

Say, "*How much would 20 biscuits cost?* (**Answer: multiply the cost of ten biscuits by two**) *How much would 30 biscuits cost?* (**Answer: multiply the cost of ten biscuits by three**) *Can anyone tell me how much 100 biscuits would cost? Talk to the person next to you.*" Some learners may need to see and use actual money in order to find the totals rather than work in the abstract. Take feedback and ask, "*How did you work out how many 100 biscuits would cost?*" (**Possible answers include: repeated addition of ten; multiply cost of ten biscuits by ten**) Record the different answers so that the class can see. Repeat for the cost of 15 biscuits, and 25. Discuss ways of finding out, record the different ways so that the class can see, and use them as discussion points. Discuss ways of recording the amounts of money.

Extend the activity by explaining that when you bought the ingredients for ten biscuits, you paid using a note of higher value than the total cost. Explain that this is a subtraction, and that they should use the methods they have learned in previous sessions. Discuss what change you will have been given. Ask learners to check their answers by adding the answer (the change) to the total cost of ten biscuits to make sure they get back to the original note value used to pay.

> ### Look out for!
> Learners who find mental calculation of money easy. *Transform one step problems into two steps, e.g. "How much would 45 biscuits cost? How much change would you have left from … ?" And change two-step problems into three-steps, e.g. "How much would it cost? How much change will you have? Show me that amount in coins/notes. Can you make the same amount in a different way?"*

Summary

- Learners can understand cooking time in minutes and hours.
- Learners should be able to recognise coins and notes in a practical context and, where appropriate, be able to use money notation.
- They can explore number problems and puzzles and make sense of simple word problems in the context of money and decide what operations are needed to solve them.

Notes on the Learner's Book
How much?(p30): requires learners to know the different coins and banknotes of US currency. They are challenged with calculating the costs of items and required change. If you have not used US currency and instead have focussed on local currency, change the questions accordingly.

Check up!
Ask
- "*If a cake takes two hours to cook, and it goes into the oven at 10 o'clock, what time will it be ready to take out of the oven?*" (**Answer: 12 o'clock**)
Repeat, changing the amount of cooking time and the time when the cake goes into the oven.
- "*If it costs $5 to make 12 biscuits, how much will it cost to make 6 biscuits?*" (**Answer: $2.50, or two dollars 50 cents**)
- "*If the ingredients for a cake cost me $11 and I pay using a $10 bill and a $5 dollar bill, how much change will I be given?*" (**Answer: $4**)

More activities

Boxed biscuits (individual or group)

```
You will need card/paper, ruler.
```

Once the dough biscuits have been made, groups or individual learners design and make a box which will hold 20 biscuits.
How many different designs are made? What are the similarities and differences between the boxes? Make a display of the boxes.

Prices (individual or group)

Make different price lists and write a set of questions to go with them: e.g. we can make 12 dough biscuits with this recipe. How much would
18 biscuits cost? Challenge the more able learners to work with higher numbers and amounts. But they have to know the answers to their questions!

Charity sale (individual or group)

Make biscuits (using the *Basic Biscuits* photocopy master rather than the *Making dough* photocopy master!). Hold a charity sale, working out the costs of
making the biscuits and deciding on a sale price. Learners could work with older learners to package the biscuits and advertise the sale as well.

Games Book (ISBN 9781107623491)

The baking game (p58) learners is a game for two to four players. Learners compare and total weights, using the standard unit of grams, and explore
number problems in the context of weight.

Measuring mass (1)

Mass can be measured in units of **kilograms** and **grams**.

There are **1000 grams in 1 kilogram**.

Mass can be measured using scales. There are many different types of scales:

Balances

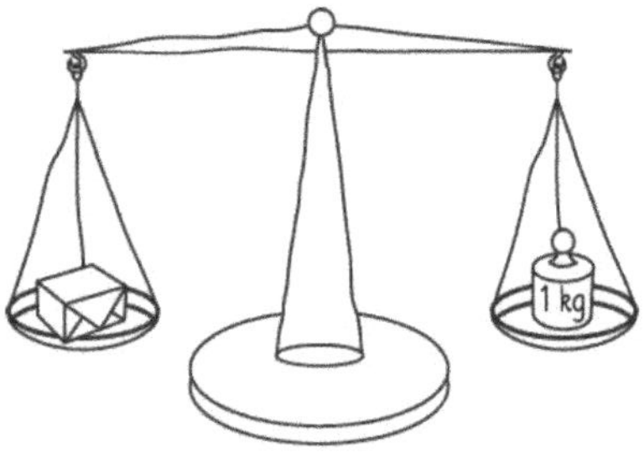

Beam balance

Top-pan balance

Weighing scales

Analogue scales

Digital scales

Spring balance

Each of these packages weighs 1 kilogram.

Instructions on page 84

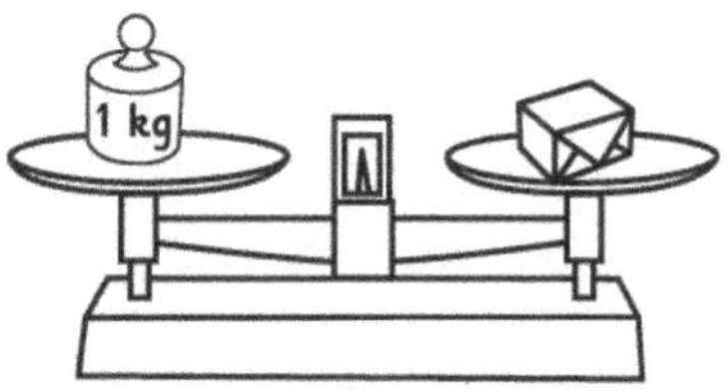

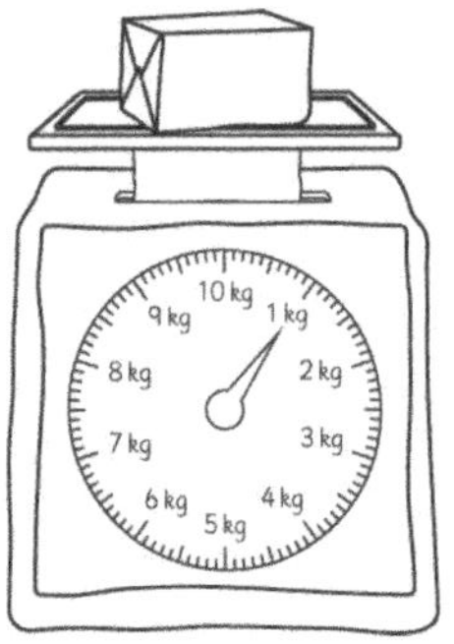

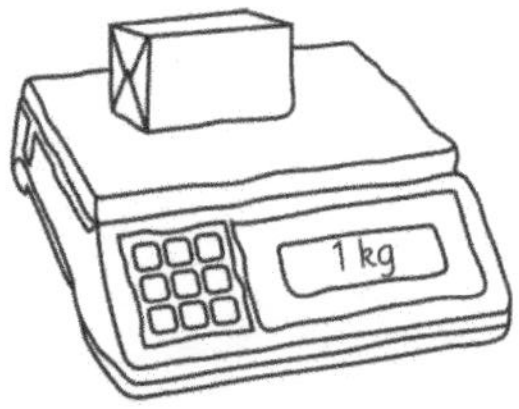

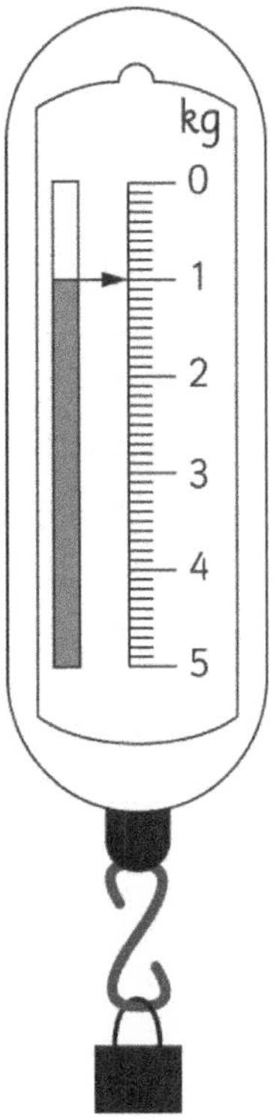

Measuring mass (2)

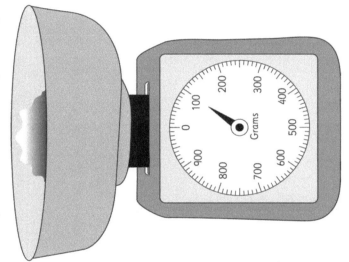

An analogue scale showing 100 grams.

A digital scale showing 100 grams.

Instructions on page 84

Quick reference

Core activity 12.1: Tens and ones to 100 (Learner's Book p31)

Learners use the 100 square and place value cards to explore what each digit in a number represents and use that understanding to order numbers.

Core activity 12.2: Comparing and ordering numbers (Learner's Book p32)

Learners explore using the < is less than and > is greater than signs to compare and order numbers.

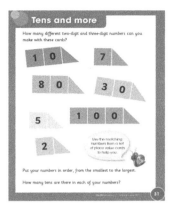

Prior learning	Objectives* – please note that listed objectives might only be partially covered within any given chapter but are covered fully across the book when taken as a whole
• Count to 100. • Experience of counting forward and back in tens. • Experience of using place value cards.	**1A: Number** (*Numbers and the number system*) 2Nn3 – Count on in ones and tens from single- and two-digit numbers and back again. **2A: Number** (*Numbers and the number system*) 2Nn6 – Know what each digit represents in two-digit numbers; partition into tens and ones. 2Nn12 – Order numbers to 100; compare two numbers using the > and < signs. **2A: Problem solving** (*Using techniques and skills in solving mathematical problems*) 2Pt2 – Explain methods and reasoning orally. 2Pt3 – Explore number problems and puzzles.

*for NRICH activities mapped to the Cambridge Primary objectives, please visit www.cie.org.uk/cambridgeprimarymaths

Vocabulary

digit • place value • partition • greater than • less than

Core activity 12.1: Tens and ones to 100

> **Resources:** *Counting cards* photocopy master (CD-ROM). *100 square* photocopy master (chapter 1, p4); large version for class display. A strip of card long enough to cover a column in the large 100 square, and a longer strip of card showing the tens column including 0 at the top (0, 10, 20, ..., 100). *How many tens?* photocopy master (p102); per learner. Scissors, glue and colouring pencils. *Tens and ones cards* photocopy master (CD-ROM); per pair of learners. *0–100 number line* photocopy master (chapter 3, p18); per pair of learners.

Begin by showing the learners the cards from the *Counting cards* photocopy master. Explain that when you show the '+1' card you would like them to count on in ones; the '–1' cards means you want them to count back in ones; '+10' means count on in tens; and '–10' means count back in tens. Choose a start number on the 100 square, such as 27, and encourage the learners to use the 100 square to help them. Begin counting in ones, displaying the +1 card. Change the counting several times. It may take a few turns before the learners all change their counting at the same time. Repeat with different starting numbers.

Ask learners what they remember about two-digit numbers from Stage 1 (Unit 3A, chapter 20). Reponses should include that they are made up of tens and ones. The number is written according to place value, with the first digit in the 'tens columns' and the second digit in the 'ones/units column'. If necessary, remind them of place value.

Remind the learners of the 100 square they made earlier in the school year (chapter 1) that was used to help them understand the decade numbers in chapter 1. Display the large 100 square. Cover up the tens column with the strip of card and place your separate tens column at the front of the 100 square, so that the 10 square is before the 11 (see chapter 20 in Stage 1 for a reminder if necessary).

> Explain that you would like the learners to make a new 100 square just like yours. Give each learner a copy of the *How many tens?* photocopy master, scissors and glue.

Once everyone has their own square, ask questions such as, "*Where are the numbers without any tens? What about the numbers with three tens?*" and so on. Make sure the learners understand that the number at the start of each row now tells them how many tens every number in that row has, so they can easily partition numbers into tens and ones.

Vocabulary

digit: a single number, e.g. 0, 1, 2, 3, 4, 5, 6, 7, 8, 9

place value: the value a digit has because of its place in terms of 10s and 1s. For example, in 43 the digit 4 is worth 4 tens (40), and the digit 3 is three ones (3). Each place (position) can only contain a single digit, e.g.

T	U
4	3

partition: to split a number into its component place value parts. For example, 43 is partitioned into 4 tens (40) and 3 ones.

Ask the learners to colour each row a different colour, then take it in turns to ask a partner questions such as, "Tell me a number with three tens in it. How many tens in 54?"

Give each pair of learners a set of the place value arrow cards from the *Tens and ones cards* photocopy master. Ask the learners to set out their place value cards with all the tens in one column, starting with ten, and all the ones in another, starting with one. They then need to use the cards to make nine different two-digit numbers and put them in order from the smallest to the largest. Ask the learners how they put the cards in order. Make sure they realise that they used the tens column and did not need to look at the number of ones because they only had one number from each decade.

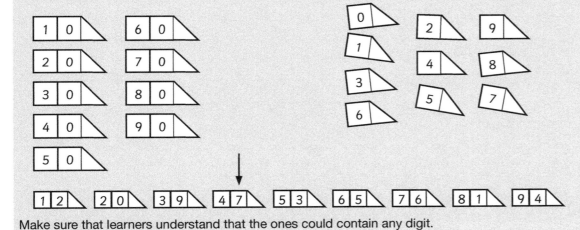

Make sure that learners understand that the ones could contain any digit.

Look out for!

- Learners who find ordering difficult. *Encourage them to use the new 100 square for support. Their first number will be on the second row, the next on the third row and so on.*
- Learners who find ordering numbers straightforward. *Give them a batch of numbers using the same digits to order, for example 86, 68, 83, 38, 63, 36. Extend to three digits, for example 234, 432, 342, 243, 324 and 423.*

Now tell the learners that each pair is going to put their numbers together with another pair so that they have 18 numbers to put in order from smallest to largest. Explain that this will be a little more challenging because they will now have two numbers from each decade. After looking at the tens column, they will need to look at the ones column to decide which number is larger. Give an example if you need to. Once the numbers have been ordered, the learners can work in pairs to mark them on a number line from the *0–100 number line* (marked in tens). More confident learners could use a 0–100 number line which has not been marked in tens (Use the *Blank 0–100 number line* photocopy master).

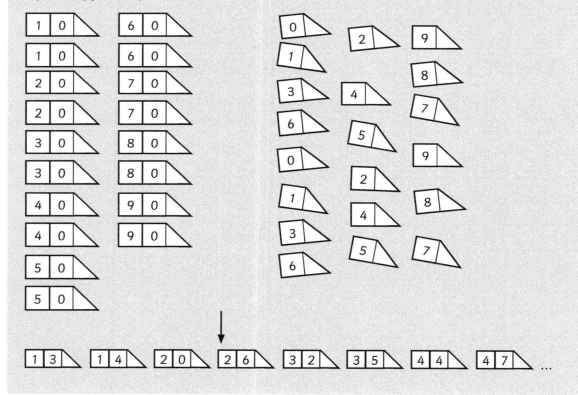

Finish the session by asking learners questions about their numbers, "*What was the highest number you could make? Did anyone make that number? What was the smallest? Did anyone make that number? What are the closest numbers to 30? Did anyone make either of those numbers? Or both?*" and so on.

Summary

Learners know what each digit in a two-digit number represents and can use their understanding of place value to put the numbers in order.

Notes on the Learner's Book

Tens and more (p31): learners use the place value cards to make numbers then put them in order. A 100 card is included to extend the numbers beyond 100 as an extension for more able learners.

Check up!

Ask learners about their door number or another number familiar to them, or give them a number.
- *"How many tens does it have?"*
- *"How many ones?"*
- *"Put these numbers into order from smallest to largest: 18, 99, 66, 87, 13, 42, 20, 78."*
  (Answer: 13, 18, 20, 42, 66, 78, 87, 99)

More activities

Clap and click (class)

Clap your hands for each 'ten', click your fingers for each 'one'. Learners respond by telling you what number they heard. You need to ensure you represent each digit in the correct place value (tens then ones). For more confident learners, you could move on to doing the actions in a different order, for example ones and tens; or extend it to include stamping your feet for hundreds.

Games Book (ISBN 9781107623491)

Place value games (p17) Game (1) is a game for two or three players. This game focuses on place value and using that understanding to order and compare numbers.

Core activity 12.2: Comparing and ordering numbers

Resources: *Counting cards* photocopy master (CD-ROM). *Tens and ones cards* photocopy master (CD-ROM); per pair of learners. *Greater than less than* photocopy master (CD-ROM); per learner. Pencils. Scissors. *0–100 number line* photocopy master (p18). (Optional: *Number sentences* photocopy master (CD-ROM); 0 – 9 digit cards (CD-ROM); *100 square* photocopy master (chapter 1, p4) per pair of learners.)

Count in ones and tens forwards and back, using the *Counting cards* photocopy master. Lay out a set of arrow cards from the *Tens and ones cards* photocopy master, showing only the tens and ones cards. Ask two learners to choose two cards each to make two different two-digit numbers, for example 37 and 63. Write or pin the two numbers where everyone can see them. Ask the learners, "*Which is the smaller number? How do you know?* **(Answer: 37 because 3 tens is less than 6 tens)** *We can say that 37 is less than 63, and that 63 is greater than 37.*" As you say the 'less than' and 'greater than' sentences, write them (in words, not using < and >) near the numbers.

Give each pair of learners a set of arrow cards from the *Tens and ones cards* photocopy master and explain that you would like them to take it in turns to make two two-digit numbers and then say two sentences about them to their partner: a 'greater than' sentence and a 'less than' sentence. Allow enough time for both learners to have at least two turns.

Explain that it was quick to say the sentence but it takes a bit of time to write, so mathematicians use a sign instead. Cross out the words 'is greater than' and replace with the sign >. Cross out 'is less than' and replace with <. Explain that, "*The signs are a bit like an open mouth, and the mouth always wants to eat the bigger number. We can use this to help us remember which is which. So, for 37 < 63, 37 is less than 63, the mouth is open at 63 because 63 is the bigger number. For 63 > 37, 63 is greater than 37, the mouth is still open at the 63 because it is bigger.*"

Give each learner a *Greater than, less than* photocopy master. Explain that the arrow is pointing to the top of the page and they must keep the page that way up as they turn the signs into creatures with wide open mouths. Ask the learners to suggest some suitable creatures – snake, lion, crocodile, alligator and so on.

Vocabulary

greater than > means is greater than, so 45 > 23.

less than < means is less than, so 23 < 45.

Look out for!

- Learners who are having difficulty in forming two-digit numbers. *They must place the arrow part of each card on top of each other to create the number correctly. This will help learners who write numbers such as 123 as 10023 to write them correctly.*
- Learners who find using the symbols straightforward. *Challenge them to use both in one longer sentence, for example 23 < 45 > 32*

Opportunity for display

Display the learners' signs with an explanation of what each sign means.

Once the learners have turned the signs into mouths, cut the sheet along the middle horizontally, so that each learner now has one of each sign. They can then use these signs to make number sentences with their arrow cards.

Finish the session by asking the learners which sign means 'is greater than' and which sign means 'is less than'. Ask them to explain how they can tell the difference between the two signs.

Summary

Learners are able to compare two-digit numbers using the 'is greater than' (>) and 'is less than' (<) signs.

Notes on the Learner's Book
Greater than, less than (p32): learners make number sentences using the digits given and the < > signs. Learners might benefit from the *0–100 number line* photocopy master (p18).

Check up!
Ask learners to tell you a number that is greater than or less than a number that you give them. Ask how they show that in writing.

More activities

Number sentences (pairs)

> You will need the *0–9 digit cards* (CD-ROM) and the *Number sentences* photocopy master (CD-ROM).

Learners create a set of number sentences using digit cards and < >.

Secret number (group or class)

> You will need the *0–9 digit cards* (CD-ROM) and the *100 square* photocopy master (p4).

One learner is designated as 'the leader'. The leader chooses a number on the 100 square. The other learners can ask questions to try to identify the number. For example, 'Is it odd? Is it even? Is it greater than 50? Is it less than 70?' The leader can only answer 'yes' or 'no'. The learner who identifies the correct number becomes the next leader and the game is repeated. Learners could cross out numbers on a 100 square to keep track of the clues.

Games Book (ISBN 9781107623491)

Place value games (p17) Game 2 is a game for two or three players. This game focuses on place value and using < and > to order and compare numbers.

How many tens

0	1	2	3	4	5	6	7	8	9	10
	11	12	13	14	15	16	17	18	19	20
	21	22	23	24	25	26	27	28	29	30
	31	32	33	34	35	36	37	38	39	40
	41	42	43	44	45	46	47	48	49	50
	51	52	53	54	55	56	57	58	59	60
	61	62	63	64	65	66	67	68	69	70
	71	72	73	74	75	76	77	78	79	80
	81	82	83	84	85	86	87	88	89	90
	91	92	93	94	95	96	97	98	99	100

Quick reference

Core activity 13.1: Estimating (Learner's Book p33)

Learners explore estimating then counting in twos, fives and tens.

Prior learning	Objectives* – please note that listed objectives might only be partially covered within any given chapter but are covered fully across the book when taken as a whole
• Count on to 100. • Beginning to count in twos, fives and tens.	**2A: Numbers and the number system** 2Nn2 – Count up to 100 objects. 2Nn4 – Count in twos, fives and tens, and use grouping in twos, fives or tens to count larger groups of objects. 2Nn13 – Give a sensible estimate of up to 100 objects, e.g. choosing from 10, 20, 50 or 100. **2A: Problem solving** (*Using techniques and skills in solving mathematical problems*) 2Pt2 – Explain methods and reasoning orally. 2Pt3 – Explore number problems and puzzles.

*for NRICH activities mapped to the Cambridge Primary objectives, please visit www.cie.org.uk/cambridgeprimarymaths

Resources: *Counting cards* photocopy master (CD-ROM). *More counting cards* photocopy master (CD-ROM). A large quantity of small counting objects such as seeds, beans, beads, small pebbles, grains of rice. Four plates/small trays of the counting object; one plate/tray should hold 10 of the items; one should hold 20; one 50 and one 100. Four labels showing the number of items on each plate/tray. A large sheet of paper with between 50 and 100 dots or crosses arranged randomly; large version for class display. Three different coloured pens and a large plate/tray; for class display. Small containers/trays/plates; per pair of learners. (Optional: *Estimating* photocopy master (CD-ROM); present wrapping paper, wall paper or other decorated paper; counters or cubes; coloured pens.)

Show the learners the +1, −1, +10 and −10 cards from the *Counting cards* photocopy master and ask them to remind you what they mean. Introduce the + 2 and – 2 cards from the *More counting cards* photocopy master. At first, make sure you change to counting in twos on an even number. As the learners grow in confidence, sometimes change on an odd number.

Show the learners the four plates and ask them which plate holds the most of the object, which holds the next most, and so on until you get to which one holds the least. Ask the learners to estimate how many of the objects are on each plate; then show them the labels one at a time (10, 20, 50 and 100), asking which plate they think the label belongs to. Once all the plates are labelled, take a handful of approximately 50 of the counting object and put them on a large plate or tray. Ask the learners to estimate how many they think there are altogether by comparing with the labelled plates. Record some of the estimates for the class to see.

Ask the learners the best way to find out how many there actually are. If they suggest counting in ones, start to demonstrate doing this but make mistakes and eventually give up. Demonstrate counting the object in twos by arranging them into groups of two; then re-count them in fives and finally count them again in tens. Make sure that the learners understand that all of these ways will give the same total. Repeat with a larger handful, aiming for over 100. Ask the learners if they would count this amount the same way as last time. There is no right or wrong answer.

Vocabulary

estimate: a sensible guess of 'how many' there are of something. For example,

Estimate: 10

Count: 12

Now ask the learners to work in pairs. One learner should take a handful of the counting items then work with their partner to agree an estimate. You may need to provide small containers for the learners to carry the handful in and a tray/plate for them to count on. After agreeing a way of counting, learners work together to calculate how many. Walk around the class as the learners carry out their count, asking pairs of learners what their estimate was, what they decided to count in and what made them choose that way. You might like to ask them to record their estimate and final count.

After the learners have completed their counts, invite them to talk about what they did. Did they find the total number quickly? Did they need to count more than once? Was their second estimate closer to the total than their first one?

Comment that it was very useful to be able to move the items and put them into groups to count them, but ask what they could do if they had a picture of lots of dots or beans instead? Show the learners your prepared large sheet containing the dots and ask them to make suggestions about what you should do to find out how many dots there are. Respond to the learners' suggestions and, if necessary, suggest that you could repeatedly draw around two, five or ten items and then count in twos, fives or tens to find out how many altogether. Use a coloured pen to circle groups of two and then count in twos with the learners joining in. If you have time, repeat for fives and tens.

Finish the session by returning to the counting cards. Introduce the + 5 and – 5 counting cards. At first, make sure you only change to counting in fives on a tens number. Then when learners are more confident, change to counting in fives on any number.

Look out for!

- Learners who find it difficult to estimate. *Give them cards with 10, 20, 50 or 100 dots/items on to use as a basis for comparison. Ask them to look at each card in turn and compare with what they have. Do they have more than what is on the card? Encourage them to keep making comparisons until they can make a link with what they have.*
- Learners who are very good at estimating. *Challenge them to be even more accurate than 10, 20, 50 and 100.*

Summary

Learners can make a reasonable estimate then count in different ways to find out how many.

Notes on the Learner's Book

Estimating (p33): learners estimate how many large and small dots there are, then match the dots with grains of rice to help them count.

Check up!

Challenge learners to count forwards or back in twos, fives or tens from a particular start number. Ask learners to estimate the number of pictures on the wall or something else that cannot be easily marked or moved and ask how they would find out.

More activities

Estimating (individuals)

> You will need the *Estimating* photocopy master (CD-ROM).

Learners tick their estimate then count the items by circling 2, 5 or 10 items.

Paper counts (pairs)

> You will need a sheet of present wrapping paper, wallpaper or other decorated paper; per pair of learners.

Ask learners to find out how many of a particular shape appears on the paper. They should place a bean, counter or cube on each shape, then arrange the beans, counters or cubes in twos, fives or tens to find the total.

Games Book (ISBN 9781107623491)

To 100 and back again! (p17) is a game for two to four players. This game focuses on counting forward and back in twos, fives and tens.

14 Number patterns

Quick reference

Core activity 14.1: Number pairs to 20 (Learner's Book p34)

Learners practise recall of number pairs for 20.

Core activity 14.2: Doubles (Learner's Book p35)

Learners explore doubles to ten and beyond, and write number stories.

Core activity 14.3: Number sorting (Learner's Book p36)

Learners begin to sort numbers according to their properties, including two criteria and negative conditions (for example, not even).

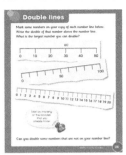

Prior learning	Objectives* – please note that listed objectives might only be partially covered within any given chapter but are covered fully across the book when taken as a whole
• Explored number pairs to 10 and 20. • Explored doubles to double five. • Explored number patterns such as odd and even. • Counting in twos, fives and tens from zero.	**1A: Number** (*Numbers and the number system*) 2Nn14 – Understand odd and even numbers and recognise these up to at least 20. 2Nc1 – Find and learn doubles for all numbers up to 10 and also 15, 20, 25 and 50. **2A: Calculation** (*Numbers and the number system*) 2Nn15 – Sort numbers, e.g. odd/even, multiples of 2, 5 and 10. **2A: Calculation** (*Addition and Subtraction*) 2Nc6 – Relate counting on/back in tens to finding 10 more/less than any two-digit number and then to adding and subtracting other multiples of 10, e.g. 75 – 30. **2A: Problem solving** (*Using techniques and skills in solving mathematical problems*) 2Pt1 – Choose appropriate mental strategies to carry out calculations and explain how they worked out the answer. 2Pt2 – Explain methods and reasoning orally. 2Pt3 – Explore number problems and puzzles. 2Pt5 – Make up a number story to go with a calculation.

*for NRICH activities mapped to the Cambridge Primary objectives, please visit www.cie.org.uk/cambridgeprimarymaths

Vocabulary

odd one out • whole • multiple

Resources: *100 square* photocopy master (chapter 1, p4); large version for class display. Two sets of 0–20 number cards from the *0–100 number cards* photocopy master (CD-ROM) per group of learners. Stopwatch or timer. *20 clock timing* photocopy master (CD-ROM). (Optional: *Target 20* photocopy master (CD-ROM).)

Begin by choosing a single digit number on the *100 square* photocopy master and counting forwards and back in tens, up and down the columns. Ask the learners to remind you what they were counting in (tens), and if they were counting up or counting back.

Demonstrate how counting up in tens is the same as 'adding ten' and counting back in tens is the same as 'subtracting ten'. Ask questions such as, "*What is 31 add 10? What about 31 take away 10?*" Once learners are confident, move on to adding and subtracting other multiples of ten. For example, ask, "*How can you use your answers to calculate 31 add 20? And to calculate 31 subtract 20? 31 add 30? 43 subtract 20?*" and so on.

Ask the learners to remind you of the number pairs for ten, then 20. Make a list of both sets and look at how they are the same and how they are different. Remind the learners that it is useful to remember the number pairs so that we can use them quickly and easily when calculating.

Explain that the learners need to work in threes for the next activity and they will need two sets of 0–20 cards from the *0–100 number cards* photocopy master. The learners have to lay one set of number cards out in a circle like a clock face, but with numbers from 1 to 20 on it. The second set of number cards is shuffled by Player 2. Player 1 places a card from the second set next to an appropriate card on the table in order to make number pairs to 20. Player 2 watches to check that Player 1 is making the number pairs correctly. Player 3 times how long it takes for Player 1 to make all the number pairs to 20. Learners then change roles so that everyone has a go at each task. Learners can have up to three turns at matching the cards, recording their times on the *20 clock timing* photocopy master.

"*Who had the fastest time? Compare fastest times and make this the challenge to beat.*"
Give the groups of learners time to repeat the activity once each.

Did the learners improve their time? Who improved their time the most?

Look out for!

- Learners who find it hard to recall number pairs. *Encourage them to practise two or three times without being timed.*
- Learners who can easily recall the number pairs to 20. *Challenge these learners to shorten their time. Set a target to reduce the time to, for example, 10 seconds. Alternatively, challenge them to work with number pairs to 30 (cards 0 to 30) or even 40 (cards 0 to 40).*

Summary

Learners learn by heart all number pairs with a total of 20.

Notes on the Learner's Book

Pairs to twenty (p34): provides further activities to practise and test learners' ability to recall number pairs to 20.

Check up!

Show or point out a number between 0 and 20 and ask:

- *"Which number makes the number pair for 20?"*

More activities

<u>**Target 20**</u> (individuals)

You will need *Target 20* photocopy master (CD-ROM); one per learner.

Learners find all the pairs of numbers which make 20. Number pairs must be next to each other. They could be across, down or diagonal. Each number can only be circled once. There are several different ways to complete the target sheet so challenge the learners to beat the best score. Even more number pairs can be found if a number can be used more than once.

Games Book (ISBN 9781107623491)

Collect 20 (p22) is a game for two to four players. This game focuses on collecting number pairs to 20. Learners could also revisit the Playing with 20 games.

> **Resources:** *100 square* photocopy master (chapter 1, p4); large version for class display. *0–20 number line* photocopy master (CD-ROM); large version for class display. *0–50 number line* (p116); one per learner. *Double lines* photocopy master (CD-ROM). (Optional: *Doubling and multiplying by 2* photocopy master (CD-ROM).)

Display the *100 square* photocopy master. Revisit counting forward and back in tens from any single-digit number. Ask questions about adding and subtracting 10, 20 or 30 from a number on the 100 square.

Ask the learners to explain what we mean by 'doubling' (they should understand that this means the same as 'multiplying by 2'). Demonstrate how we can record doubling as adding a number together twice, or as multiplying a number by two.

Display the *0–20 number line* photocopy master; the double of 0, 2, 5 and 10 have already been marked above the number line. Start at 0 and read aloud the doubles that have already been marked. Ask the learners to tell you some doubles they know and mark them in above the number line. (For example: double 2 is 4, write 4 above the 2 on the number line.) As you build up the doubles, ask questions such as, "*What is double 5? Is that the same as two lots of 5? What is two times 6?*" and so on. Complete four or five doubles, then ask, "*How do we find double 20?*" Talk about two lots of 20 but also ask the learners to think about this in terms of place value: if double 2 is 4, then double 2 tens must be 4 tens.

Talk through using their knowledge of place value to double 15: learners should partition 15 into 10 and 5, then double 10 and double 5 and add the two numbers together. Move on to say, "*I know that double 15 is 30. How could you use this to work out double 16? What about double 17? What about double 14?*" **(Possible answers include: 16 is one more than 15, so double 16 would be two more than double 15, so 30 + 2 = 32; 17 is two more than 15 … 30 + 4 = 34; 14 is one less than 15, so this time subtract 2, 30 – 2 = 28)**

Give each learner a number line from the *0 to 50 number line* photocopy master and ask them to mark the numbers between 0 and 10 on it. Ask them to calculate the double of each number between 0 and 10 above the number line. Then ask learners to mark 15, 20, 25 and 50 on the number line. Again, ask them to write the double above each of these numbers.

Once the learners have completed their double lines, ask questions such as, "*Which number must I double to get 20?*" **(10)** *14?* **(7)** *30?* **(15)** *I double a number and get 20. What number did I start with?* **(10)** *What is the opposite to doubling?*" **(Answer: halving)**

Explain that it is fun to make up a story to go with a calculation. Tell a simple story such as, "*I needed five apples so that I could take one to school every day. But then I remembered that I would not be able to go shopping next Saturday, so I had to buy double my usual number of apples, enough for two weeks. I needed ten apples.*" Or, "*When I go and visit my mother, I take her two magazines because she likes to read them. I haven't been to see her for a while so I think I will take her double the usual number, that is four magazines.*"

Ask the learners to work in pairs. They need to look at their double lines and make up a story to go with one of their double calculations. It could be a shopping story, a money story, something they did with a friend or something completely different.

Finish the session by sharing some of the stories.

Summary

Learners will recall doubles of numbers to ten and begin to work out doubles of larger numbers.

Notes on the Learner's Book
Double lines (p35): learners mark some numbers on number lines and double them. Give each learner a copy of the *Double lines* photocopy master to write down their answers.

Check up!
Tell the learners that you have a special pair of invisible glasses. When you put them on you see double!
- "*I can see eight now. What number will I see when I put my doubling glasses on?*"
- "*I've put my doubling glasses on and I can see number 20. What number will I see if I take my doubling glasses off?*"

Share your glasses with the learners. Point to a number, give them the doubling glasses and ask them what the number is now.

More activities

Doubling and multiplying (individuals)

You will need the *Doubling and multiplying* photocopy master (CD-ROM); one per learner.

Learners compare the effect of doubling and multiplying by two.

Games Book (ISBN 9781107623491)

Doubles game (p22) is a game for two to four players. This game focuses on doubles and identifying which number has been doubled (and then halving it).

Resources: *100 square* photocopy master (chapter 1, p4); large version for class display. *Blank Carroll diagram* photocopy master (p117); per group of learners. *0–100 number cards* photocopy master (CD-ROM); per two–three groups. *Number sort cards* photocopy master (CD-ROM); per group of learners. Scissors. *Blank Venn diagram* photocopy master (p118). (Optional: *Missing labels* photocopy master (CD-ROM); *Number box* photocopy master (CD-ROM).)

Begin by counting in fives from 0 to 100 and back again, using the 100 square. Tell the learners that they are going to count in fives again, but this time they are going to start on six. Ask what the next number will be. What about the number after that? Either write the list of numbers or mark them on the 100 square: 6, 11, 16, 21, 26, 31.

Ask the learners what patterns they can see. Draw out that when you start on six, you are starting on one more than five, so each number is one more than what we usually say when we count in fives starting from five. With the beginning of the count written or marked to help them, challenge the learners to count in fives from 6 to 96.

Remind the learners that there are lots of patterns in numbers and ask them to suggest some. They might talk about odd and even, the patterns produced when you count in fives or tens, or other patterns they have noticed.

Draw a simple Carroll diagram for the whole class to see. It should have two spaces and be labelled for odd and even numbers. Make sure the learners remember what a Carroll diagram is from Stage 1 (Unit 3C, chapter 28); it is a way of representing data and sorting it into sets of similar properties. Ask the learners to suggest numbers to go in each box. If necessary remind learners of the work they did in Stage 1 on odd and even numbers (Unit 2A, chapter 11); even numbers are numbers that can be grouped into twos, with none left over. Odd numbers cannot be grouped into twos, they have a remainder (one left over).

After putting a few numbers in the boxes, ask the learners if they can change one of the labels without needing to move any of the numbers. Odd could be changed to 'not even' or even could be written then crossed out to mean not even.

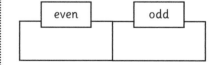

Vocabulary

odd one out: different to the others.

whole: not split into parts.

multiple: when you start counting at 0 and count in steps of equal sizes, you find numbers that are multiples of the step size.

0, 2, 4, 6, 8 … are multiples of two and are all in the two times table.

0, 5, 10, 15, 20, 25…are multiples of five and are all in the five times table.

Example: simple odd and even Carroll diagram.

even		odd	

Ask questions such as, "*Could I do the same with odd, and make the labels odd and not odd? Are there any numbers that belong in both boxes? What about in neither box?*"
Make sure the learners understand that all whole numbers are either odd or even.

Sort the learners into groups of three or four. Each group will need the *Blank Carroll diagram* photocopy master, some number cards and a set of cards from the *Number sort cards* photocopy master. Learners use the number sort cards to create labels for their Carroll diagram. The number sort cards should be used in pairs, for example 'odd' and 'not odd', 'even' and 'not even', 'multiples of 5' and 'not multiples of 5' etc.

Learners then place appropriate cards from the *0 – 100 Number cards* photocopy master into each box of their Carroll diagram. After the learners have explored the pairs of sorting cards, ask them to try labelling one box 'multiples of 5' and the other 'multiples of 10'. Remind the learners what we mean by 'multiples of five' and 'multiples of 10'.

After a while, stop everyone and explain that you have noticed a problem. "*Some of the numbers belong in both parts of the Carroll diagram. Where have you put 10, 20 or any other multiple of 10, because a multiple of 10 is also a multiple of 5?*" Discuss the learners' ideas. Show the learners the *Blank Venn diagram* photocopy master. Explain that this is also a way of sorting data into sets but that by overlapping the circles you can create sections that have more than one property. Ask learners to label the first circle 'multiples of 5' and the second circle 'multiples of 10'. Explain that the overlap has numbers that are multiples of five AND multiples of ten. Numbers which do not belong in either circle should be placed outside the circles but within the box.

Explain that these numbers can be considered to be the 'odd ones out', they do not fit in either category and are different to the other numbers. Learners should begin to use number properties to identify, and to explain why, numbers that do not fit the categories are considered the 'odd ones out'.

Learners should continue to place numbers where they think they belong.

Ask the learners to talk about what they have noticed. There should be numbers in all areas except the part of the 'multiples of 10' circle that does not overlap the 'multiples of 5' circle. Remind the learners that the reason they needed to change diagrams was because there was nowhere to put the numbers that were both multiples of five and multiples of ten. Now they go in the overlap to show they belong in both circles. There are no numbers which are multiples of ten but not multiples of five.

Example: Venn diagram showing multiples of 10, and multiples of 5 to 100 (only partially filled).

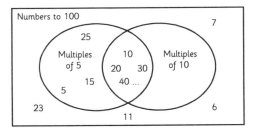

Ask the groups of learners to explore other combinations of labels, thinking carefully about where they place their numbers. After giving the learners time to explore, ask each group to stop without removing any of their numbers. Groups should then move around the room to look at each other's arrangements.

When the learners return to their own arrangement, each group should take turns to explain what they did and what they noticed about the numbers.

Summary

Learners begin to sort numbers according to their properties, including into two criteria and negative conditions (for example, 'not odd').

Notes on the Learner's Book
Odd one out (p36): learners decide which number could be 'the odd one out' and explain their reasoning.

Check up!

Tell the learners that you have a special wooden number box and only some numbers will pass through the lid into the box. Explain and ask questions such as "*If 7 is in my box but 4 cannot go in my box, what could you say about the numbers in the box?* (**They are odd numbers**) *What could you say about the numbers that are not allowed in box?* (**They are even numbers**) *Tell me another number to put in the box. Tell me a number that would not go in the box*". Change the numbers according to the properties of the numbers you put into the box. Learners will find this more engaging if you use some numbers and a real box.

More activities

Odd One Out (pairs)

You will need the *0–100 number cards* photocopy master (CD-ROM).

Player 1 shuffles and displays three cards. Player 2 has to decide which one is 'the odd one out' and explain why by providing a property pattern that is shared by all the numbers except for the odd one out. Possible properties could be that they are (or are not) odd, even, multiples of five, multiples of ten etc. It could even be that for two of the numbers, the digits add up to the same total and the third one does not. No answer is wrong, provided the learner can explain why that number could be the odd one out.

Missing labels (pairs)

> You will need the *Missing labels* photocopy master (CD-ROM).

The labels have fallen off the Carroll and Venn diagrams. What could they be? Ask the learners to work in pairs to partly complete a Carroll or Venn diagram. They can then remove the labels and challenge another pair to work out what they were.

Number box (pairs)

> You will need the *Number box* photocopy master (CD-ROM).

Player 1 has a selection of number cards. The cards are handed one at a time to Player 2 who decides on a rule and places each card inside or outside the box in accordance with that rule. Player 1 must work out why the numbers are in the box and can have one guess after each number has been placed. Player 1's score is the number of cards in the box. Players then switch roles. The winner is the person with the highest score after each player has had three turns at each role.

0–50 Number lines

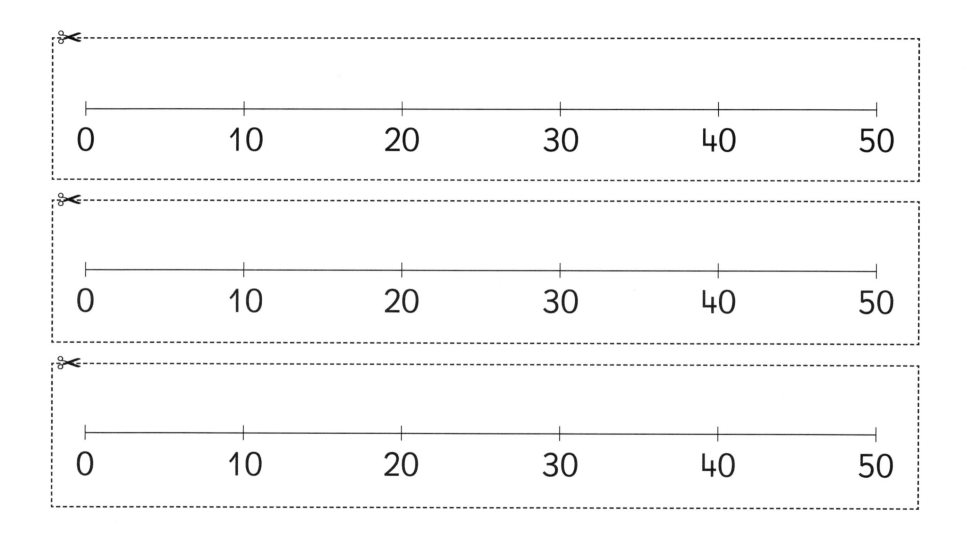

Blank Carroll diagram

Blank Venn diagram

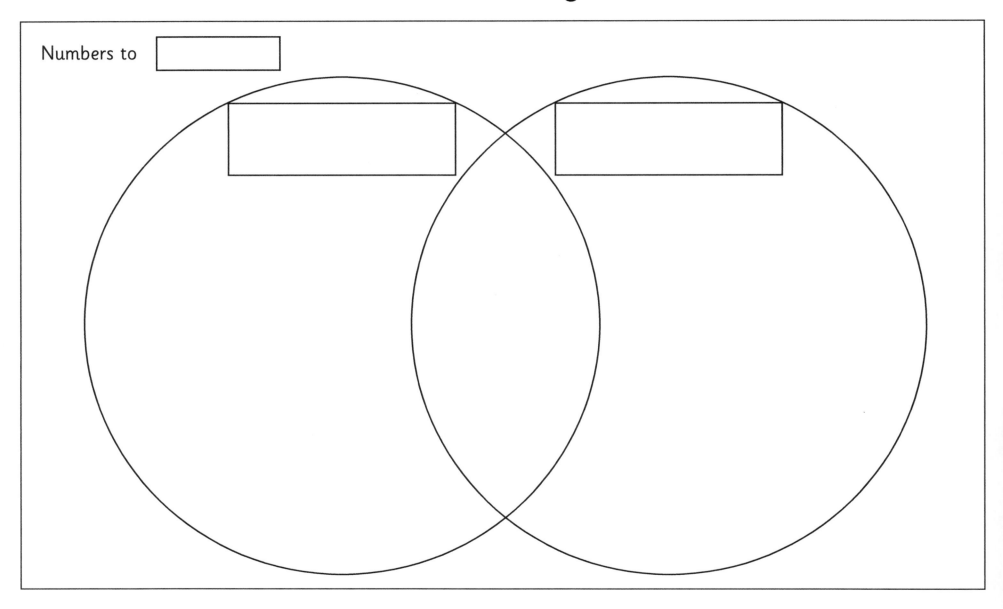

Numbers to

15 Adding and subtracting (2)

Quick reference

Core activity 15.1: Single-digit and two-digit numbers (Learner's Book p37)
Learners develop a strategy using ten for adding and subtracting a single-digit number from a two-digit number.

Core activity 15.2: Two-digits numbers (Learner's Book p38)
Learners partition two two-digit numbers into tens and ones in order to add them together.

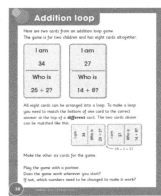

Prior learning	Objectives* – please note that listed objectives might only be partially covered within any given chapter but are covered fully across the book when taken as a whole
• Adding and subtracting single-digit numbers. • Using place value cards to partition two-digit numbers.	**1A: Number** (*Numbers and the number system*) 2Nn7 – Find 1 or 10 more/less than any two-digit number. **2A: Calculation** (*Addition and subtraction*) 2Nc11 – Add and subtract a single digit to and from a two-digit number. 2Nc12 – Add pairs of two-digit numbers. **2A: Problem solving** (*Using techniques and skills in solving mathematical problems*) 2Pt1 – Choose appropriate mental strategies to carry out calculations and explain how they worked out the answer. 2Pt2 – Explain methods and reasoning orally. 2Pt6 – Check the answer to an addition by adding the numbers in a different order or by using a different strategy, e.g. 35+19 by adding 20 to 35 and subtracting 1, and by adding 30+10 and 5+9.

*for NRICH activities mapped to the Cambridge Primary objectives, please visit www.cie.org.uk/cambridgeprimarymaths

Vocabulary
strategy • adjusting • loop game

Resources: *Tens and ones cards* photocopy master (CD-ROM); per pair of learners. (Optional: *Subtraction stars* photocopy master (CD-ROM); scissors.)

Give each pair of learners a set of arrow cards from the *Tens and ones* photocopy master (exclude the 100 card). Learners set them out in two columns in front of them, with 10 and 1 closest to them. These columns need to be ordered numerically. Choose a single-digit number, such as 7, and ask the learners to count in tens, starting from 7. Explain that they can use the 7 card to help them. They should match the arrow on the 7 card with the 10 card to show 17, then move the 7 along the tens column, making 27, 37, 47 and so on.

Count back from 97 in the same way. Repeat the count with a different single-digit number. Ask the learners to explain what is happening as they move the single-digit number up and down the column of tens. Check that they understand that they were adding or subtracting ten. Explain that we can use this to help us add or subtract any single-digit number because we know our number pairs to ten so well.

Ask the learners to make 38. "*What will the total be if we add 10?*" **(48)** "*What if we only wanted to add nine?*" Take suggestions from the class and discuss each one. If necessary, draw out that we know that $9 + 1$ is 10, so we could add 10 to 38 then take away one: $38 + 10 = 48$, $48 - 1 = 47$.

"*What if we needed to subtract 9 from 38?*" Again, take suggestions from the class and draw out that we know that $9 + 1$ is 10, so we can take away 10 then add back 1: $38 - 10 = 28$, $28 + 1 = 29$. Explain that the process of adding or subtracting too much and then adding or subtracting a smaller number from the solution to get the correct answer is known as '**adjusting**'. This can make the calculation easier, by adding or subtracting an easier number first. Choose another two-digit number to add and subtract nine from as a class.

If learners struggle with the idea of adjusting, for example, accepting that adding 10 and subtracting 1 is the same as adding 9, demonstrate it to them practically using objects such as cubes.

Put 8 cubes of one colour together, then add 9 cubes of a different colour to the end of the block of 8 one at a time, counting on as you do so. 9, 10, 11, 12, 13 … until you've added on 9

Vocabulary

strategy: the way we choose to do a calculation.

adjusting: adding or subtracting too much and then adding or subtracting a smaller number so that overall we have carried out the correct calculation. For example, adding ten then subtracting one in order to add nine.

cubes. Establish that you have 17 cubes, so 8 + 9 is 17. Then discuss that it would be quicker to have just added 10 to the 8 cubes and subtracted 1, rather than counting on each new cube. To prove that it works, set up a block of 8 cubes and a block of 10 cubes of a different colour and line them up under your block of 17 cubes. Count the 10 cubes, then remove one cube, to show that the second block of cubes is the same length as the first, i.e. 8 + 9 = 8 + 10 − 1 = 17.

As per the diagram

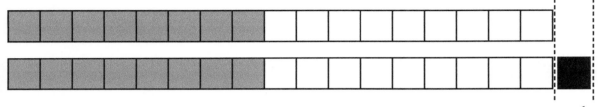

$$- 1$$

Ask pairs of learners to take it in turns to make a two-digit number and tell their partner how to find nine more and nine less by first adding or subtracting ten. After both partners have had a turn, repeat the process for adding and subtracting eight; using the number pairs to ten, the learners need to add or subtract ten from their intermediate solution in order to get the correct answer.

It might be useful to focus on adding and subtracting seven, six and five in another session. Alternatively, once both partners have had a turn, explain that we could do the same for adding and subtracting seven, six and five. Remind them that this is called **adjusting**. We deliberately add or subtract too much because it is an easier calculation to do, then we adjust our total by a small number so that, altogether, we have carried out the correct calculation.

Look out for!

- Learners who find it hard to recall the number pairs to ten. *Provide them with a list or help them to make their own. Looking up the number pair will help to develop recall.*
- Learners who find number pairs straightforward. *Encourage them to explore adding and subtracting a single-digit number to and from a three-digit number.*

Ask the learners if they would add (or subtract) one in the same way. The learners should be able to tell you that it would be easier to just count on (or back) one. Ask the learners what they would do to add or subtract three and four. Discuss when it is easier to count on and back and when it is better to switch to the using the adjusting strategy. There is no right or wrong answer for five, but learners are likely to see that the adding or subtracting ten strategy is useful for six, seven, eight and nine but counting on (or back) is quicker for adding or subtracting one, two, three and four.

Towards the end of the session, remind the learners that they were exploring one way to add or subtract a small number but it is not the only way. Sometimes the way in which you do the calculation will depend on both numbers. Write two number sentences where the learners can see them. For example: $22 + 5$ and $28 + 5$.

Ask the learners to talk with their partner about how they might do each calculation.

Finish the session by looking at each calculation in turn, exploring different ways of solving it. For example,
$22 + 5$: $5 + 2$ is 7, so $22 + 5 = 27$.
No need to add 10 and adjust because you can swap the ones around to make it $5 + 2$.
$28 + 5$: $28 + 10 = 38$, $38 - 5 = 33$
Or, $28 + 2 = 30$ (using the number pair for 10) $30 + 3 = 33$

The learners may have other ideas too. Encourage learners to check their answers by adding the numbers in a different way or using a different strategy.

Summary

Learners begin to develop a strategy for adding/subtracting a single digit to/from a two-digit number by adding or subtracting ten and adjusting.

Notes on the Learner's Book

Number stories (p37): learners make up a story to match a number sentence.

Check up!

Keep some slips of paper with simple addition and subtraction number sentences on. Ask learners to tell you a story for the calculation. If necessary, model one yourself then give the learners a different one to use. Or ask questions such as, "*How would you add 5 to 27? What if you were adding 5 to 22?*"

More activities

Subtraction stars (individuals)

> You will need the *Subtraction stars* photocopy master (CD-ROM).

Learners cut out the star then fold all the star arms in to the middle so that the numbers cannot be seen. They then fold open one arm and subtract the smaller number in the middle of the star from the larger number on the point of the star. After three calculations, they fold out two arms and subtract the number in the middle of the star next to one arm from the number on the point on the other arm. Each time they unfold two arms, there will be two subtractions to carry out.

Games Book (ISBN 9781107623491)

Make 100 (p14) is a game for two players. Learners add and subtract numbers to get as close as they can to 100.

Resources: *Number pair cards* photocopy master (CD-ROM). *0–100 number line* photocopy master (chapter 3, p18); large version for class display, and one per pair of learners. *100 square* photocopy master (chapter 1, p4); large version for class display. *Tens and ones cards* photocopy master (CD-ROM); per pair of learners. Base 10 apparatus (if available). Paper or mini whiteboards (if available); per pair of learners. (Optional: *Adding stars* photocopy master (CD-ROM); *Addition loop cards* photocopy master (CD-ROM); 1–6 dice (if not available use the net on the CD-ROM).)

Begin by shuffling the cards from the *Number pair cards* photocopy master. Show the learners each card in turn and ask them to tell you the number pair to ten. Turn the cards over and reshuffle them before going through them again.

Show the learners two two-digit numbers such as 25 and 32. Ask them how best to add the numbers together; work together as a class to draw up a list of useful reminders. These might include:
- Start with the bigger number.
- Look for number pairs to ten.
- Find the bigger number on the number line and count on the right number of spaces.
- Find the bigger number on the 100 square and count on.

Work through two or three examples using the *0–100 number line* photocopy master, counting on in ones first, then repeat the calculation counting tens and ones. Then work through two or three examples using the *100 square* photocopy master, moving down a square to add on each ten, then count on the ones.

Explain that these are all very useful but there is an easier way. Remind the learners that they know how to partition (split) numbers into tens and ones. Explain that this is very useful when adding. Give each pair of learners a set of arrow cards from the *Tens and ones* photocopy master and ask them to find the cards to make 25 and 32. Discard the other cards for the moment. Split both numbers into tens and ones, so that the learners have 30 and 20, and five and two. Some learners may find it useful to make the numbers with base ten apparatus to support their partitioning (so, 25 would need two ten sticks and five cubes). Ask the learners to add 30 and 20.

Vocabulary

loop game: a game which can start and finish anywhere because it is one continuous loop.

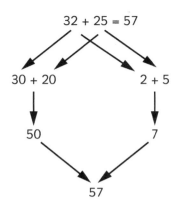

32 + 25 = 57

Remind the learners that they know $3+2=5$, so they also know that 3 tens and 2 tens must be 5 tens, so $30+20=50$. Ask the learners to add 2 and 5 and record it on the diagram. Show the learners how to turn the diagram into a number sentence:
$32+25=30+20+2+5=50+7=57$

Write some numbers where all the learners can see them. For example: 13, 32, 16, 24, 27 and 35. Ask the learners to work in pairs, choosing any two numbers to add together. They should make each number using the arrow cards from the *Tens and ones* photocopy master, then draw what they do, as you did earlier. The learners could use mini whiteboards or paper to record. They could also use a 100 number line or 100 square to help them if they need to.

Towards the end of the session, write six short number sentences where everyone can see them, for example, $32+25=57$. Remind the learners that the total was found by partitioning the numbers and adding. Ask the learners to pick a number sentence and check if it is correct using any method they choose. After a few minutes, talk through some of the different methods used.

Summary

Learners partition two-digit numbers to help add them together.

Notes on the Learner's Book
Addition loop (p38): learners make the six cards to create a loop game; they will need blank cards, scissors and pens.

Check up!

- *"How would you partition 27 to add it to another number? Why is that a useful thing to do?"*
- *"Add 34 and 57 together. How did you do this?"*
- *"Add 13 and 89 together. How did you do this?"*

More activities

Adding stars (individuals)

> You will need the *Addition stars* photocopy master (CD-ROM).

Learners cut out the star then fold all six of the star arms in to the middle so that the numbers cannot be seen. They then fold open two arms and add those numbers together, drawing a diagram to show what they did.

Addition loop (groups, ideally four or six players)

> You will need the *Addition loop cards* photocopy master (CD-ROM). A 1–6 dice.

Share the cards between learners so that each player has the same number of cards. Players turn their cards face up and arrange them how they wish, taking note of the 'I am' numbers. Players take it in turns to roll the 1–6 dice; the player who rolls the lowest number starts. They choose one of their cards, read it out and turn the card face down. Everyone works out the calculation and looks to see if the total is one of their 'I am' numbers. The player who has the matching number reads out that card.

Play continues in this way until all cards are turned face down. As a check, the calculation on the last card should have the 'I am' number of the first card as its total. The game is a loop so it does not matter where it starts but all cards should have been turned over when the game is complete.

16 Finding the difference

Quick reference

Core activity 16.1: Find small differences (Learner's book p39)

Learners count on and back, and compare quantities to find the difference, linking this with subtraction and take away.

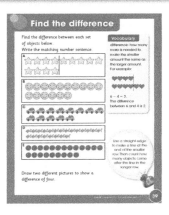

Prior learning	Objectives* – please note that listed objectives might only be partially covered within any given chapter but are covered fully across the book when taken as a whole
• Counting to 100. • Experience of take away and subtraction.	**2A: Calculation** (*Addition and subtraction*) 2Nc13 – Find a small difference between pairs of two-digit numbers. 2Nc15 – Understand subtraction as both difference and take away. **2A: Problem solving** (*Using techniques and skills in solving mathematical problems*) 2Pt2 – Explain methods and reasoning orally. 2Pt7 – Check a subtraction by adding the answer to the smaller number in the original subtraction.

*for NRICH activities mapped to the Cambridge Primary objectives, please visit www.cie.org.uk/cambridgeprimarymaths

Vocabulary

difference

Resources: *100 square* photocopy master (chapter1, p4); large version for class display. *Counting cards* photocopy master (CD-ROM). *More counting cards* photocopy master (CD-ROM). *0–100 number line* (chapter 3, p18); large version for class display. Beadstrings; per pair of learners (if not available use the *Beadstrings* photocopy master (p131), one per learner). (Optional: *Find the difference* photocopy master (CD-ROM); *Talk cards* photocopy master (CD-ROM).)

Remind the learners how to respond to the counting cards from the *Counting cards* and *More counting cards* photocopy masters. Include the +1, –1, +2, –2, +5, –5, +10 and –10. Choose a start number on the 100 square, such as 34, and encourage the learners to use the 100 square to help them. Repeat with different starting numbers.

Remind learners of the term '**difference**' that they encountered in Stage 1 (Unit 2A, chapter 13), and what it means.

Display the *0–100 Number line* photocopy master for the whole class to see, keep this up for reference if required. Give each learner a beadstring if available, or a copy of the *Beadstrings* photocopy master. If using real beadstrings, learners will need to work in pairs, comparing their beadstrings. Point out 18 on the beadstring or on the displayed number line. Ask the learners to find it on their first beadstring (if they are using the photocopy master, they could quickly label it or colour it in). Ask the learners to find 15 on their second beadstring. Ask, *"Which set of beads is longer, the 18 or 15 beads? So which set is shorter? How can we find the difference between them?"*

Discuss the learners' ideas. If no one suggests it, write 18 – 15 where everyone can see it and suggest counting back from 18 to 15. Then show the learners how to draw a line from after the 15 bead to the same point on the second beadstring and again for the 18 bead. Point out the gap and explain that it is now very easy to see that the difference between 18 and 15 is 3. Explain that when the two numbers are close together, we can easily find the difference by looking at the gap.

Ask the learners to use their first two beadstrings again to find the difference between 39 and 37, then 56 and 52, and finally 83 and 78.

Vocabulary

difference: how many more is needed to make the smaller amount the same as the larger amount.

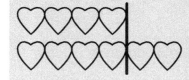

6 – 4 = 2. The difference between 6 and 4 is 2.

Explain that they found the difference by comparing the two amounts, but it is just as easy to do that on one beadstring or Number line. Ask the learners find 32 and 36 on their third beadstring. Ask how many beads they count when they count on from 32 to 36; they should count 4, so the difference between 36 and 32 is 4, and $36-32=4$.

Once the differences have been agreed, remind the learners that what they were doing was subtraction, or 'take away' calculations: $18-15$; $39-37$; $56-52$; $83-78$; and $36-32$. Ask them to check their answers by adding the difference to the smaller number in the original calculation.

List some more small differences for the learners to find using their beadstrings; ask learners to check their answers as before. After agreeing the answer for each calculation, collect the beadstrings.

Ask the learners to explain what they did each time to find the answer. Sum up the explanations given by saying that what they did was to start from the small number and count on how many more to get to the bigger number. Explain that they could also count back from the bigger number to the smaller number, but counting on is usually easier.

Write $28-25$ where everyone can see it. Tell the learners that they will not always have a beadstring, or even paper and pencil, when they want to do a calculation, so it is a good idea to think about how to do them mentally. Demonstrate using $28-25$: they need to start with 25 in their heads, then count on to 28, i.e. 26, 27, 28. Learners may find it helpful to extend a finger for each number they say. Ask the learners how many numbers they said, (**Answer: 'three'**). So, $28-25=3$. "*The difference between 28 and 25 is 3; 28 take away 25 is 3; and 28 subtract 25 is 3. It does not matter how we say it, we are doing the same thing each time.*" Explain that we could check that we had found the right answer by adding the answer to the smaller number in the original subtraction, in this case, $25+3=28$. Repeat the process with $23-18$, including checking by adding. If there is time, work through a few more small differences together.

Look out for!

- Learners who are having difficulty 'counting on'. (When some learners count on from 32 to 36 on a beadstring they count '5' because they are including bead number 32 as 1.) *Remind them that the first bead was part of the starting number, so it has already been counted. What they are doing is counting how many **more** to get to 36.*
- Learners who recognise early on how useful it would be to count on. *Give them more difficult numbers to find the difference between, for example, those on the last two rows of the Find the difference photocopy master.*

Summary

Learners are able to count on to find a small difference and they begin to recognise 'difference' and 'take away' as subtraction.

Notes on the Learner's Book

Find the difference (p39): learners write a number sentence for each difference picture.

Check up!

- *"What is the difference between 13 and 17?* **(4)** *How did you work this out?"*
- *"What is the difference between 31 and 29?"* **(2)** *How did you work this out?"*
- *"If I found the difference between 27 and 19 would I get the same answer as if I took 19 from 27? Why?"* **(Yes, because finding the difference and taking away are the same thing, they are both subtraction calculations.)**

More activities

Find the difference (individuals, pairs or groups)

You will need the *Find the difference* photocopy master (CD-ROM) and the *Talk cards* photocopy master (CD-ROM).

Learners take it in turns to take a difference card and a talk card. The talk card tells the learner how to read the calculation to the rest of the group. Learners could work in pairs or a small group. Alternatively, learners could complete the cards as an individual challenge. The bottom two rows of difference cards are more challenging and could be omitted if necessary.

Games Book (ISBN 9781107623491)

10 Difference (p25) is a game for two or three players. Learners find the difference between two small numbers, aiming for a total of up to three differences of 10.

Beadstrings

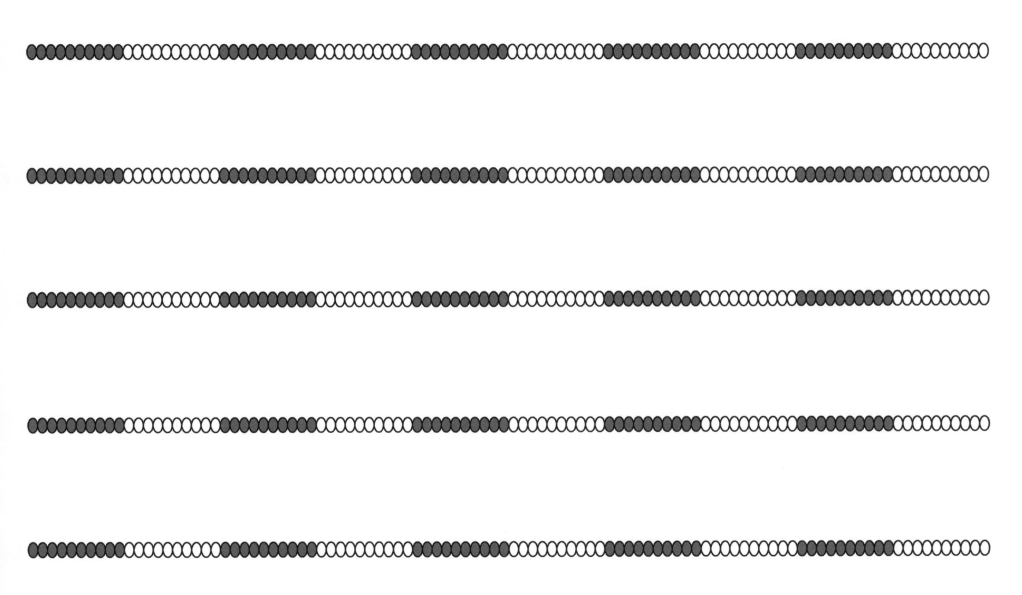

Blank page

Quick reference

Core activity 17.1: Arrays (2) (Learner's Book p40)
Learners explore multiplication and addition by making different arrays with the same number of objects.

Core activity 17.2: Counting to twos, fives and tens (Learner's Book p41)
Learners count in twos, fives and tens to solve practical problems.

Core activity 17.3: Division (Learner's Book p43)
Learners begin to understand division as grouping, use the division sign and recognise that sometimes there will be some left over.

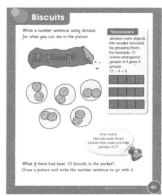

Prior learning	Objectives* – please note that listed objectives might only be partially covered within any given chapter but are covered fully across the book when taken as a whole
• Counting in twos, fives and tens. • Explored representing repeated addition in an array.	**2A: Calculation** (*Multiplication and division*) 2Nc17 – Understand multiplication as describing an array. 2Nc18 – Understand division as grouping and use the ÷ sign. 2Nc23 – Understand that division can leave some left over. 2Nc19 – Use counting in twos, fives or tens to solve practical problems involving repeated addition. **2A: Problem solving** (*Using techniques and skills in solving mathematical problems*) 2Pt1 – Choose appropriate mental strategies to carry out calculations and explain how they worked out the answer. 2Pt2 – Explain methods and reasoning orally. 2Pt3 – Explore number problems and puzzles. 2Pt4 – Make sense of simple word problems (single and easy two-step), decide what operations (addition or subtraction, simple multiplication or division) are needed to solve them and, with help, represent them, with objects or drawings or on a number line. 2Pt5 – Make up a number story to go with a calculation.

*for NRICH activities mapped to the Cambridge Primary objectives, please visit www.cie.org.uk/cambridgeprimarymaths

Vocabulary

divide/division • grouping • remainder

Resources: *100 square* photocopy master (chapter 1, p4); large version for class display, and one per learner. *Counting cards* photocopy master (CD-ROM). *More counting cards* photocopy master (CD-ROM). *Array cards* photocopy master (CD-ROM); large version for class display. Each pair of learners will need: 12, 18 or 24 cubes or counters and squared paper.

Remind the learners how to respond to the large counting cards from the *Counting cards* and *More counting cards* photocopy masters. Include +1, –1, +2, –2, +5, –5, +10 and –10. Choose a start number on the 100 square such as 34 and encourage the learners to use the 100 square to help them. Repeat with different starting numbers.

Ask the learners if they can remember what an array is. Show them the *Array cards* photocopy master. Ask if they can remember how to label an array. Choose one of the array cards to label as repeated addition and as multiplication. Rotate 90 degrees and write the new labels. Make sure the learners realise that the labels are all for the same array.

Ask the learners to work in pairs. Give each pair 12, 18 or 24 cubes (or counters) as appropriate. Ask them to arrange their cubes in an array and then record it on squared paper, writing the matching number sentences next to it. Each X below represents a cube.

X	X	X	X		3	+	3	+	3	+	3	=	12		
X	X	X	X		4	×	3	=	12						
X	X	X	X		4	+	4	+	4	=	12				
					3	×	4	=	12						

Challenge the learners to find as many different arrays as they can for their cubes. If the learners feel they have found all the possible arrays for their number, ask them to choose their own number to investigate. Can they make an array with their chosen number of cubes? Remind them that every row must have the same number of cubes in it. Every column must also have the same number of cubes in it, but the number in each row and each column do not have to be the same.

Look out for!

Learners who find arrays straightforward. *Challenge them to choose a number and predict what arrays they will be able to make. They can then check with that number of objects to see if their predictions were correct.*

Opportunity for display

Display all the different arrays for each number. Use the heading *Arrays* then label each group *Arrays for 12; Arrays for 18; Arrays for 24.* Ask questions such as, "*Have we found all the different arrays for these three numbers? Can you think of any more?*"

Finish the session by drawing or listing all the different arrays for 12, 18 and 24. Did each pair find all the possible arrays? Discuss what learners have noticed about other numbers they have explored. For example, we can make an array with one in each column or one in each row for any number.

Summary

- Learners understand arrays as representing multiplication.
- They recognise that a particular number of objects can sometimes be arranged in different arrays.

Notes on the Learner's Book

Where are the arrays? (p40): learners draw arrays to match the repeated addition and multiplication number sentences.

Resources: *Counting cards* photocopy master (CD-ROM). *More counting cards* photocopy master (CD-ROM). *100 square* (chapter 1, p4); large version for class display, and one per learner. (Optional: *Counting grid* photocopy master (CD-ROM); '*2*', '*5*', '*10*' *stamps* photocopy masters (CD-ROM).)

Count with the learners using the counting cards from the *Counting cards* and *More counting cards* photocopy masters. Discard +1 and −1. Choose a start number on the 100 square such as 25 and encourage the learners to use a 100 square to help them. Repeat with different starting numbers.

Ask the learners how many eyes there are in the classroom today. "*How can you find out?*" Discuss ideas such as counting how many people there are in the classroom and then doubling the number; or counting every person in twos. Work out how many eyes there are using both methods.

Remind the learners that doubling means two lots of something, so it is the same as multiplying by two. Ask the learners how many hands there are in the classroom. We already know because it will be the same as the number of eyes in the class, if everyone has two eyes and two hands.

Ask, "*How many fingers are there in the classroom today? We know how many hands, but how many fingers?*"

> Ask the learners to work in pairs to find out how many fingers. Challenge them to work out how many toes too.

Compare methods. Did the learners count in fives to find how many fingers? Or did they realise that everyone has 10 and count in tens? Did they recognise that there would be the same number of toes?

> Challenge the learners to estimate how many fingers there are in school today. Discuss how they arrived at their estimates. **(Possible answers include: multiplying the number of fingers in their classroom by the number of classes in the school)** Are the estimates reasonable? Ask the learners to work with a partner to discuss how they could find out.

Share ideas on how to find out. If you have time (or as part of another session), choose a method and find out the number of fingers in the whole school. Compare the result with the estimates.

Look out for!

- Learners who find it hard to maintain their counting in twos, fives or tens to sufficiently high numbers to answer the questions. *Give them a copy of the 100 square for support, or a class list to record their count beside each name.*
- Learners who find counting in twos, fives and tens straightforward. *Ask them to estimate and then to find out how many legs in the classroom, including chair, table and any other legs. They could go on to find out how many legs in school today.*

Summary

Learners have used counting in twos, fives and tens to solve practical problems.

Notes on the Learner's Book

Shoe boxes (p41): learners calculate how many shoes there are by counting in twos.

Hands up! (p42): learners calculate how many fingers there are by counting in fives.

Check up!

Give learners a start number and challenge them to count on (or back) in twos, fives or tens as appropriate.

More activities

Counting grid (individuals)

> You will need the *Counting grid* photocopy master (CD-ROM).

Learners complete the grid by counting in twos, fives and tens. They circle a number in the grid then draw the matching array. This can be extended by learners counting down the column in the appropriate number, then drawing the array for one of the numbers in the grid.

Two, five, ten fish stamps (pairs)

> You will need the *2, 5, 10 fish stamps* photocopy master (CD-ROM).

Label envelopes or parcels with a particular amount in the local currency. Challenge learners to put the correct amount of stamps on the envelope or parcel.

Games Book (ISBN 9781107623491)

2, 5, 10 game (p27) is a game for two to four players. Learners collect twos, fives and tens then count in twos, fives and tens to find their total.

> **Resources:** (Optional: *Division stories* photocopy master (CD-ROM); *Mixed division stories* photocopy master (CD-ROM).)

Ask the class how many learners are present in the classroom today. If necessary, ask the learners to sit still while one learner counts and another checks using a different method. Once the number is confirmed, ask the learners, "*Do you think you will be able to arrange yourselves into groups of one? Do you think anyone will be left over?*" If the learners have any doubts, get them to arrange themselves in ones to check. (**Answer: there will be no one left over**)

Write the number of learners as a calculation, where everyone can see it. For example, say there are 25 learners in the classroom: $25 \div 1 = 25$, read out what you have written. Point out the division sign and explain what it means: it is used to show that we have put something into groups.

Ask, "*Do you think you will be able to arrange yourselves into groups of twos? Do you think anyone will be left over?*" If necessary, encourage the learners to consider whether the number of learners is odd or even. Remind them that an even number can be divided by two with none left over but an odd number cannot.

Ask the learners to arrange themselves in twos and record what they discover. For example, if there are 24 learners in the classroom then they would write $24 \div 2 = 12$. If there is an odd number of learners, such as 25, then they will discover that someone is not part of a two, they are 'left over'. Explain that this can be written as $25 \div 2 = 12r1$. We write what is left over after division with an 'r' for remainder.

Continue to ask the learners to divide the class into threes, fours, fives and sixes. You could go as far as grouping the learners into tens. Record each calculation with the help of the learners. Talk about the fact that sometimes you can put things into groups with none left over but sometimes there will be some left over.

Point to one of the number sentences and tell a matching story such as, "*There were 25 learners in Class P. The learners got into twos to walk to the shops. There were 12 groups of two and one child left over.*"

Vocabulary

divide/division: sorting a quantity into smaller, equally sized groups.

grouping: sorting objects together into sets of the same size.

remainder: what is left over after division.

Look out for!

- Learners having a problem with the concept of a remainder, particularly if the remainder always seems to be one. (If the number of learners present is 25, the remainder will be 1 when dividing by 2, 3 and 4. If the remainder is always the same number, learners may be left thinking that the remainder is always one.) *Make sure you continue the grouping until a different remainder occurs.*
- Learners who find division as grouping straightforward. *Encourage them to write some division word problems for a friend to solve.*

Invite a child to tell a story for one of the other number sentences. Can the rest of the learners identify which number sentence they used?

Opportunity for display

Take photographs of each grouping and display with the matching division sentence. You could label the display *Dividing our class*, *Dividing Class P* or something similar.

Summary

- Learners begin to understand division as grouping.
- Learners begin to recognise and use the division sign.
- Learners recognise that following some divisions there will be a remainder.

Notes on the Learner's Book
Biscuits (p43): learners write the matching division number sentence for the picture.

Check up!
When a different number of learners are present ask questions such as:
- *"Could we divide the class into twos today? Would there be a remainder? How do you know?*
- *"Could we divide the class today into fives? Would there be a remainder? How do you know?"*

More activities

Division stories (individuals)

You will need the *Division stories* photocopy master (CD-ROM).

Learners model the division using objects, then write the number sentence for a division story. There are no remainders for these stories.

Mixed Division stories (individuals)

You will need the *Mixed division stories* photocopy master (CD-ROM).

Learners write the number sentence for the division stories. Some of these stories will leave a remainder.

Games Book (ISBN 9781107623491)

Remainders game (p27) is a game for two to four players. Learners use counters to create a division calculation with a particular remainder.

Blank page

18 Handling data

Quick reference

Core activity 18.1: Block graphs (Learner's Book p44)
Learners collect and sort data, then represent it using a block graph.

Core activity 18.2 Comparing data (Learner's Book p45)
Learners compare data across two different representations and draw conclusions about the data.

Core activity 18.3: Venn diagrams (Learner's Book p46)
Learners sort and compare data using a Venn diagram.

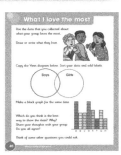

Prior learning	Objectives* – please note that listed objectives might only be partially covered within any given chapter but are covered fully across the book when taken as a whole
• Some knowledge and understanding of collecting data. • Some knowledge and understanding of block graphs. • Early understanding of simple problem solving.	**2B: Handling data** (*Organising, categorising and representing data*) 2Dh1 – Answer a question by collecting and recording data in lists and tables, and representing it as block graphs and pictograms to show results. 2Dh2 – Use Carroll and Venn diagrams to sort numbers or objects using one criterion; begin to sort numbers and objects using two criteria; explain choices using appropriate language, including 'not'. **2B: Problem solving** (*Using techniques and skills in solving mathematical problems*) 2Pt2 – Explain methods and reasoning orally. 2Pt3 – Explore number problems and puzzles. 2Pt4 – Make sense of simple word problems (single and easy two-step), decide what operations (addition or subtraction, simple multiplication or division) are needed to solve them and, with help, represent them, with objects or drawings or on a number line. 2Pt11 – Consider whether an answer is reasonable.

*for NRICH activities mapped to the Cambridge Primary objectives, please visit www.cie.org.uk/cambridgeprimarymaths

Vocabulary

represent • set • sort

Resources: *What I love the most survey* photocopy master (CD-ROM); one per learner. Paper, pencils, and masking tape.

Introduce the topic title of 'What I love most'. "*We are going to look at the things that you love the most. Talk to the person next to you about what you love the most. I want you to draw a quick picture of what you love the most.*" Give learners a few minutes to finish their drawing and then ask some of the learners to share their ideas with the rest of the class. "*We'll put your drawings* [suitable location] *so that everyone can see them and then we'll need to sort them into different sets.*" Explain what is meant by a 'set'; it is the mathematical term used for a 'group' of items that are of the same/similar type.

Invite the learners to say what they have drawn, and as they do so, give them some masking tape so that they can stick their picture up for the class to see.

"*Let's look at all of these pictures and see if we can sort them into different sets. Remember that all the pictures have to have something that is the same about them in order for them to be in the same set. Can anyone give me the title of a set that we can put some of these pictures in?*"

Learners will have to think about names for their categories; explain that in order to do this, they will also need to think about what fits into which category. "*You will need to think about which things go together. You may find it easier to group the things first and* **then** *think of a name for each set based on how you have grouped them. Talk to the person next to you about your ideas.*"

Take ideas from the class. There may be lots of different categories or only a few. (Mother, Father, family, favourite animals, toys, hobbies, food etc.). Encourage learners to assess if their answers are reasonable, for example, you might get some classifications such as 'has two legs', but explain that this could include a person and a bird, which could also fit into 'family' or 'favourite animals', so explain that the name of the set needs to be relevant to the original question that was asked, 'What I love the most'.

Discuss sets with the class and make any changes that they suggest. As the learners begin to agree on the sets, move the pictures into the sets so that they can see which pictures have been classified and which are still left to sort. Students need to try to give good reasons for their ideas.

Vocabulary

represent: to show/display/present/describe something.

set: a group of items that are the same type or that share a property.

sort: grouping items together that are of the same/similar type or that share properties.

Explain that by grouping their pictures into sets and giving each set a name, they have been 'sorting' data. Once data has been sorted, it is a good idea to find a way to represent that data so that it is organised neatly and we can look for any patterns. Explain what is meant by 'represent'.

"Now all of the pictures have been sorted, we're going to make a giant block graph. Can you remember what we need to make the block graph?" Choose some learners to share their ideas and gradually construct the graph as they tell you what you need to do.

If necessary, remind them that a block graph has a straight flat (horizontal) line (called an axis) labelled with the name of each set. A block is used to represent an item of data; in this case one block represents one learner. Make sure learners understand the importance of writing the name of each set under the stacked blocks; explain that this is called 'labelling the graph' and is very important.

The finished block diagram should list the sets across the bottom of the board and there should be blocks (the learners' pictures in this case) stacked vertically above the name of the appropriate set. Each block represents one learner's picture (and therefore represents one learner). There may be one or two pictures that do not fit into any of the sets and need one of their own. *"We have these few pictures left. We need to find a set or make a new one for these. What label do you think we could put on them?"*

Start to introduce the idea of using the block graph to find patterns and/or make statements about the data they have collected.

Ask, *"What does the block graph tell you about what we love the most?"* Encourage answers such as: 'We love [enter set name here] the most'; 'We love [set name] the least'; 'The same number of us loved [set name] and [set name]'. Ask learners to explain their answer: 'Because [set name] has the most blocks.'; 'Because [set name] has the least blocks'; 'Because [set name] and [set name] have the same number of blocks'. Discuss whether or not learners' answers seem reasonable given the graph.

Invite the learners to ask each other questions by using the block graph, for example, 'How many learners love [set name] the most?'

Display the graph in a place where it can be seen during the next two sessions. Use the block graph to make a statement/hypothesis such as, *"We love [set name] the most, so I think that the adults at home must also love [set name] the most."*

Look out for!

- Learners who find it hard to make a block graph or discuss categories. *Put them into a group where others can support them. Allow them to listen to the ideas of others.*
- Learners who may wish to collect more data from learners their own age. *They can ask one or two other learners after school or at playtime. Add the new data to the giant block graph.*

Opportunity for display

Display the giant class block graph as this will be needed for future sessions.

Ask the learners to collect data from the adults in their home in order to test if your statement is true. "*Use the 'What I loved the most survey' sheet and ask the adults you live with to help you fill it in.*" Show the class the *What I love the most* photocopy master survey sheet and explain what you want them to do.

Ask the class to bring back the sheets for the next session.

Summarise what the learners have done in the session. If you want, you could show them the steps in a flow diagram like that below. This is beyond the scope of the framework and not necessary but it might be a nice way to help the learners understand what they've been doing:

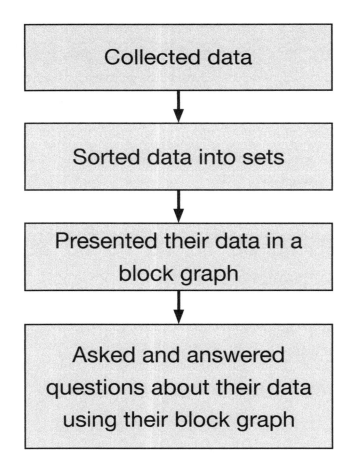

Summary

- Learners are able to answer a question by collecting and recording data in lists and tables, and representing it as a block graph to show results.
- They have explored problems and are able to explain their methods, thinking and reasoning orally.
- They have had the opportunity to consider whether their answer is reasonable, giving reasons if they change their mind.

Notes on the Learner's Book

Block graphs (p44): reinforces the core activity by using different data that can be interpreted and discussed. It also gives learners the opportunity to ask their own questions.

Check up!

- *"What do we mean by sorting data?"*
- *"What do we mean by representing data?"*
- *"How could you collect, sort and represent the class's favourite colour?"*
- *"What do we need to remember when we make a block graph?" "What do all block graphs need?"*
  (Answers include:
  - **sort the data into sets**
  - **put the sets along a straight (horizontal) line (axis)**
  - **make sure the block graph is labelled and it is indicated what each block represents)**
- *"What words do we use when we talk about graphs"?*

More activities

More data (individuals, pairs or groups)

Some students can collect data from another class, either the same age or different, and bring the results back to be sorted and graphed. What are the similarities to the class graph and what are the differences? Why might this be? Ask them to collect data from home using different criteria. They can make this into a block graph to share with the rest of the class.

Resources: A large sheet of paper, sticky notes and pencils; per group of learners. (Optional: 10 interlocking cubes of the same colour; per learner (but so that pairs of learners have different colours); a 1–6 dice (CD-ROM) or a 1–9 spinner (p40).)

"This session, we will look at and discuss the data that you collected from the adults you live with." Some learners may not have brought any information back to school but there should be enough from the others to make the session work, or you could prepare some results yourself.

"What did you find out? Did you find some of the most loved things were the same as in our bar graph? What were the things that were different?" List all of the 'most loved things' collected from adults on a board. Learners will use this list for later work in the session.

"When we put our most loved things on the block graph we decided how we could put them together in sets. The titles were [read out sets from previous session]. *Do you think the same sets will work for the adult data? Do you see any of the adults' most loved things that would fit in with our sets? Do you see any that don't fit?"* Allow time for the class to find and comment on similarities and differences between their own data and the adult data. There may be some that will fit and some that don't.

Put learners into small groups and ask them to sort the adult data into appropriate sets; they may or may not be the same sets as used in the previous session. *"In your small groups, you'll have to make some decisions about which things go together from the adult data. Sort the adult data and think about what you will call each set."*

Give each group a large sheet of paper to create a block graph and some sticky notes on which they draw or write the adult data, one note per 'most loved thing'. *"You can draw or write the adult 'most loved things' on the sticky notes. Decide where to put them on your graph. You can change your mind if you want to."* Allow time for each group to discuss the data, sort it and represent it as a block graph.

Each group has a chance to share their graph with the rest of the class giving their reasons for the grouping and set titles. Ask questions such as, *"Can you describe your method or rule to us all? Can you explain why it works? What have you learned or found out today? If*

Look out for!

- Learners who are having problems when discussing and making the graph. *Allow learners to discuss some ideas for the graph in pairs or with an adult.*
- Learners who have successfully completed a graph for the adult data. *Ask them to make comparisons between the class and adult graphs and combine the two to make a complete graph of both.*

Ask them to record what they found out and give possible reasons for the differences and the similarities. They should be ready to share their findings with the rest of the class.

you were doing it again, what would you do differently? Did you change your mind while you were working? Why?" Emphasise interesting differences so that the learners are aware of alternative ways of sorting the data.

Ask learners to make some statements about what adults love the most, based on the data shown in their block graphs. For example, 'Adults love [enter set name here] the most, I know this because that set has the most blocks'; 'They love [set name] the least; I know this because that set has the least number of blocks'; 'The same number of adults love [set name] and [set name]; I know this because both sets have the same number of blocks.'

Now tell the class that you want to compare the things that the class loves the most with what the adults loved the most. Ask how you might do this. Collect suggestions from the class and encourage the learners to understand that in order to do the comparison, they need to collect all the adult data together into one block graph. Decide on the sets for another giant block graph as a class and sort the adult data accordingly.

Once the giant adult block graph is complete, compare it with the block graph made in the previous session. Ask the class to decide if your statement from the previous session is correct: "*We love [set name] the most, so I think that the adults at home must also love [set name] the most.*" Is the adult data the same as the class data? If not, why not? Discuss similarities and differences.

Ask how many adults were asked and how many learners were asked in the previous session; discuss how having a larger/smaller total number of data items might impact the results. For example, if one household contained four adults, who might be more likely to all like the same thing, it might make a set seem more popular than it really is. Or if many more adults were asked than learners, it might not be fair to compare the data.

At the end of the session ask, "*Do different graphs show different things about the adult data?*"

Explain that in the next session they will be using their data and the data from adults to graph the results in a different way.

Opportunity for display
Large block graph from the class and the adult block graphs developed by the groups.

Summary

- Learners are able to answer a question by collecting and recording data in lists and tables, and representing it as a block graph to show results.
- They can explain their methods, thinking and reasoning orally.
- They have explored problems and have had the opportunity to consider whether their answer is reasonable and if they want to change their mind, giving reasons.

Notes on the Learner's Book

Comparing data (p45): learners interpret two graphs and then compare them. Encourage learners to discuss the way the information is displayed and what information is shown by the graphs.

More activities

Noughts and crosses (pairs)

> You will need 20 interlocking cubes, ten of one colour, ten of another.

Learners draw a 3 × 3 grid to give nine spaces which can be filled. Players each decide whether they are a nought (O) or a cross (X). Taking turns, each player puts a nought or cross in each box. When one player has three in a row, vertically, horizontally, or diagonally, then they are the winner. Players make a graph as they play. Each pair needs 20 interlocking cubes on the table in front of them, ten of one colour and ten of another. They decide who is going to be each colour. The winner of each game takes a cube in their colour. They join their cubes to form a block graph showing who has won most games.

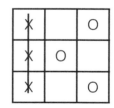 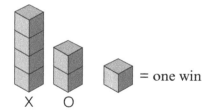

= one win

Play ends when one player has used all of their cubes.
Ask, *"Can you work out from your graph how many games you played?"*
Can you find a winning strategy? Many players start from the middle. Try starting from a corner and put your next two turns in a corner as well, and see what happens."

Cubes (pairs)

You will need a 1–6 dice (CD-ROM) or a 1–9 spinner (p40) and two different coloured interlinking cubes.

Learners each throw a dice ten times. Every time they throw an even number, they take a blue cube. Every time they throw an odd number take a red cube. Learners join the cubes of the same colour together and determine if they threw odd or even numbers the most. They should explain how they know. Ask them to explore that would happen if they threw the dice 11 times. Would that make any difference to the possible scores of each type of number? Why? Learners compare their answers.

Games Book (ISBN 9781107623491)

Track the Trolls (p83) is a game for two to four players. This game gives practice in, and reinforcement of, constructing and interpreting a bar graph.

Resources: *Venn diagram* photocopy master (p153); per pair of learners. Paper and pencils.

Remind learners of how they compared the 'class' block graph to the 'adult' block graphs in the previous session. Explain, "*This session is about representing our data in a different way. We are going to use a Venn diagram to do this. What can you tell me about Venn diagrams?*"

Draw a large Venn diagram for the whole class to see in order to help their thinking, and for responses. Answers should include things such as: data is grouped into circles; circles/other shapes are used to contain sets; overlapping circles are used to show items that fit into two sets.

Ask the class to think about the class data for the 'What I love the most' survey and the giant block graph of the adult data. "*Are there the same sets in each graph? Which set was the most popular for our class? What was the most popular set in the adults' graph? Are there any sets in the class graph that are not in the adult graph? Are there some sets in the adult graph that we do not have for the class data? Why might that be? What is the least popular set for both sets of data?*"

Allow time for discussion. Encourage the class to make simple comparisons such as the labels for same/different sets, if there are the same or a different number of blocks in set with the same name. During this discussion, the different ways in which different groups of learners sorted their data can be discussed again. Explain that the two block graphs show the detail of how many people liked each set, but what if we wanted a more clear picture of what only the adults liked, or what only the class liked? Or what both groups liked?

Explain that it would be easier to compare the two lots of data in this way if they were all on the same graph; explain that we can use a Venn diagram to do this. "*We can label our Venn diagram with titles to compare our class data with the adult data in a different way. We can label this side 'Adults' and this side 'Us' and put the 'set' names in the circles to show who liked what. We need to look very carefully at the data. What could we put in the 'Adult' circle that is not in the 'Us' circle? What could we put in the 'Us' circle that isn't in the 'Adult' circle?*" Give time for discussion and sharing of ideas.

Example: a typical Venn diagram

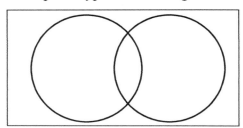

Look out for!

- Learners who have difficulties understanding a Venn diagram where the two circles overlap. *Give them two circles with no overlap. This could be done using hoops and physical resources to make a more concrete example. The data that doesn't fit in either goes round the edge. Slowly introduce the idea of them crossing.*
- Learners who are confident and competent with a Venn diagram. *Introduce the idea of using a Carroll diagram to show the same data. Use just two boxes at first, increasing to four.*

"Using the giant block graphs, I want you to work with a partner to sort both sets of data onto your own Venn diagram. You will need to think about where you will put data that is the same for adults and us. You can use words or pictures to show the information."

Give each pair one copy of the *Venn Diagram* photocopy master and, as they are working, walk round the room to make sure that they all understand the task. Remind them how important it is to label their Venn diagram so that we know what each set is.

Invite learners to talk about their Venn diagrams, including explaining what labels they used and where they sorted the data. Ask them to make statements about the data based on their Venn diagram. For example, 'No adults loved [set name] because it is only inside the 'Us' circle'; 'Both the class and the adults love [set name] because it is within the overlap of the two circles'; 'There are more sets for the adults than there are for the class' (or vice versa).

Ask the learners to think of reasons why the data is grouped how it is. For instance, if 'Video games' is a set that is only in the 'Us' circle this might be because most adults have grown out of playing computer games. If 'driving' is a set in the 'Adults' circle, it won't be in the 'Us' circle because we are too young to drive. Sets that overlap might be because they are activities the whole family does together, or a shared interest (such as pets, family etc.).

At the end of the session, ask some of the pairs to share what they did and what they found out.

Ask questions such as, *"What have you learned or found out today? If you were doing it again, what would you do differently? Did you change your mind while you were working? Why?"*

> ### Opportunity for display
> Group/pair Venn diagrams to be displayed with the block graphs.

Summary

- Learners are able to use a Venn diagram to display sets of data with up to two criteria.
- They are able to explain choices using appropriate language, including 'not', and be able to explain methods and reason orally.

Notes on the Learner's Book
What I love the most (p46): can be used as a reference to the work during the sessions but also as a starting point for learners to come up with their own ideas and questions.

Check up!
Ask:
- *"How could we find out what is the most popular subject in the class?" "How could we collect, sort and represent the data?"*
- *"What do we need to remember when we make a Venn diagram?"*
- *"What do all Venn diagrams need?"*
- *"What words to we use when we talk about graphs?"*
- *"What words do we use when we talk about a Venn diagram?"*

More activities

Sorting (class)

Use other familiar items to sort into a Venn diagram. Use learners' ideas, such as what fish are in the fish tank compared to what fish are likely to be in a local lake or aquarium (without taking them out of the water!). Discuss ways of representing the fish by drawing or writing. If you have a garden, you could use butterflies or birds. Favourite food is another area where learners can relate real-life experiences to representing the data.

3-criteria

Use a Venn diagram with three overlapping circles where learners are asked to sort using three criteria.

Venn diagram

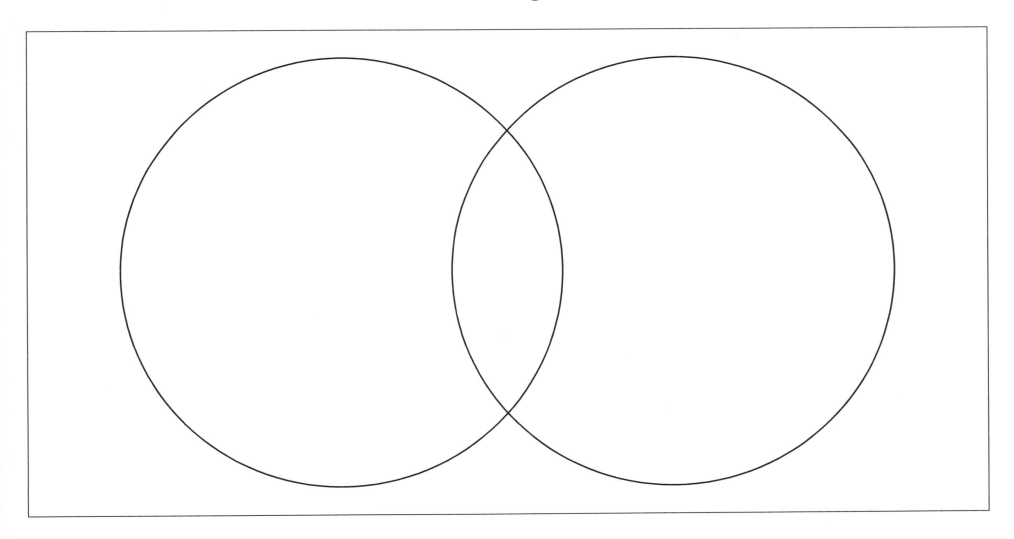

Blank page

19 Length, height and capacity

Quick reference

Core activity 19.1: Length and capacity (nesting shapes) (Learner's Book p47)
Learners are introduced to nesting shapes. They estimate, measure and
compare length, height and capacity by making their own 'Russian dolls'.

Core activity 19.2: Length and time (distance travelled) (Learner's Book p48)
Learners measure the distance travelled by paper aeroplanes, in centimetres, using standard
measures. They record how long the planes fly, in seconds.

Core activity 19.3: Following instructions (measuring in centimetres) (Learner's Book p49)
Learners continue to develop their listening skills by following a series of verbal instructions
to make a paper puppet. They are required to measure lengths accurately in centimetres.

Prior learning	Objectives* – please note that listed objectives might only be partially covered within any given chapter but are covered fully across the book when taken as a whole
• Knowledge and understanding of simple measures. • Knowledge and understanding of vocabulary associated with measures. • Understanding and use of estimation.	**2C: Measure** (*Length, mass and capacity*) 2Ml1 – Estimate, measure and compare lengths, weights and capacities, choosing and using suitable uniform non-standard and standard units and appropriate measuring instruments. 2Ml2 – Compare lengths, weights and capacities using the standard units: centimetres, metres, 100 g, kilogram and litre. **2C: Measure** (*Time*) 2Mt4 – Measure activities using seconds and minutes. **2C: Problem solving** (*Using techniques and skills in solving mathematical problems*) 2Pt2 – Explain methods and reasoning orally. 2Pt10 – Make a sensible estimation for the answer to a calculation. 2Pt11 – Consider whether an answer is reasonable.

*for NRICH activities mapped to the Cambridge Primary objectives, please visit www.cie.org.uk/cambridgeprimarymaths

Vocabulary

vertical • horizontal • nesting shapes

> **Resources:** Russian (Babushka) dolls or a set of boxes or shapes that fit inside each other (e.g. pastry cutters, gift boxes, shoe boxes, packaging). Learners should be asked to bring in any type of doll from home (if available). *Making Russian dolls* photocopy master (CD-ROM); large version of the instructions for class display, and one per learner. Paper/card, sticky tape, rulers and a pair of scissors; per learner of pair of learners. (Optional: *Russian doll outlines* photocopy master (CD-ROM); *Paper strips* photocopy master (CD-ROM); paper/card; glue.)

Using the collection of dolls (encourage learners to bring some in if they can) ask, "*What do you notice about these dolls? Are they all the same or are they different? Tell the person sitting next to you something about one or more of these dolls.*" Allow a few minutes for discussion. Choose some learners to share what they have noticed.

Show the learners the closed Russian doll (i.e. just the larger doll with the smaller ones still hidden inside) and ask, "*Has anyone seen a doll like this before? What is special about this doll?*" Ask some learners to share what they think is special. If no one can answer, gently shake the doll so that learners can hear the others inside. "*Listen very carefully. What can you hear when I shake the doll?*" Leave some time for all learners to hear. "*Can you hear it rattling? What do you think could be inside?*" Choose some learners to tell you what they think.

"*How could we find out?*" Take ideas from the class and agree that you could open it. Slowly open the doll to show another one inside. "*Do you think this is the last one? We have one, two dolls. Listen.*" Shake the dolls again. "*Let's open the next one. Now we have one, two, three dolls. I wonder how many there will be in total? Talk to the person next to you.*" Ask learners to give their estimates and record them on the board. Look at the least and the most. Ask, "*How could we find out how may there are in total?*"

By now most learners will suggest opening the dolls. When all of the dolls are shown, line them in order of size. Explain that shapes that fit inside each other in this way are known as **nesting shapes**. Make sure that the learners are able to relate this activity back to their work on capacity: how much an object can hold.

In order to create a set of nesting shapes, each smaller shape has to have a smaller capacity than the one before it. Relate this to length and width by reminding learners that if they make a 3D shape from a 2D net, one of the lengths on the 2D net will fold to create the width/depth of the 3D solid: so as a given length on the 2D net changes, so does the size of the 3D solid.

Vocabulary

nesting shapes: shapes of increasing/decreasing size that fit inside one another.

Explain the task to the learners. "*On your table is a pair of scissors, rulers, blank sheets of paper, sticky tape and some Russian Doll templates.*" Display the first page of the *Making Russian dolls* photocopy master for the whole class to see and talk them through the instructions of how to construct a 3D doll. Do not give them any clues about how to create the different capacities (they should find through trial and error that decreasing the length of the paper strip allows them to make a doll with a smaller 'capacity'). "*I want you to talk to your partner and find a way to make your own set of five nesting dolls using the templates.* As the learners are working, walk round to make sure that they all understand the task.

Opportunity for display
Make a display out of the nesting dolls made by the learners. If possible, include some dolls brought in from home. The owners could write a few sentences about their doll and use it as a label.

Look out for!
Learners who find the task easy. *Suggest that they make some instructions in words, pictures or diagrams to make a set of nesting shapes that can be used by others. What different 3D shapes can they make? Can they make a set of nesting dolls where each doll is a different shape?*

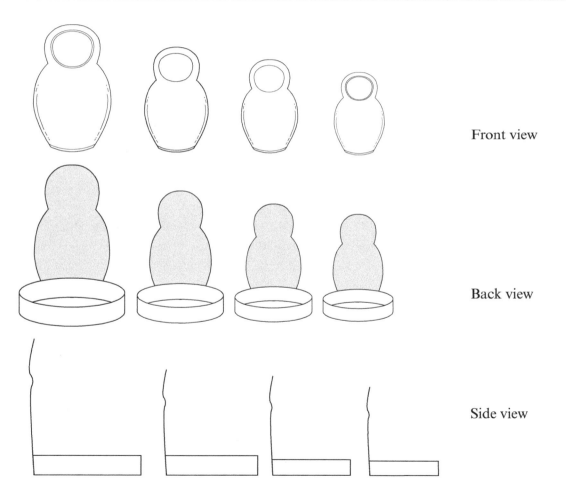

Front view

Back view

Side view

Towards the end of the session, choose some learners to show their set of 'dolls'. "*Can you tell us what you did? How did you make sure that they fitted inside each other? Can you explain why it works? What have you learned or found out today? If you were doing it again, what would you do the same or would you do something different? What did you find easy/most difficult?*"

Learners *should have* (if they haven't already) made the largest doll first (or the smallest), making a note of how long the paper strip for that doll was. Then, for each smaller doll (or larger doll), they should measure shorter and shorter (or longer and longer) strips of paper so that the circle is smaller (or larger) each time.

Summary

- Learners have consolidated and developed their understanding of length and height by making the paper strips to create different 'capacities' when looking at the properties of nesting.
- Learners have had the opportunity to discuss and refine their ideas and then share them with the rest of the class.

Notes on the Learner's Book

Nesting shapes (p47): can be used to begin a discussion; as a reference during the instruction stage of the lesson; or as support.

Check up!

- "*If we are making a set of nesting boxes what are some of the things that we need to remember?*"
  (Possible answers include:
  - **there needs to be a set of objects of different sizes that can fit inside each other, i.e. of decreasing capacity**
  - **it doesn't matter how tall they are, but they must be the same shape**
  - **we need to measure one box against the size of the one next to it)**

More activities

Different Russian dolls (individuals)

You will need the *Russian doll outlines* photocopy master (CD-ROM).

Use the set of blank templates so that learners can create their own design.

Nesting 3D shapes (individuals)

Learners create nesting shapes of their own choice. Explain that, "*They don't have to look like the Russian Dolls. You can use cylinders, pastry cutters, open boxes or any other shape. They don't all have to be the same height but they can be if you want. These will be your 'nesting shapes' and they can look how you want them to. But you must make five in your set, they must each be the same shape, and they must fit inside each other.*"

Nesting 2D shapes (individuals)

Learners measure and cut out a rectangle that is half the size of an A4 sheet of paper. They measure and cut out a rectangle that is half the size again. Learners repeat this until they have three or four rectangles of different sizes.

Place the largest rectangle on top of a fresh sheet of A4 paper, one on top of joined at one corner. Add each of the smaller rectangles in the same way, so that the rectangle on the top is the smallest. You should be able to line up a ruler from the matched corner through all the diagonal corners.

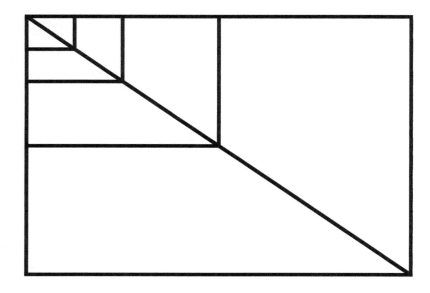

Resources: Pictures/posters/models of aeroplanes; large version for class display. An A4 sheet of paper; for class display. A sheet of A4 paper and a pair of scissors per learner. Linear measuring resources such as a ruler, tape measure, metre stick/rule, and a timer that shows seconds such as stop watches, clocks with a second hand or digital clocks; per pair of learners.

Show the pictures/models/posters to the class. Ask, "*Who has been on an aeroplane or knows someone who has been on an aeroplane? How high did you fly? Did you go higher than I am tall? Higher than the school? What could you see out of the window?*" Spend a few minutes discussing planes and flight.

Explain that today you are going to make a paper aeroplane. "*We're going to try to make a plane that flies for a long time and flies a long way.*"

Show the class a piece of A4 paper and ask, "*Would this piece of paper fly well just as it is? Why not? What do you think I need to do first?*" Fold the paper in different ways according to the learners' instructions. Or, if necessary, do your own folding to create a basic paper plane: fold the paper in half horizontally when holding the paper in the portrait orientation, to create a long and thin piece of paper. Fold back the top corners until they touch the central fold of the paper.

When your demonstration plane is finished, launch it by throwing it across the classroom (or hall, or playground). You could have a 'launch zone' marked with distances. "*What do you think? Was that a good design? What could have made it fly better?*" Discuss ideas before the learners make their own planes.

Explain the task to the learners. "*I want you to work with a partner to make a paper aeroplane that will fly. When you have made it, test it. If you want to change the design you can. Make sure you fly the plane in a safe place.*" Allow some time for the learners to make and test their planes. Then say, "*When everyone has finished making and testing their planes, work in groups to see which plane flies the longest distance and which plane flies for the longest time. You will need to think about how you will measure the distance and how you will measure the time. Talk to everyone in your group. You will need to keep a record of what you find to share with the rest of the class.*"

Look out for!

- Learners who are struggling to read centimetres and metres using the measuring equipment provided. *Support them when measuring distance or time and encourage learner-learner support.*
- Learners who find measuring time and distance easy. *If they were able to record in a systematic way, add another 'rule' to the task. Estimate both time and distance before each throw. How close were their estimates to the actual measurements? How can they record this?*

As the learners are working, walk round and make sure that they all understand the task and are working as groups to find and record the information. At the end of the session choose groups to share what they did and what they found out.

Learners should be able to choose appropriate measuring instruments to measure the distance each plane flies: a metre stick/rule or tape measure would be best but a 15/30 cm ruler would also work. Learners should be able to record the time in seconds; support them in doing so if required.

"How far was the furthest distance? Was the plane that flew the longest distance also the plane that was in the air for the most amount of time? How did you record those measurements? In your group which was the 'best' plane. Why? What was the best way to launch your paper aeroplane? Which way made it go the furthest/highest/lowest?"

Choose all of the 'best' planes from each group and fly them as a class. Find out which one goes the furthest and which one stays in the air the longest. Label this one 'Champion plane of the day'. These may be the same plane or two different planes, one for time, the other for distance.

Summary

- By the end of this session learners will have measured and compared lengths, using the standard units: centimetres, metres.
- They will also have had experience of measuring the passage of time using seconds.

Notes on the Learner's Book

Paper aeroplanes (p48): can be used to reinforce and practise the content of the core activity. It encourages learners to think about what they have learnt and to apply it in a different context.

Check up!

Discuss the following statements, asking learners whether they are reasonable statements or not. Encourage them to explain their answers. **(Answers should be based on the learners' own experiences following the *Core activity*, and they should use these as justification for their responses)**

- *"A paper aeroplane can . . .*:
    - *fly for 12 hours* **(Answer: not reasonable because the planes only flew for a few seconds, not even minutes, so hours is not very likely)**
    - *fly for a distance of 50 cm* **(Answer: reasonable, as most of the planes flew for at least [x] cm)**
    - *fly for a distance of only 1 cm"* **(Answer: not reasonable because all the class data shows that every plane flew at least [x] cm (because of how they are released, i.e. arm back + thrust forward as you let go).)**

Ask the learners to develop their own statements about planes.

More activities

Plane challenge (individuals)

Challenge the class to make a plane at home in order to fly it against the class 'Champion' plane in the next session.

Core activity 19.3: Following instructions (measuring in centimetres)

LB: p49

Resources: *Paper puppet instructions* photocopy master (CD-ROM); large version for class display. A collection of puppets/pictures of puppets. A4 paper, a pencil, a ruler, scissors, glue and other coloured paper to decorate; per learner. (Optional: box and other items to serve as puppet theatre scenery etc; materials to make other types of puppet, such as string, felt, paper, colouring pens/pencils.)

Show the puppets/pictures of puppets. "*Who can tell me what I have here? Do any of you have puppets at home? Do you know anyone who has a puppet? Who can tell us something about a puppet they have or a puppet they have made?*" Allow some time for class discussion. Then explain the task, "*You are all going to make your own puppet today. You will need a piece of paper and a ruler.*"

Display the *Paper puppet instructions* photocopy master, show the class the required resources and talk through how to make the puppet:
"*You will need to measure 7 cm from this edge and make a mark where 7 cm is. Move the ruler so that zero is on that mark and measure another 7 cm and make another mark.*" Some learners may be able to measure 14 cm in one go. "*Turn the paper round so that the top is at the bottom and the bottom is at the top. Do the same thing again.*" Demonstrate.

"*Now, using the ruler, join the marks at the top of the page to those at the bottom (vertically) or from side to side (horizontally).*" Demonstrate.

"*Fold the paper from the edge into the middle line on both sides. Open it up and you can see three different parts to the paper.*" Demonstrate.

"*Fold it back again. Now fold it in half from top to bottom.*" Demonstrate.

"*Now the last fold. Fold each of the two end pieces up and back so that they are on top of the middle fold. Put your hands in holes at the ends. You have a puppet!*"

"On your table you have all that you need to make your own puppet. When you have made it you can decorate it how you want to." While the learners are working, walk round to make sure that they all understand the task and are able to measure accurately.

Vocabulary

vertical: perpendicular, upright, going up and down in a straight line.

horizontal: going side to side in a straight line.

Look out for!

- Learners who are unable to measure accurately. *Allow them to use strips of card with the measurements already marked as a guide. Give these learners more practice in using a ruler.*
- Learners who can use a ruler for accurate measurement confidently and competently. *Use different length and width papers and different measurements to make different puppets. Make a 'family' of puppets, each one smaller (or bigger!) than the next. Ask questions such as, "Which one did you start with? Why? Would you have found it easier to start with a different one? Why/why not?"*

At the end of the session, choose some learners to share their puppets with the rest of the class.

Summary

- Learners can work with the length and width of a standard piece of A4 paper in order to follow instructions to make a puppet.
- They can measure centimetres accurately using a ruler.

Notes on the Learner's Book

Making puppets (p49): is a visual explanation of the puppets made during the lesson. This page can be used alongside the verbal instructions or as a reminder for learners as they make their own puppets.

Check up!

- *"What do you think would happen if we didn't measure accurately when:*
  - *Building a house?*
  - *Cooking a meal?*
  - *Making the door for our classroom?"*

More activities

Design and make a puppet theatre (class)

> You will need a box, a ruler, materials for scenery.

This will allow all learners to be involved in practical tasks using length, width and sometimes weight. You could: choose a box as the theatre; use a table top; think about height/width of scenery; think about the use of curtains (width/length).

Designer puppets (individuals, pairs or groups)

> You will need paper, string, glue, materials for decoration, a ruler.

Learners design and make their own puppets using different materials, such as string, their hand, their finger. Learners write a play to perform. They will need to think about: length, weight, width, area, (to fit over hand).

Puppet performance (individuals)

> You will need paper, pens, glue, materials for decoration.

Learners can make invitations and envelopes; design and make posters of different shapes and sizes; find a way of numbering the seats; design and make a programme for the performance; put times on the posters (when the performance will start and when it will finish) and so on.

Blank page

Quick reference

Core activity 20.1: Volume (Learner's Book p50)

Learners are introduced to the concept of volume and litres. Learners estimate and compare relative volumes using objects and one litre of water.

Core activity 20.2: Making a litre (Learner's Book p51)

Learners improve their estimating skills and begin to visualise the volume of one litre.

Core activity 20.3: A litre and a half-litre (Learner's Book p52)

Learners gain further practice in estimating and developing their knowledge and understanding of a half-litre and one litre, and the link between them.

Prior learning	Objectives* – please note that listed objectives might only be partially covered within any given chapter but are covered fully across the book when taken as a whole
• Some experience and knowledge of liquid measures. • Understanding of reasoning.	**2C: Measure** (*Length, mass and capacity*) 2Ml1 – Estimate, measure and compare capacities choosing and using suitable uniform non-standard and standard units and appropriate measuring instruments. 2Ml2 – Compare lengths, weights and capacities using the standard units: centimetres, metres, 100 g, kilogram and litre. **2C: Problem solving** 2Pt2 – Explain methods and reasoning orally. 2Pt11 – Consider whether an answer is reasonable.

*for NRICH activities mapped to the Cambridge Primary objectives, please visit www.cie.org.uk/cambridgeprimarymaths

Vocabulary

litre • volume

> **Resources:** Transparent jug with a capacity of more than 1 litre, with litres and half-litre markings (alternatively use a plastic bottle with the top cut off and add the appropriate markings). Objects for putting in the water, such as an apple, a stone, a ball, cubes, corks; for class display. A jug containing a litre of water and six objects; per group of learners. (Optional: different size/shape jugs.)

Make sure that the concept of capacity is fully understood before introducing volume.

Fill the jug to one litre. Ask the learners to look at the water level. Point to the one litre mark and ask, "*Does anyone know what this means? Has anyone seen it before? You might have seen it in school, at home or in a shop?*" Explain that the mark shows one litre of water. Write this on a board so that all of the class can see. Explain that this is a standard measure of capacity and volume and that volume is how much space something takes up.

Make sure they understand it is different from capacity, which is how much an object **can** contain, not how much is does contain. A jug with a capacity of three litres might only contain a volume of liquid of two litres.

This jug has a capacity of 1 litre. The water inside has a volume of 1 litre.

This jug has a capacity of 1 litre. The water it contains has a volume of less than 1 litre.

Vocabulary

volume: how much space a 3D object takes up.

capacity: the amount that something can contain.

litre (*l*): a litre is a standard (metric) unit for measuring volume and capacity. It is mostly used to measure the volume of liquids.

Say, "*This jug has a capacity of [x] litres. The volume of water in the jug is one litre. I have some objects here that are going to be put in the jug of water. What do you think will happen to the level of the water when the apple goes in? Talk to the person next to you.*"

Give a few minutes for discussion to take place. Then choose a learner to put the apple into the water. "*Look at the level of the water before the apple goes in. Now put the apple in and look again at the water level. What has happened?*" Choose some learners to respond. **(Answer: The level rose.)** "*Why do you think that has happened?*" Take responses.

"*When we put the apple in the water, the level of the water got higher. Does this mean that we have more water in the jug, less water, or the same amount of water? Why?*" Allow time for discussion. Mark the new level of the water on the jug. Take the apple out. Ask, "*What happens to the water when I take the apple out? Why is that? So, do we have the same amount of water, more, or less water? How do we know?*" Allow time for discussion.

Learners should reason that there is not more water because you have not added more, and if none has spilled out then there can't be less water, so there must be the same amount of water each time.

Choose another learner and another object to repeat the activity and ask the same questions. (It is a good idea to check that the jug still has one litre of water in it before the new objects are put in.) Before adding the object, ask, "*When this goes into the water do you think the level will be higher than the level with the apple in, or lower? Why?*" (Suggestions might include that the object is smaller/larger, or lighter/heavier.) Put the object in the water and check. Mark the level of the water again. Then ask, "*Do you think that whatever object we put into the water will make the level rise to above the one litre mark? Why?*"

Observe that adding an object to the jug of water pushes the level of the water up because the object has pushed some of the water out of the space that the object now takes up, moving the water up so that the total volume inside the jug increases; note that it isn't the volume of water that increases, but rather the total volume of material inside the jug.

"On your table you have a jug with one litre of water in it and some objects from the classroom. Before you put the objects into the water, estimate where you think the level of the water will rise to. Make a record of your estimate and the actual level of the water after adding the object. Note down what you have found out". You can tell the learners to look at *Jugs* in the Learner's Book (p50) for ideas of how to record what they have found out. While the learners are working, walk round to make sure that they all understand the task and are able to record what they find out.

At the end of the session, ask the learners to use their recordings to share what they have found out with the rest of the class. Ask questions such as, *"Were there any surprises when you put something in the water? What was it and why were you surprised? Do you think the weight of the object made any difference?"* Learners should discover that the weight of an object is not significant (unless it is so light it floats, see point below); it is the size of the object that matters. The larger the object, the bigger its volume (it takes up more space) and so the higher the level of water will rise.

Some learners might have used objects that float (corks, empty cups or bottles) while others might use objects that sink. It is important to encourage learners to discuss how floating objects affects the level of water; if an object floats then they are sitting on the surface of the water and therefore does not push any of the water out of the way and will not cause the level of water to rise.

Look out for!

- Learners who are unable to make sensible and reasonable estimations about how much water will be displaced by different objects. *Allow them a lot more practical experience and let them work within a group so that they can see and hear the thoughts and experiences of others.*
- Learners who can make reasonable and accurate predictions and give reasons. *Give them different challenges such as changing the shape and size of the container whilst still using one litre of water and the same objects.*

Summary

- Learners begin to understand the concept of volume and litres.
- Learners have estimated and compared the volume of objects and of water, working logically and systematically to record their findings.
- Learners have shared their findings and given reasons for them.

Notes on the Learner's Book

Jugs (p50): can be used as a discussion page at the end of the session or as a support during the activity.

Check up!

- *"How is the capacity of a jug different to the volume of water the jug contains?"* **(Answer: the capacity is how much the jug can hold, the volume of water is the amount of water it is actually holding at the time of measurement)**
- *"What would happen to the level of water if I put a large stone in it?"*
- *"What would happen if I put something heavier than the stone but the same size?"*

More activities

What if . . . ? (pairs)

Repeat the core activity, using a larger/smaller/wider/narrower container. Learners to put in the same objects and predict how much the water level will rise this time. (For example, the same object will cause the water to rise higher if a narrower container is used.) Mark 2 cm above the one litre mark and tell learners to put in objects and sort them into three sets: objects that didn't make the water rise enough to meet the mark; objects that made it rise above the mark; and objects that made it rise to just about the mark.

What did they notice about each set of objects? (E.g. the weight of an object does not affect the rise in water level.)

Core activity 20.2: Making a litre

Resources: *Making a litre* photocopy master (CD-ROM); per learner. A waterproof pen, water (or sand), a range of containers (plastic bottles, jugs, bowls, eggcups), a cup (transparent if possible), litre measure (jug or bowl), funnel, spoon, washing up bowl or other large bowl and cloths or mops; per group of learners.

This activity allows learners to explore liquid measures and develop an understanding of one litre, more than one litre and less than one litre. It is an ideal activity for small groups of up to four learners.

Demonstrate the activity to the whole class before each group investigates their own containers. *"I have some empty containers here and a cup. I want us to think about where the level of water would be in this container if I filled the cup with water and then poured it in."* Show the cup and the container to the class. Gather responses.

Learners should reason that as the cup is smaller than the container it has a smaller capacity than the larger container. So whilst the cup is full, the level of water will **not** fill the larger container. Mark on the outside of the container the agreed estimate of where the water level will be based on the size of the cup relative to the container. Pour in the water.

"How close is our estimate to the actual volume? Is there enough water in the container to reach our mark, or do we need some more?"

Repeat with two more (different) containers. Ask, *"Where do you think the water will come to? Why do you think that? Where would you put the mark for two cups of water, or three cups of water?"*

Learners should reason that the level of the water will be different in a different sized/shaped container even though we are using the same cup to pour each time. So, the actual amount of water is the same but its level in the container might be different; this should help learners begin to understand that objects can have the same volume even if they are a different size/shape. Learners should reason that two cups of water will reach a level twice as high as one cup of water and three cups of water will reach a level three times as high as one cup of water.

When the learners are confident about the activity, arrange them into small groups to investigate their own containers.

Look out for!

Learners who do not realise that, for accurate measurement, the cups need to be filled to the same level each time. *Let them try using different levels of water each time and see how the results vary.*

After they have worked together for a while, stop the learners and introduce the idea of using a litre measure such as a jug or a bowl. Explain that they have a capacity of one litre. *"How many cups of water do you think it would take to fill the jug to the one litre mark? What will you do if there is too much?"* Allow discussion in the groups and gather feedback.

Explain the next stage of the task. *"You have other containers on your table. Could you use those to make exactly one litre? What if you don't have enough water to make a litre just using cups? Could you use some cups and then a different container? Discuss it in your groups."* Show and explain the Making a litre photocopy master. *"Find as many different ways of making a litre as you can. The first column is to draw or write your estimate. Then you need to talk as a group. The next column is what the group decides to do. Then do it. The last column is for what actually happened and what you did about it. You may have more or less than a litre so you must find ways to adjust that amount."*

As the learners are working, walk round the class to make sure that all groups understand the task and also understand the recording you want them to do. This activity will help learners to gain an understanding of how much one litre of water is and to enhance their estimating skills.

At the end of the session, ask learners what they did and what they found out when they were measuring a litre. *"Can you tell us what you did and what you found out? What have you learned today? Do you think it was important to have every cup filled the same amount each time? Why? If you were doing it again, what would you do differently? Why? Did you all agree in your group about what to do? What did you find difficult? What helped you?"*

Look out for!

Learners who are confident and competent in filling, pouring and measuring to 1 litre. *Ask them to predict and check for two litres or half litre.*

Summary

Learners get more practice of estimating non-standard units as well as developing knowledge and understanding of one litre and ways to make it.

Notes on the Learner's Book
Making a litre (p51): reinforces the work done in the *Core activity* by giving further opportunities for discussion both in the class and in small groups.

Check up!

- *"If I wanted to fill this one litre jug with water, which would be quicker, using cups of water or spoons of water? Why? How do you know?"* **(Answer: cups because they have a larger capacity and therefore can contain a larger volume of water)**
- *"What would happen if the cup wasn't filled to the same point every time?"*
- *"Would it take more or fewer cups of water to fill the jug to half a litre? To two litres? Why? How do you know?"* **(Answer: less time to fill to half litre as this is a smaller volume than one litre; more time to fill to two litres as it is a larger volume)**

More activities

Cups and eggcups (class)

> You will need containers of varying sizes, e.g. cup, eggcup, bowl etc.

Collect containers of different shapes that hold more than, less than and the same as one litre. Discuss similarities and differences of the containers in each set (some have corners, some do not). Ask, *"What if . . .*

- *you used an eggcup and the same containers. Would you use more cups or eggcups? How do you know?"*
- *you used a jug instead of a cup and the same containers?"*
- *you used a two litre jug and investigated ways of making two litres?"*

Resources: *Estimate record* photocopy master (CD-ROM); per learner. A bucket with a capacity of at least 2 litres; per group (before the session, mark a line on the inside of each bucket at $\frac{1}{2}$ litre, 1 litre, $1\frac{1}{2}$ litres, 2 litres or $2\frac{1}{2}$ litres, depending on the size of the bucket). A water tray (if working inside). A 1 litre measuring jug, water (or sand), a waterproof pen, a $\frac{1}{2}$ litre measuring jug, a 1 litre jug, a $\frac{1}{2}$ litre jug, a 2 litre jug; per group of learners. (Optional: jug of drink and drinking glasses.)

You may prefer to do this activity outside. If not, stand the bucket in a water tray or use dry sand instead.

Show learners a bucket and a one litre measuring jug. Ask, "*I want to calculate the capacity of the bucket. How many jugs of water do you think it will take to fill the bucket?*" Record learners' estimates on the board and discuss them. Use the greatest and the least amounts and compare them, giving the learners opportunity to change their mind after they have considered whether their answer is reasonable.

Explain, "*Before we start to fill the bucket we need to think about some things. Do we need to start with the jug full or just filled to the one litre mark? Why?* (Answer: fill the jug to the one litre mark so that it is easier to calculate the volume of water poured into the bucket, and hence the capacity of the bucket)* Do we need to fill the bucket right to the top? Or is there another way we can call the bucket full? Talk to the person next to you and decide.*" Allow time for discussion and then take feedback.

Some learners may think that the bucket needs to be full to the top. Others may think almost to the top because it would be difficult to lift and move without spilling. Draw out that it is best to choose a suitable level just below the top (otherwise the water might spill out when carried). "*We can make a mark inside the bucket and fill the water level to that mark.*"

Fill the jug to the one litre mark and choose a learner to pour it into the bucket. Then ask, "*Is the bucket full?*" Establish that it isn't and that you need to put another litre in. Choose learners to pour the water in, checking after each litre whether or not the bucket needs more water. When the level has almost been reached ask, "*What do you think will happen if we put another litre of water in?*" Pour it in. "*The water has gone over the level. What does that mean? The last litre was too much. What do we need to do?*" Most learners will say take it out again!

Look out for!
- Learners who do not understand that they will get different results if they fill the measure partly rather than filling it properly. *Allow them to try using different levels of water each time and see how the results vary.*
- Learners who can measure accurately in litres and half-litres. *Offer them the two litre jug, or challenge them to find how many different ways they can make two litres, or three litres, where they will need to use their knowledge and understanding of equivalence (e.g. $\frac{1}{2}+\frac{1}{2}+1+1=3$ litres or $\frac{1}{2}+\frac{1}{2}+\frac{1}{2}+\frac{1}{2}+1=3$ litres).*

Take out one litre of water then say, "*Now we don't have enough. What could we do about that?*" Allow time for discussion then conclude that we need to use a smaller measure than one litre.

Show learners the half-litre jug. "*This jug holds less than one litre.*" Fill the half-litre jug to the half litre mark and pour it into the one litre jug. "*What do you notice?* **(Answer: the one litre jug is filled to half of its capacity)** *We call this measurement half a litre. What do you think will happen if I put another half a litre of water into the one litre jug?*" Do it and ask, "*What do you notice?*" Establish that you now have two half-litres of water, which is the same as one litre, and the jug is filled to its capacity.

Explain the task to the learners. "*On your table you have a half-litre jug, a one litre jug and a bucket with a 'full' level marked inside. Use the one litre jug to fill to that mark. You will need to think about whether you need to also use the half-litre jug. You will need to keep a record of how many one litre and how many half-litre jugs of water you use. How will you do that? Decide in your groups.*"

As the learners are working on the activity, walk around the classroom. Encourage them to make estimates about the number of litres and/or half-litres they will need before doing the activity and write them on the estimate sheet. Some learners may want to change their mind during the activity and make a second guess or even a third and fourth guess.

At the end of the session ask learners what they did and what they found out when they were measuring a litre and/or a half-litre. Ask, "*Can you tell us what you did and what you found out? What have you learned today? If you were doing it again, what would you do differently? Why? Did you all agree in your group about what to do? What did you find difficult? What helped you?*"

Summary

- Learners developing knowledge and understanding of one litre and half a litre and the link between them.
- They practice their estimating skills.

Notes on the Learner's Book
Fill the bucket (p52): provides the opportunity for practice and reinforcement. The final questions can be used for more able learners or to encourage discussion in small groups of learners.

Check up!
- "*If I wanted to fill a bucket with water very quickly, should I use a litre jug or a half-litre jug? Why?*" **(Answer: a litre jug as it has a larger capacity and therefore you can fill the bucket with a larger volume of water with each pour)**
- "*If I wanted to fill a small vase would I use a litre or a half-litre jug? Why?*" **(Answer: a half-litre jug because a small vase is not likely to have a capacity of as much as a litre)**

More activities

Pouring drinks (groups)

> You will need a jug of drink and some drinking glasses.

Learners have one litre of water to share equally amongst their group. Learners estimate how much would be in each glass. Encourage learners to see how much the level has gone down after pouring out one glass. Does this fit with their original estimate? Would they like to change their mind? How could they record what they did, what they found out and what they changed?

Games Book (ISBN 9781107623491)

Slide, slip and spill (p62) is a game for two to four players. This game uses learners' knowledge and understanding of the equivalence between two half-litres and one litre.

21 Investigating weight, length and time

Quick reference

Core activity 21.1: Weight (Learner's Book p53)

Learners practise measuring and ordering weight using comparison and the standard units of grams.

Core activity 21.2: Length (Learner's Book p54)

Learners measure the distance travelled in metres in a given amount of time.

Core activity 21.3: Time (Learner's Book p55)

Learners measure the time in seconds that it takes to travel a given distance in metres.

Prior learning	Objectives* –	please note that listed objectives might only be partially covered within any given chapter but are covered fully across the book when taken as a whole
• Some knowledge and understanding of measuring length. • Some knowledge and understanding of measuring time. • Some knowledge and understanding of measuring weight. • Some experiences of using measuring equipment for length, weight and time.	**2C: Measure** (*Length, mass and capacity*)	
	2MI1 –	Estimate, measure and compare lengths and weights choosing and using suitable uniform non-standard and standard units and appropriate measuring instruments.
	2MI2 –	Compare lengths and weights using the standard units: centimetres, metres, 100 g, kilogram, litre.
	2C: Measure (*Time*)	
	2Mt1 –	Know the units of time (seconds, minutes, hours, days, weeks, months and years).
	2Mt2 –	Know the relationships between consecutive units of time.
	2C: Problem solving (*Using techniques and skills in solving mathematical problems*)	
	2Pt1 –	Choose appropriate mental strategies to carry out calculations and explain how they worked out the answer.
	2Pt2 –	Explain methods and reasoning orally.
	2Pt3 –	Explore number problems and puzzles.
	2Pt4 –	Make sense of simple word problems (single and easy two-step), decide what operations (addition or subtraction, simple multiplication or division) are needed to solve them and, with help, represent them, with objects or drawings or on a number line.

*for NRICH activities mapped to the Cambridge Primary objectives, please visit www.cie.org.uk/cambridgeprimarymaths

Vocabulary

gram (g) • kilogram (kg)

Resources: *Measuring mass (1)* photocopy master (chapter 11, p93). A set of four identical containers with a lid (or home-made cardboard lids) such as plastic cups or beakers, yogurt pots, tubes, tubs; per pair or group of learners. Sand (wet or dry), labels, pens or pencils, and weighing/balance scales; per group of learners. (Optional: *Comparing weight and volume* photocopy master (CD-ROM); scales; cups; plastic bags for weighing different objects; a variety of materials such as sand, dirt, pebbles, bark chips, rice, and flour.)

Remind the learners of the work they did on weight when they baked biscuits (Unit 1C). They were introduced to the standard metric units, grams and kilograms. Display the *Measuring mass (1)* photocopy master.

Explain the task. *"Work with a partner. You have four containers, label them 1, 2, 3 and 4. One of you measure out four different weights of sand. Put a different amount of sand in each container; make a note of what weight of sand is in each container. Don't let your partner see. Put the lids on. Ask your partner to lift each container by hand and then put them in order of weight from lightest to heaviest. Ask them, 'which is the heaviest, which is the lightest?' When all of the containers have been put in order, your partner weighs each of them and records the results. Tip all the sand out again and swap roles with your partner. Do the same as before."*

Remind the learners that they should have two sets of results, one from each learner. As the learners are working, walk round the classroom to make sure that they all understand the task and have a way of recording their results.

Towards the end of the session, choose the containers from one group and a set of scales. In front of the class, choose a learner to estimate the weights and put them in order. *"Let's weigh the containers and see if the results match what you have done."* Weigh the first one and tell the class the result. *"Is that more than 100 grams or less?"* Record the weight and weigh the next one. Ask the same question. Repeat for the remaining two containers.

Vocabulary

gram (g): a standard measure of weight.

kilogram (kg): one thousand grams.

Look out for!

- Learners who need more experience of ordering relative weights. *Learners can improve their skill in ordering weight by starting with containers of very different weights and gradually making the weights more similar.*
- Learners who have a problem reading scales accurately. *Provide them with balance scales.*
- Learners who can estimate and check results, and record their results systematically. *Use more precise measures such as the exact amount of grams above/below 100 g instead of 'about', 'just over' or 'just under' during the activity.*

"Looking at these results, which was the heaviest container 1, 2, 3, or 4? How do you know? Which was the next heaviest … (and so on)? Some of these are more than 100 grams and some are less. Which is the closest to 100 grams? How do you know? Which weight is the closest to 1 kilogram? How do you know?"

Summary

- Learners practise estimating and measuring weight accurately.
- Learners devise a systematic way to record their results.

Notes on the Learner's Book

Number balance (p53): takes the concept of weight and uses it in the context of number and balance. It is designed to support those who are not yet confident, as well as challenging the more able by adding in more rules.

Check up!

- *"Which weighs more, one kilogram or one gram?"*
- *"Which weighs less, one kilogram or one gram?"*
- *"How many grams are in a kilogram?"*

More activities

Different ways of comparing (individuals)

> You will need scales, a variety of sand, dirt, pebbles, etc.

Compare weights (masses) by lifting, using a variety of scales and by measuring to the nearest 10 or 100 grams.

At home (individuals)

Learners make a list of objects at home that they would measure in kilograms (rather than grams).

Comparing weight and volume (pairs)

> You will need scales, a cup, plastic bag, materials to weigh.

Learners investigate the weight of the same volume (a cup) of different materials/objects (less than 1 kg) to discover if they have the same weight. Ask learners to fill a cup with the first material and tip it into a plastic bag. Tie the top of the bag to seal it. Repeat for the other materials. Learners compare the weight of a cup of two materials at a time by holding one bag in each hand. They decide which bag is lighter and which bag is heavier and record the results. Then choose another two bags and compare. Continue until all of the bags have been ordered from the lightest to the heaviest and the order recorded.

Weigh the bags to confirm that the order is correct. Record the weights in grams. Discuss the results. *"What was the order of the materials from the lightest to the heaviest? How do you know which was the heaviest or the lightest material? Did any bags seem to be about the same weight in your hands? Which ones? Each bag contained a cup of a material. Why did the weights differ if the materials all took up the same space?"*

Core activity 21.2: Length

Resources: *Investigating distance and time* photocopy master (CD-ROM); per group of learners. Tape or chalk. Paper and pencil. Metre sticks/rule. Stopwatch (alternatively, analogue clocks with second hand or digital clocks showing seconds).

This session will investigate the measurement of distance and time. Before the start of the session, use tape or chalk to mark a starting line and a line at right angles to this (to show the direction of movement).

Ask the learners to look at *'Moving time'* (p55) in their Learner's Book. Discuss what the activity involves (**measuring how far the learners can travel in a given amount of time**). *"Look at the picture. The learners are moving in different ways. What can you see?* **Possible answers include: one boy is walking so that on each step the back of one foot is up against the toe of the other; the girl is hopping on one leg; the other boy is taking long strides.** *Can you think of a different way that you could move?"* Allow time for discussion and feedback. Record the different ways on the board.

Explain what learners need to do. *"Moving in your chosen way you will need to choose a length of time that will be same for you all and see how far you can move in that time. How long will you choose, one second, one minute, one hour, one day? Would it be a good idea to use one day as your time? Why not? Would it be a good idea to use one second as your time? Why not? You will need to talk to each other in your groups and choose a sensible time. You will also need to think about how you will measure how far you have moved."*

Allow time for discussion, record their thoughts and discuss. Emphasise that this activity is not a race but is a way of measuring time and distance.

Show and explain the *Investigating distance and time* photocopy master. *"Each group will have a recording sheet to write down what you did and what you found out."* As the learners are working, walk round to make sure that they all understand the task and have a way of recording their results. *"How are you going to tackle this? What information do you have? What do you need to find out or do?"*

Look out for!

- Learners who had difficulty in measuring distance accurately. *Give them more opportunities to measure using cm as well as metres. For example, they can measure the length of their book, the height of their table, the distance to the door.*
- Learners who are finding the activity easy. *Suggest recording the information using a block graph:*

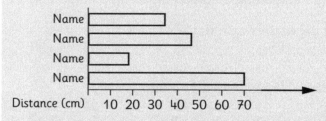

Ask, *"What does your graph show? Why did you choose this type of graph? What do you think would happen if you chose a different type? Do you think the information will be the same?"*

Opportunity for display

Any photos taken during the activity.

At the end of the session, groups share with what they did and what they found out with the rest of the class. *"How did you get your answer? Can you describe your rule to us all? Can you explain why it works? What have you learned or found out today? If you were doing it again, what would you do differently? Why?"*

Summary

- Learners measure and compare lengths in centimetres and metres choosing and using suitable uniform non-standard and standard units and appropriate measuring instruments.
- Learners used units of time (seconds, minutes) and developed further understanding of the relationships between consecutive units of time.
- Learners chose appropriate mental strategies to carry out calculations and explain how they worked out the answer.

Notes on the Learner's Book

Time travel (p54): asks learners to work out the time taken for a journey; and then to calculate the distance travelled of another journey, relating time to distance.

Check up!

- *"If I wanted to run a kilometre would you time me in seconds, minutes, hours or days?"*
- *"Could you use a combination of those times? What could you use?"*
- *"If I wanted to time a tortoise walking a kilometre what would I use? Why?"*

Learners should devise some questions of their own to ask the class.

More activities

Sports day (groups)

> You will need a stopwatch, a metre rule.

Plan and set up different activities such as walking backwards, a three-legged race, egg and spoon race, and so on to practise and reinforce the links between time and distance. Each activity will need a time keeper and a distance marker. Learners work in groups and the roles are changed at each activity.

Daily routine (individuals)

Ask learners to time or measure different activities they do whilst at home. For example, how long does it takes to brush their teeth, how far to walk to the shop. Ask them to consider what they could you use to measure time and distance when they are at home. Ask, *"What do you spend most/least time on? What is the shortest/longest distance from your house? Make some graphs to show us what you do, how long it takes, and how far you travel. What if you go in a car or on a bus?"*

Resources: *Investigating time and distance* photocopy master (CD-ROM). Metre stick/rule for each group. Tape or chalk. A stopwatch (alternatively, an analogue clocks with second hand or digital clocks showing seconds for each group.)

The aim of this lesson is to measure and record time intervals and to present and interpret data to the rest of the class. This is similar to the last session but here learners will be considering how long it takes them to move a certain distance instead of focusing on how far you can move in a given amount of time.

Ask the learners to look at '*Moving time*' (p55) in their Learner's Book. Talk about the different ways they can move discussed in the previous session. Allow time for discussion and feedback. Record the different ways on the board.

Explain what the learners need to do. "*Last time, we saw how far you could move in a given time that we decided. Now we are going to look at how long it takes you to move a distance that we decide. Before you can begin the activity, talk with the rest of your group and decide how far you want to move. Measure it with the metre stick. You can move one, two, three metres or more. Mark the start point and end point of that distance using tape or chalk. When you start to move, the time starts. When you reach the end point of the distance, the time stops.*"

Emphasise that this activity is not a race but is a way of measuring time and distance. If necessary, explain the *Investigating time and distance* photocopy master again.

"*Each group will have a recording sheet to write down what you did and what you found out. Think about how you will do this differently from last time.*" As the learners are working, walk round to make sure that they all understand the task and have a way of recording their results. "*How are you going to tackle this? What information do you have? What do you need to find out or do?*"

At the end of the session, choose groups to share what they did and what they found out with the rest of the class. "*How did you get your answer? Can you describe your rule to us all? Can you explain why it works? What have you learned or found out today? If you were doing it again, what would you do differently? Why?*"

Look out for!

- Learners who have difficulty timing the activity. *Give these learners more opportunities to time other events such as the time spent getting ready for PE, or tidying a table. Use a stopwatch, second hand or digital clock.*
- Learners who find the activity easy. *Suggest recording the information using a block graph:*

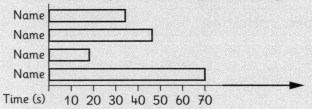

Ask, "*What does your graph show? Why did you choose this type of graph? What do you think would happen if you chose a different type? Do you think the information will be the same?*"

Opportunity for display

Any photographs that were taken of the activity.

Summary

- Learners have measured lengths choosing and using appropriate measuring instruments and using the standard units: centimetres and metres.
- They have have developed and used the units of time (seconds, minutes) and developed further understanding of the relationships between consecutive units of time.
- They have chosen appropriate mental strategies to carry out calculations and explain how they worked out the answer.

Notes on the Learner's Book

Moving time (p55): can be used as a discussion page before the activity, but also as a support during the activity.

Check up!

- *"If I had one minute, what could I do? Could I run a kilometre? Could I write my name 20 times? Think of some other things that you could do in one minute."*
- *"What about one second. What could I do in one second?"*

More activities

Interpreting data (individuals, pairs, groups or class)

Prepare some data using time and distance that has no title. Ask the class to give possible contexts for the data. Ask learners/pairs/groups to produce data using time and distance that can be interpreted by the rest of the class.

Games Book (ISBN 9781107623491)

Hare and Tortoise (p65) is a game for two players This game links the ideas of time and distance.

Blank page

Quick reference

Core activity 22.1: Doubling two-digit numbers (Learner's Book p56)

Learners explore patterns produced by doubling. They double any two-digit number by partitioning, doubling the tens and ones and then adding these together.

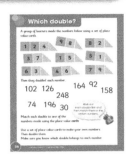

Prior learning	Objectives* –	please note that listed objectives might only be partially covered within any given chapter but are covered fully across the book when taken as a whole
• Doubles to double 5 and beyond.	**1A: Numbers and the number system**	
• Experience of using place value cards.	2Nn1 – Count, read and write numbers to at least 100 and back again.	
• Counting in fives, forwards and back.	2Nn14 – Understand odd and even numbers and recognise these up to at least 20.	
	3A: Numbers and the number system	
	2Nn6 – Know what each digit represents in two-digit numbers; partition into tens and ones.	
	3A: Calculation (*Multiplication and division*)	
	2Nc20 – Find doubles of multiples of 5 up to double 50 and corresponding halves.	
	2Nc21 – Double two-digit numbers.	
	3A: Calculation (*Mental strategies*)	
	2Nc5 – Find and learn doubles for all numbers up to 10 and also 15, 20, 25 and 50.	
	3A: Problem solving (*Using techniques and skills in solving mathematical problems*)	
	2Pt1 – Choose appropriate mental strategies to carry out calculations and explain how they worked out the answer.	
	2Pt2 – Explain methods and reasoning orally.	
	2Pt3 – Explore number problems and puzzles.	
	2Pt8 – Describe and continue patterns which count on in twos, threes, fours or fives to 30 or more.	

*for NRICH activities mapped to the Cambridge Primary objectives, please visit www.cie.org.uk/cambridgeprimarymaths

> **Resources:** *100 square* photocopy master (chapter 1, p4); large version for class display and one per learner. *Double 5 strip* photocopy master (CD-ROM). *Tens and ones cards* photocopy master (CD-ROM). (Optional: *200 square* photocopy master (CD-ROM) *Hundreds cards* photocopy master (CD-ROM)).

Give each learner a set of place value cards from the *Tens and ones cards* photocopy master, including the card for 100. Ask them to lay the cards out in front of them in two columns, so that the 1 and 10 are closest to them and the 9 and 100 are furthest away.

Explain that they are going to work their way up each column, doubling every number. Begin working up the ones column, saying, *"Double one is two, double two is four, double three is six,"* and so on. Repeat if some of the learners need the practice. Explain that, in many ways, doubling the tens column is just the same. Ask the learners to join in with you as you work your way up the column saying, *"Double one ten is two tens, double two tens is four tens, double three tens six tens,"* and so on. When you get to the top of the column, ask the learners to explain how it was the same as doubling the ones. **(Answer: you are still doubling a single digit)**

Go on to explain, *"The numbers we said have names of their own, so let's do that again, saying the number names. Double 10 is 20, double 20 is 40, double 30 is 60,"* and so on. Repeat if necessary. Explain that now that they can double any of the ones numbers and any of the tens numbers, they can also double any two-digit number. Call out a number such as 24 and ask the learners to make that number with the place value cards. Pull the two parts of the number apart and explain that, *"Double 20 is 40 and double 4 is 8, so double 24 is 40 + 8 which is 48."*

Give each learner a copy of the *Double 5 strip* photocopy master and display the *100 square* for the whole class to see. Count in fives to 100 as a class, asking the learners to quickly complete the list of numbers they say when counting in fives in the first column of the *double 5* grid. Once the list is complete, ask the learners to write the double of each of those numbers in the column on the right. Ask learners to put this to one side as they will need it again later.

Ask the learners to work with the person next to them, taking it in turns to say a number with up to four tens and up to five ones. After several turns, ask the learners why they think you asked them to only use those particular numbers.

Example. Using the *Tens and ones cards* to double two-digit numbers.

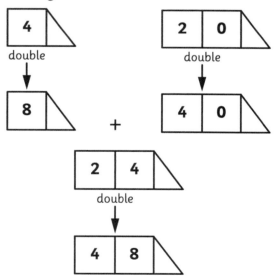

Explain that they managed very well to add the doubles they made so far, because none of the single-digit numbers doubled to more than ten and none of the two-digit multiples of ten doubled to more than 80. Ask, "*What is double 50?*" Explain that as soon as the learners double numbers 50 and over, they will be working with numbers over 100. Ask them to double 7 (**Answer: 14**) "*What would double 57 be?*" (**Answer: 100 + 14 = 114**)

Show the learners how to use the place value cards to help them write the number correctly. Tell the learners that they did so well doubling numbers below 50, that they are now ready to double the higher numbers.

Challenge them to take it in turns, as before, but this time with numbers over 50 and any amount of ones. Remind them to make the number with the place value cards then double each part. Support any pairs who find this difficult.

Ask learner to look again at their completed double 5 strip. Ask, "*Can you see a pattern in the coloured numbers? Describe what you notice.*" Give support if required but the learners should very quickly notice the pattern: as double 5 is 10, each time we increase our number by 5 we increase the double by 10.

Look out for!

- Learners who find doubling higher numbers difficult. *Suggest that they could focus on doubling numbers over 50 but with up to five ones, so that the total does not cross a ten. They should use a 100 or 200 place value card to help them write the doubled number correctly.*
- Learners who find doubling very straightforward. *Give them 200, 300 and 400 place value cards from the Hundreds cards photocopy master and ask them to double some three-digit numbers.*

Summary

- Learners can double any two-digit number by partitioning the number, doubling the tens column, doubling the ones column, then recombining to find double the original number.
- Learners understand the pattern produced when doubling multiples of five.

Notes on the Learner's Book
Which double? (p56): learners match each number to its double.

Check up!

Ask learners questions such as:
- "*What is double 15? How do you know?*"
- "*What is double 33?*"
- "*What is double 49?*"

More activities

Double trouble (pairs)

Doubles are always even. Is this always, sometimes, or never true? Learners work in pairs to answer the question and show how they reached their answer.

Counting to 200 (pairs)

For more able learners, extend counting in fives to 200. Give pairs of learners a copy of the *200 square* photocopy master. Ask learners to look at the 101 to 200 squares. Ask, "How is the 200 square the same and how is it different to the usual 100 square?" (**Answer: the numbers are the same, they just have 100 in front of them and 100 becomes 200**) Use place value cards from the *Tens and ones* cards and *Hundreds cards* photocopy master to show how numbers such as 124 and 179 are made from hundreds, tens and ones. Ask learners to use the two number squares to help them count in fives from 0 to 200 and back again.

Games Book (ISBN 978110762349)

Dice doubles or Spinner doubles (p70) is a game for two players. Players double numbers 1 to 6 if using a dice, or 1 to 10 if using the spinner.

23 Threes and fours

Quick reference

<u>**Core activity 23.1: Counting in threes**</u> (Learner's Book p57)
Learners count in threes and explore the patterns produced.

<u>**Core activity 23.2: Counting in fours**</u> (Learner's Book p58)
Learners count in fours and explore the patterns produced.

Prior learning	Objectives* – please note that listed objectives might only be partially covered within any given chapter but are covered fully across the book when taken as a whole
• Counting in twos, fives and tens. • Counting to 100.	**1A: Numbers and the number system** 2Nn14 – Understand odd and even numbers and recognise these up to at least 20. **3A: Numbers and the number system** 2Nn5 – Begin to count on in small constant steps such as threes and fours. **3A: Problem solving** (*Using techniques and skills in solving mathematical problems*) 2Pt3 – Explore number problems and puzzles. 2Pt8 – Describe and continue patterns which count on in twos, threes, fours or fives to 30 or more. 2Pt9 – Identify simple relationships between numbers and shapes, e.g. this number is double…; these shapes all have…sides.

*for NRICH activities mapped to the Cambridge Primary objectives, please visit www.cie.org.uk/cambridgeprimarymaths

> **Resources:** *100 square* photocopy master (chapter 1, p4); large version for class display. *Threes* photocopy master (CD-ROM). Colouring pencils. A4 paper. Cubes/counters. (Optional: *0–50 number lines* photocopy master (chapter 14, p116); squared paper; scissors.)

Begin the session by telling the learners you are going to count in fives, but that you will start at 4. Display the *100 square* photocopy master. Ask them to listen carefully to the numbers you say because you will be asking them to talk about the pattern they hear. Explain that they are welcome to join in too. Count, "*4, 9, 14, 19, 24, 29, 34, 39, 44, 49,*" pointing to the numbers on the 100 square as you say them. Repeat if necessary.

Ask the learners to talk to a partner about what they noticed. Ask some pairs of learners to explain what they talked about. Either write the numbers where everyone can see them or highlight them on the 100 square, to confirm the patterns that the learners talked about.

Learners should notice that the last digit in each number has a repeating pattern of 4, 9, 4, 9, 4, 9, 4, 9. They should reason that this is sensible because the pattern of multiples of 5 when starting at 5 is 5, 0, 5, 0, 5, 0 so when they start at 4, which is one less than 5, the repeating pattern is digits that are one less.

Tell the learners that they are getting very good at noticing patterns, so you would like them to explore what happens when they count in threes on the 100 square. Give each learner a copy of the *Threes* photocopy master and show them that the first three numbers, 3, 6 and 9 have been shaded for them. Explain that they should choose a coloured pencil and continue counting in threes, colouring in every third square. After the learners have had time to explore, ask them to talk to a partner about the patterns they can see.

Most learners will be able to count in threes beyond 30 using a 100 square for support. Although this extends beyond what is expected in Stage 2, it will help learners to see the pattern more easily. Bring the learners back together and ask two or three learners to talk about what they noticed. The learners will have noticed the diagonal lines but ask them to look more closely at one of the diagonals. Ask, "*How does the number change each time you move down the column onto the next row? What about when you move up to the row above? Is the pattern the same?*"

Give the learners five to ten minutes to talk to their partner.

Look out for!

- Learners who lose track when they are counting in threes, particularly when moving onto the next row. *Give them three cubes or counters to use. After colouring in a square, they place the counters on the next three squares, counting to three (1, 2, 3) as they put them on the 100 square. They can only colour in the square they put the last counter on, i.e. the one they placed when they said 'three.'*

- Learners who have mastered counting in threes. *You could also give these learners a 100 square and ask them to find out if the same pattern will be produced if you start counting in threes from 1 or 2. Ask them to explain why.*

Check that the learners have noticed that each time you move down (or up) to the next row, the number increases or decreases by nine.

1	2	3	4	5	6	7	8	9	10
11	12	13	14	15	16	17	18	19	20
21	22	23	24	25	26	27	28	29	30
31	32	33	34	35	36	37	38	39	30
41	42	43	44	45	46	47	48	49	50
51	52	53	54	55	56	57	58	59	60
61	62	63	64	65	66	67	68	69	70
71	72	73	74	75	76	77	78	79	80
81	82	83	84	85	86	87	88	89	90
91	92	93	94	95	96	97	98	99	100

This is because you move onto another row after three lots of three, which is nine. When you move on nine squares, you need to move down a square to the next row and back one, because $10 - 1 = 9$. When moving up a row, the pattern is the same, but this time you move up a square and forward one, again because $10 - 1$ is 9. Count along in threes together to 50 and then 100.

Finish the session by playing 'three-bingo'. Give each learner an A4 sheet of paper and ask them to fold it in half three times: half, then half again and then half again. When they open it up, they can see eight spaces. They must choose eight of their coloured numbers and write one in each space. Call out random numbers from the three pattern. When a learner hears one of their numbers they cross it out. The winner is the first learner to cross out all their numbers; to show they have done this, they need to call out *Bingo!* Or *House!*

During the game, occasionally call out a number which is not in the threes pattern. If no one notices, tell the learners that you did not notice anyone crossing off that number and comment, "*I wonder why?*" Check that the learners now realise the number was not one they coloured. It was not in the threes pattern so no one would have written it on their bingo card.

If you have time, talk to the learners about the fact that tri- means 'three' in English, so a triangle has three angles (corners) and three sides, a tricycle has three wheels and triplets are three brothers or sisters born at the same time. Ask if they can think of some more words, either in English or in their native language, that have a similar pattern.

Summary

- Learners are beginning to count on in threes and starting to recognise the sequence produced.
- They can talk about the patterns in the numbers.

Notes on the Learner's Book
Planet Tribly (p57): encourages counting in threes using aliens that have one head but three arms, legs, fingers, toes and so on. Learners have to work out the number of legs and toes behind a wall.

Check up!
Begin to count in threes:
- "*3, 6, 9....*" If the learners do not join in, ask, "*What comes next?*"

More activities

Three in a line (individuals)

You will need the *0–50 Number line* photocopy master and learners' completed *Threes* photocopy master.

Leaners use the Number line to show jumps of three from zero. They might like to use their completed *Threes* photocopy master for support.

Three-strip (individuals)

You will need squared paper.

Cut a strip of squared paper 3 squares wide. Learners write the digits 1, 2 and 3 in the squares of the first row. Learners continue to write the sequence of counting numbers along each row; so row two will contain 5, 6, and 7; row three will contain 8, 9 and 10, and so on. Ask learners to look at the patterns in each **column**. Most learners will begin to recognise the pattern in the last column (counting in threes from 3), but some will also see that the first column is also counting in threes, but from 1 and the second column is counting in threes starting from 2.

> **Resources:** *100 square* photocopy master (chapter 1, p4); large version for class display. *Fours* photocopy master (CD-ROM). Colouring pencils. A4 paper. Cubes or counters (Optional: *0–50 number lines* photocopy master (chapter 14, p116); squared paper; scissors; *Mazes* photocopy master (CD-ROM).)

Begin the session by revising counting in threes from 0 to (at least) 30 with the learners. Ask if they can describe the pattern they saw on the 100 square in the previous session.

Remind the learners that they are very good at noticing patterns, so you would like them to explore what happens when they count in fours on the 100 square. Give each learner a copy of the *Fours* photocopy master and show them that the first three numbers, 4, 8 and 12 have been shaded for them. Explain that they should choose a coloured pencil and continue counting in fours, colouring in every fourth square.

Remind them that this was what they did with three, but explain that they need to be careful because the pattern will be different. After the learners have had time to explore, ask them to talk to a partner about the patterns they can see.

Bring the learners back together and ask two or three of them to talk about what they noticed. The learners will have noticed that the pattern is very different to the threes pattern. They may describe it as 'a patchwork' where every other square is coloured in some columns and none in others. They may find it more difficult to describe than the threes pattern. Ask the learners to look at the pattern to 20, then 40, then 60, 80 and 100. They should also look at the ones digit in each number to see if they can notice another pattern.

Give the learners five to ten minutes to talk to their partner. Check that they have noticed that the pattern repeats itself after each 20. They should also notice that only the even numbers, 2, 4, 6, 8 and 0 are found in the ones place value column. Give the learners a few more minutes to talk to their partner about the patterns.

Check that the learners have noticed counting in fours is like counting in twos, just missing every other number out. When we count in twos we are saying the even numbers and even numbers are made up of twos. Four is two twos, so counting in fours also makes only even numbers. Five lots of 4 is 20, so each twenty is another five lots of four, so the pattern repeats itself. Count along in fours together to 60 and then 100.

Look out for!

- Learners who lose track when they are counting in fours, particularly when moving onto the next row. *Give them four cubes or counters to use. After colouring in a square, they place the counters on the next four squares counting to four (1, 2, 3, 4) as they place them. They can only colour in the square where they put the last counter, i.e. when they said 'four'.*
- Learners who have mastered counting in fours. *You could also give these learners a 100 square and ask them to find out if the same pattern will be produced if you start counting in fours from 1, 2 or 3. Ask them to explain how the pattern is the same or different.*

Finish the session by playing 'four-bingo'. Give each learner an A4 sheet of paper and ask them to fold it in half three times: half, then half again and then half again. When they open it up, they can see eight spaces. They must choose eight of their coloured numbers and write one in each space. Call out random numbers from the four pattern. Learners cross of their numbers as they are called and the winner if the first person to cross off all their numbers. They call out *Bingo!* Or *House!*

During the game, occasionally call out a number which is not in the fours pattern. If no one notices, tell the learners that you did not notice anyone crossing off that number and comment, "*I wonder why?*" Check that the learners now realise the number was not one they coloured. It was not in the fours pattern so no one would have written it on their bingo card.

If you have time, tell the learners that quad- means four in English. Ask, "*How many wheels are there on a quad bike? If I am a quad, how many brothers and sisters were born at the same time as me?*" Ask if they can think of some more words, either in English or in their native language, that have similar patterns.

Summary

- Learners are beginning to count on in fours and to recognise the sequence of numbers produced.
- They can talk about the patterns in the numbers.

Notes on the Learner's Book
Planet Quadling (p58): provides opportunities for learners to count in fours using aliens called 'Quadlings'. Learners have to count in threes and fours when the Qualidings' friends from Tribly are introduced.

Check up!
Begin to count in fours, "*4, 8, 12 . . .* " If the learners do not join in, ask, "*What comes next?*" Ask questions such as, "*What is special about the numbers when we count in fours? Can you remember when the pattern repeats itself?*"

More activities

Four in a line (individuals)

You will need the *0–50 Number line* photocopy master and learner's completed *Fours* photocopy master.

Learners show jumps of four from 0. They might like to use their completed *Fours* photocopy master for support.

Four-strip (individuals)

> You will need squared paper.

Cut a strip of squared paper 4 squares wide. Learners write the numbers 1, 2, 3, 4 in the first row. Ask the learners to continue writing the counting numbers along each row; so in row two they would write 5, 6, 7, 8 and in row three they would write 9, 10, 11, 12 and so on. Ask them to look at the patterns in each column. Most learners will recognise the even numbers in the last column and might also notice the even numbers in the second column.

Mazes (invidiuals)

> You will need the *Mazes* photocopy master.

Learners count in threes or fours to find their way through the mazes.

Games Book (ISBN 978110762349)

3 and 4 race (p31) is game for two players. Players count in threes or fours to race to the finish.

24 Sums and differences

Quick reference

Core activity 24.1: Next door numbers (Learner's Book p59)
Learners add two consecutive two-digit numbers and explore the resulting pattern.

Core activity 24.2: Missing numbers (Learner's Book p60)
Learners find the difference between two two-digit numbers. They begin to identify a missing number within a number sentence by counting on or using number pairs to 10 or 20.

Core activity 24.3: Add or subtract? (Learner's Book p61)
Learners begin to spot clues to help them identify when to add and subtract in word problems that involve adding/subtracting single-digit numbers to/from a two-digit number.

Prior learning	Objectives* – please note that listed objectives might only be partially covered within any given chapter but are covered fully across the book when taken as a whole
• Counting to at least 100. • Explored number patterns. • Explored addition, and subtraction as take away and difference.	**1A: Numbers and the number system** 2Nn14 – Understand odd and even numbers and recognise these up to at least 20. **3A: Calculation** (*Mental strategies*) 2Nc1 – Find and learn by heart all number pairs to 10 and pairs with a total of 20. **3A: Calculation** (*Addition and subtraction*) 2Nc6 – Relate counting on/back in tens to finding 10 more/less than any two-digit number and then to adding and subtracting other multiples of 10, e.g. $75 - 30$. 2Nc9 – Recognise the use of a symbol such as or Δ to represent an unknown, e.g. $\Delta + \square = 10$. 2Nc10 – Solve number sentences such as $27 + \square = 30$. 2Nc11 – Add and subtract a single digit to and from a two-digit number. 2Nc12 – Add pairs of two-digit numbers . 2Nc13 – Find a small difference between pairs of two-digit numbers. **2B: Problem solving** 2Pt9 – Identify simple relationships between numbers and shapes, e.g. this number is double . . .; these shapes all have . . . sides. **3A: Problem solving** 2Pt2 – Explain methods and reasoning orally. 2Pt3 – Explore number problems and puzzles. 2Pt4 – Make sense of simple word problems (single and easy two-step), decide what operations (addition or subtraction, simple multiplication or division) are needed to solve them and, with help, represent them, with objects or drawings or on a number line. 2Pt5 – Make up a number story to go with a calculation, including in the context of money. 2Pt6 – Check the answer to an addition by adding the numbers in a different order or by using a different strategy, e.g. $35 + 19$ by adding 20 to 35 and subtracting 1, and by adding $30 + 10$ and $5 + 9$. 2Pt7 – Check a subtraction by adding the answer to the smaller number in the original subtraction.

*for NRICH activities mapped to the Cambridge Primary objectives, please visit www.cie.org.uk/cambridgeprimarymaths

Vocabulary

consecutive (or next door numbers) • word problem

Resources: *100 square* photocopy master (chapter 1, p4); large version for class display and one per learner. *Tens and ones cards* photocopy master (CD-ROM). *0–100 number line* (chapter 3, p18). (Optional: *Number wordsearch* photocopy master (CD-ROM). *0–200 number line* photocopy master (CD-ROM). *200 square* photocopy master (CD-ROM).)

Begin by choosing any number on the *100 square* photocopy master and count forward and back in tens. Ask the learners question such as, "*What is 10 more than 26? How do you know?*" Ask several '10 more', '10 less' questions to check understanding, then move on to '20 more', '20 less' and '30 more or less'.

Next, introduce them to the term 'consecutive' and use the *100 square* to show examples of consecutive or 'next door numbers'. Each number is one more than the number before it.

Tell the learners that they are very good at noticing patterns so you have a challenge for them. Explain, "*I would like you to choose two numbers next door to each other on the 100 square (for example, 23 and 24 or 47 and 48, any numbers you like) and add them together. You could use place value cards, a number line or anything else to help you. Don't forget to add the numbers in a different order or in a different way to check that you were right. Choose whether to work on your own or with a partner. After five lots of additions, look at your answers to see if you notice anything. If you don't see a pattern, try a few more additions and look again. If you add numbers below 50, your total will be on the 100 square. You might like to cross the total numbers out on the 100 square to help you spot any patterns, or you could just write a list.*"

Give the learners plenty of time to explore, then ask them to tell you anything they have noticed. If necessary, ask if all the numbers are even. The learners should be able to tell you that all the totals are odd. Ask if this will always happen when you add two next door numbers. Discuss their responses until agreement is reached. Challenge them to explain why the total will always be odd. **(Answer: there is a pattern in consecutive numbers of odd-even-odd-even-odd-even, i.e. alternating odd and even numbers. So, when two consecutive numbers are added, one of the numbers will always be odd and the other will always be even, and 'even + odd' will always be odd.)**

Divide the class into two teams and have a vocabulary quiz to check that learners understand words such as 'consecutive/next door numbers', 'total', 'double', 'column', 'row', 'cube', 'square' and so on. Ask teams to explain what a word means to earn a point.

Vocabulary

consecutive (or next door numbers): are numbers that are next to each other; each number is one more than the one before. For example, 23, 24, 25, 26 are consecutive numbers.

Look out for!

- Learners who might write numbers greater than 100 as they sound. For example, writing one hundred and twenty four as 10024. *Remind them that they know how to use the place value cards to make 24 and show them how to use the 100 card to turn 24 into 124 so they can write it correctly.*

- Learners who are confident writing numbers greater tan 100. *Challenge them to work with numbers over 50, so their total will be over 100. They could also use the 0–100 Number line, 0–200 Number line and the 200 square photocopy masters to help them to see any patterns.*

Summary

Learners explore patterns when adding two consecutive numbers.

Notes on the Learner's Book

Odd? (p59): learners write three correct sentences using the words 'odd' and 'even', and the symbols '+' and' ='.

Check up!

Ask questions such as:
- *"Give me some examples of next door numbers."*
- *"Are 10, 20, 30, 40 and 50 next door numbers?"* **(Answer: no, the difference between them is ten each time, not one. They are decade numbers.)**
- *What sort of total do you get if you add two next door (consecutive) numbers together?"* **(Answer: an odd number)**
- *"What sort of numbers would you need to add to get an even total?"* **(Answer: even numbers or an even number of odd numbers, because odd + odd = even)**
- *"Is there another way to get an even total?"*

More activities

Number wordsearch (individuals)

> You will need the *Number wordsearch* photocopy master (CD-ROM).

Learners find the number words zero to ten in a wordsearch.

Games Book (ISBN 978110762349)

10 plus 10 minus game (p36) is a game for two players. Game 1: Players add and subtract tens numbers from a two-digit number. Game 2: Players add and subtract tens numbers from a three-digit number.

Core activity 24.2: Missing numbers

> **Resources:** 100 square photocopy master (chapter 1, p4). *Tens and ones cards* photocopy master (CD-ROM); per pair of learners, *0–9 spinner* or *0–9 digit cards*, photocopy master (CD-ROM); per pair of learners. *Multiples of 10* photocopy master (CD-ROM); per pair of learners. (Optional: 3 cm piece of flattened cardboard tube; strips of card.)

Begin by asking the learners what we mean by 'find the difference'. Learners should recognise this as a subtraction or take away calculation (Unit 2A, chapter 16). Ask questions involving two two-digit numbers such as, "*Find the difference between 23 and 27*". Remind the learners that when the two numbers are close together, it is easier to count on from the smaller number to the larger number.

Learners can start at 23 and count on 4 to get to 27, or start at 27 and count back 4 to get to 23. Some people will do it one way, some people will do it the other way. Repeat with several other pairs of numbers. Some learners may find a *100 square* helpful.

Explain that we could write an addition number sentence to help us find the difference. Write the last calculation that the learners did with an empty box for the missing number, for example, $23 + \square = 27$.

Ask the learners what they did to find the missing number. Go on to show them a difference where they can use their number pairs to 10, for example $24 + \square = 30$. Ask the learners if they needed to count to find the missing number this time.

> Give each pair of learners a set of *Tens and ones cards,* a part set of decade cards (20 to 100) from the *Multiples of 10* photocopy master, and a 0–9 dice or set of digit cards. The place value cards should be placed randomly on the table, face down. Learners turn over a place value card. This is their total. Then they subtract 10 from the place value card and roll the dice to find the ones part of the number. For example, if they turn over 40 and then roll 3, they know that their calculation will be $33 + \square = 40$. They write the calculation with the missing box, then write in the missing number using the number pairs to 10. Challenge the learners to write at least 10 missing number sentences and then solve them.

Look out for!

- Learners who find it difficult to work out what the missing number is when it comes before the equals sign. *Model a simple number sentence with counters or cubes, then cover up the first or second number and talk through how we can work out what is under the cover.*
- Learners who find it straightforward to work out where the missing number is when it is before the equals sign. *Challenge them by giving them three missing numbers to work out. For example,*

$$\square + \triangle + \hexagon = 120$$

or

$$\square + \triangle - \hexagon = 34$$

Towards the end of the session, remind the learners that 10 is a very important number and keeps appearing in most of our number work. Ask the learners if they know their number pairs to 10. Quickly list them with the help of the learners, encouraging them to suggest the number pairs in order so that they can be sure they have not missed any. Finish off the session by showing them the following number sentences:

$$\square \ + \ \triangle = 10 \qquad \qquad \triangle \ + \ \square = 20$$

Ask the learners what they think the triangle and square might mean. Make sure that the learners understand that they both mean that we do not know what number is in the box. Ask the learners to choose a number to go in the first empty box. Once that number is chosen, do they have a choice about what goes in the second box? Make sure the learners understand that once a number is written in one of the boxes, there can only be one number that goes in the second box.

Challenge the learners to write all the number pairs that could go in the boxes before the end of the session.

Summary

- Learners have developed their understanding of 'difference'.
- They understand that an empty box, whatever the shape, represents a missing number.

Notes on the Learner's Book
What goes where? (p60): learners write some number sentences using the numbers given. The learners should notice a number pair to 20 for the first three numbers 20, 13 and 7.

Check up!
Ask questions such as:
- *"What is the difference between 27 and 30? How do you know?"*
- *"If I have 43, how many more do I need to make 48? How do you know?"*

More activities

Slide number strips (pairs)

You will need a 3 cm piece of flattened cardboard tube (such as that used within a roll of kitchen paper towels), strips of card or paper.

Learners take it in turns to write a number sentence across a strip of card/paper. They slip the flattened tube over the number strip to cover any one of the numbers in their number sentence. The hidden number is the unknown number. Learners show their partner their number sentence with a number covered and the other learner has to decide what the missing number is, and explain how they know.

Games Book (ISBN 9781107762349)

Peek a boo! (p38) is a game for two players. This game helps players to develop a strategy to solve missing number calculations.

Core activity 24.3: Add or subtract?

Resources: *Tens and ones cards* photocopy master (CD-ROM); per pair of learners. *Solve it!* photocopy master (p205); per pair of learners. (Optional: *Solve it! extra* sheets 1 and 2 photocopy master (CD-ROM); *Domino dilemmas* photocopy master (CD-ROM); sets of double six dominos (CD-ROM); a set of double nine dominos for checking (CD-ROM); counters.)

Give each pair of learners a set of place value cards from the *Tens and ones cards* photocopy master. Remind them how to add or subtract a single-digit number from a two-digit number by adding or subtracting 10, then adjusting the total using ones; as they did in Term 2 (Unit 2A, chapter 15). Call out some additions and subtractions for the learners to work out. Ask various learners how they found the answer.

When you are confident that the learners can use this particular method, remind them that there are other ways of finding the answer. For example, they could notice and use a number pair to 10, or use doubles or perhaps something else. Call out two or three more additions or subtractions of a single-digit number from a two-digit number for the learners to find the solution in their own way.

Ask the learners how they know when they need to add or subtract. They will probably talk about the addition and subtraction signs, but ask, "*What if there are no signs because the question is written in words?*" Write up a simple word problem where everyone can see and read it out loud. For example:

"*There are 27 learners in the class. 8 are away today. How many learners are here?*" You could change the numbers to be true for your class.

Ask the learners to talk to their partner about what they could do to find out the answer.

After giving the learners a little time to discuss, ask if they think they need to add or subtract. How do they know? What is it in the word problem or number story that tells them? Check that they realise that the word 'away' helps them to recognise that it is a subtraction and they need to take away eight here. Write the matching number sentence and solve it together. Other helpful clues include words such as 'were' and 'left'.

Write and read out another word problem. "*19 learners are playing football. Seven are watching. How many learners altogether?*"

Vocabulary

word problem: another name for a number story.

Ask the learners to talk with their partner again. Are there any clues that tell them if they need to add or subtract? After giving the learners a little time to discuss, check that they recognised that the word 'altogether' tells them that they needed to add. 'Altogether' is another way of saying 'in total'. Other helpful clues are words such as 'more'.

Write the matching number sentence and solve it together.

Give each pair of learners one of the pages from the *Solve it!* photocopy master. Ask them to decide whether each problem is asking them to add or subtract. They should then work together to write the matching number sentence and find the answer to the problem.

After giving the learners enough time to have a go at several questions, work through some of the problems together, talking through how we know whether to add or subtract.

Look out for!

- Learners who find it hard to identify when they need to add or subtract. *Model going through the word problem one step at a time, looking at what each part is saying to show how you know what to do. If a learner continues to find this hard, get them to write a simple adding problem and look at the words they use to make sure the reader adds. Do the same with a subtraction problem.*
- Learners who find it straightforward to know when to add or subtract. *Suggest that they move on to two-step problems, for example, "Rani had 30 sweets. 12 of them were red, the rest were green. Soriah had double the amount of green sweets Rani had. How many green sweets did Soriah have?"*

Summary

- Learners are able to add or subtract a single digit from a two- or three-digit number.
- They can make sense of simple word problems, deciding correctly whether to add or subtract.

Notes on the Learner's Book
Add or subtract? (p61): learners decide when to add or subtract to solve word problems. They also write a problem to match a number sentence.

Check up!

Make up a simple word problem for the learners to solve. Ask them to identify if it requires addition or subtraction, then ask them to write the number sentence and solve the calculation.

More activities

Solve it! (individuals)

> You will need the *Solve it! extra (1)* and *(2)* photocopy masters (CD-ROM).

Give learners the *'extra'* question sheets to explore.

Domino dilemmas (individuals)

> You will need the *Domino dilemmas* photocopy master (CD-ROM).

Print out enough copies of the *Domino dilemmas* questions for the learners to have a choice. Cut up the cards and ask the learners to choose a question to investigate or play the game. They can record what they find out in any way they choose.

Solve it!

There are 32 apples in the box. If we eat 6, how many will be left?	All 26 learners in the class take a lolly from the jar. There are 8 lollies left. How many lollies were in the jar at the start?
34 people are on the bus. 7 more get on. How many people on the bus now?	There were 56 birds on the lake. 9 flew away. How many are left?
There are 148 beads in a pack. I have 7 left. How many have I used?	I have 36 marbles. My friend gives me 7 more. How many have I got now?

Blank page

3A 25 Fractions

Quick reference

<u>**Core activity 25.1: Parts of a whole**</u> (Learner's Book p62)

Learners explore the concept of fractions as parts of a whole. They find
$\frac{1}{4}, \frac{1}{2}$ and $\frac{3}{4}$ of a shape or small amount, and learn that $\frac{1}{2}$ and $\frac{2}{4}$ are equivalent.

<u>**Core activity 25.2: Parts of an amount**</u> (Learner's Book p62)

Learners explore $\frac{1}{2}$ as a number and find $\frac{1}{2}$ and $\frac{1}{4}$ of a small amount.

Prior learning	Objectives* – please note that listed objectives might only be partially covered within any given chapter but are covered fully across the book when taken as a whole
Explored half of a shape and a number.	**3A: Numbers and the number system** 2Nn16 – Recognise that we write one-half $\frac{1}{2}$, one-quarter $\frac{1}{4}$ and three-quarters $\frac{3}{4}$. 2Nn17 – Recognise that $\frac{2}{2}$ or $\frac{4}{4}$ make a whole and $\frac{1}{2}$ and $\frac{2}{4}$ are equivalent. 2Nn18 – Recognise which shapes are divided in halves or quarters and which are not. 2Nn19 – Find halves and quarters of shapes and small numbers of objects. **3A: Problem solving** (*Using techniques and skills in solving mathematical problems*) 2Pt3 – Explore number problems and puzzles.

*for NRICH activities mapped to the Cambridge Primary objectives, please visit www.cie.org.uk/cambridgeprimarymaths

Vocabulary

half • quarter • three-quarters

Core activity 25.1: Parts of a whole

Resources: *Circles and squares* photocopy master (p215) printed on coloured paper. Scissors, plain paper and glue for each learner. Cubes or counters. (Optional: *Fraction folders* photocopy master (CD-ROM); *Is it a half? Is it a quarter?* photocopy master (CD-ROM); scissors.

Ask the learners to remind you what a half is. Fold some paper shapes to demonstrate a half. Explain that you are going to fold each shape to create two pieces; start doing this with the first shape and fold it to create two pieces that are clearly **not** the same size. Learners should object and inform you that is not correct. Respond to the learners' suggestions of what a half is.

Draw out that a half is one part of something that has been split into two **equal parts**. Make sure that the learners really do understand that a half is one part of two **equal** pieces, not just two pieces, by drawing some shapes for the whole class to see, and then showing them what half of the shape is.

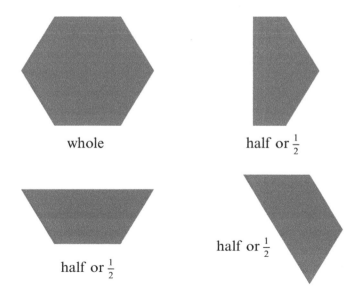

whole

half or $\frac{1}{2}$

half or $\frac{1}{2}$

half or $\frac{1}{2}$

Label the shape with the word 'half' and explain that we can also write it using the symbol $\frac{1}{2}$.

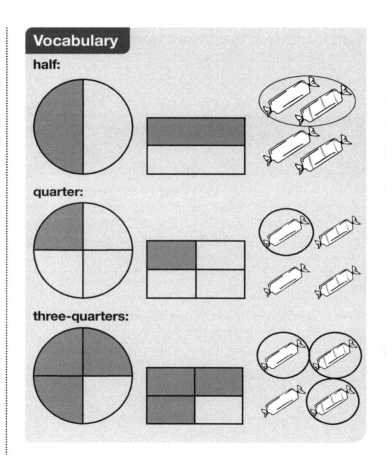

Vocabulary

half:

quarter:

three-quarters:

Ask the learners if you can have half of a number. Again, accept their ideas and illustrate them by drawing a given number of crosses for the whole class to see, and grouping them into two equally sized sets. You could do the same with a number of counters or cubes. If any of the learners are unsure, ask them to take four interlocking cubes and make a tower. Ask them to break the tower into two equal halves, so that each half has two cubes. Explain that this demonstrates that half of 4 is 2.

Write $\frac{1}{4}$ near $\frac{1}{2}$ for the whole class to see. Ask the learners to talk to their partner about what it means.

Respond to the learners' ideas by drawing and folding some shapes to show $\frac{1}{4}$. Ask the learners if you can have $\frac{1}{4}$ of a number. Explore their ideas as before.

Give each learner a copy of the *Circles and squares* photocopy masters and ask them to cut out the squares and circles. Ask the learners to find different ways to show $\frac{1}{2}$ and $\frac{1}{4}$ using the shapes. Explain that, *"After folding and cutting each shape, you must label the pieces. Then glue them onto plain paper as if you were putting the squares and circles back together again. We need to see that each shape started off as a whole one and how you have cut them up."*

Look at some examples of the learners' work as a class. Take the opportunity to check that the learners understand that two-halves make a whole and that four-quarters make a whole.

$\frac{1}{2} + \frac{1}{2} = \frac{2}{2} = 1$ $\frac{1}{4} + \frac{1}{4} + \frac{1}{4} + \frac{1}{4} = \frac{4}{4} = 1$

Cut a circle from the *Circles and squares* photocopy master into half, then cut **one** of the halves into quarters. Demonstrate that one half and two quarters makes a whole. Explain that this shows us that $\frac{1}{2}$ and $\frac{2}{4}$ are the same size, i.e. they are equal/equivalent. Remind learners of the term 'equivalent' if necessary (Unit 1A, chapter 6).

Finish the session by exploring $\frac{3}{4}$ together. Write $\frac{1}{4}$ and $\frac{3}{4}$ for the whole class to see and ask the learners to talk with their partner about what $\frac{3}{4}$ might mean. Share ideas as before. Draw out that it means 'three-quarters'. The bottom number tells us how many equally-sized pieces the 'whole' has been split into and the top number tells us how many of those pieces we have.

Reinforce this by returning to $\frac{1}{2}$ and $\frac{1}{4}$. The '2' tells us that the whole has been split into two equal parts and the 'one' tells us we have one of those parts. The '4' tells us that the whole has been split into four equal parts and the '1' tells us we have one of those parts.

Look out for!
- Learners who find $\frac{1}{4}$ difficult. *Focus on the fact that $\frac{1}{2}$ is one whole cut into two equal pieces and that a quarter is one whole cut into four equal pieces. This is shown in how we write them. Avoid describing $\frac{1}{4}$ as half of a half with learners who find the idea of a quarter difficult, as this is likely to increase their confusion.*
- Learners who find $\frac{1}{4}$ and $\frac{1}{2}$ straightforward. *Challenge them to cut $\frac{3}{4}$ of a shape in one piece, rather than three separate quarters.*

Opportunity for display
Display cut shapes next to a label giving the fraction. Such displays can act as a helpful reminder of the different fractions.

Summary

- Learners begin to find $\frac{1}{2}$, $\frac{1}{4}$ and $\frac{3}{4}$ of a shape and a small amount.
- They know that $\frac{2}{2}$ make a whole, that $\frac{4}{4}$ makes a whole and that $\frac{1}{2}$ and $\frac{2}{4}$ are equivalent.

Notes on the Learner's Book

Fraction parts (p62): learners find $\frac{1}{2}$, $\frac{1}{4}$ and $\frac{3}{4}$ of 12 socks. This page could be used with *Core activity* 25.2 as well / instead.

Check up!

Ask learners questions such as:

- *"If I cut a circle into two equal-sized pieces, what would each piece be called?"*
- *"If I had four sweets and I gave you half of them, how many would you get?"*
- *"What if there were eight sweets and you and your brother got half each? How many would you get?"*
- *"If I have a chocolate bar made of four squares and I eat three, how much of the whole bar have I eaten?"*

More activities

Is it half? Is it a quarter? (individual, pairs or group)

> You will need the *Is it half? It is a quarter?* photocopy master.

Learners check if each shape correctly shows a half or a quarter.

Fraction Folders (individual or pairs)

> You will need the *Fraction folders* photocopy master.

Learners cut out each strip of paper. They keep the first as one whole: eight squares. They fold and cut the second strip in half, colouring each half a different colour to create two-halves: two lots of four squares. Check that they see that two-halves are the same as one whole. They fold and cut the third strip in half, then cut each one of the halves in half in order to make four-quarters: four lots of two squares.

Show the learners how to align two $\frac{1}{4}$ strips underneath one $\frac{1}{2}$ strip to show that they are equivalent (i.e. the same size). Then align one $\frac{1}{2}$ and $\frac{1}{4}$ strip side-by-side (to create one strip) and then line up three of the $\frac{1}{4}$ strips underneath to show that $\frac{1}{2}$ and $\frac{1}{4}$ make three-quarters.

Games Book (ISBN 978110762349)

Fraction game (p40) is a game for two to four players. Players complete four squares using different fractions ($\frac{1}{4}$, $\frac{1}{2}$ and $\frac{3}{4}$) of a square.

Core activity 25.2: Parts of an amount

Resources: A large 0–10 number line for display. Cubes or counters. (Optional: *Fraction Circles* photocopy master (CD-ROM); prepare some bags of objects with labels such as 'Find $\frac{1}{2}$', 'Find $\frac{1}{4}$' or 'Find $\frac{3}{4}$').

Remind the learners that they know that a half is one of two equal pieces. If necessary, fold a shape to show this. Explain that $\frac{1}{2}$ is also a number. Draw a number line and label the ends 0 and 1. Mark a point half way between the 0 and the 1. Ask the learners what this could be. After some discussion, label it $\frac{1}{2}$.

Extend your number line to 2. Say, *"I am marking a point half-way between 1 and 2. It is not 1. It is not 2. It is half way between them. How can I label it?"* If the learners find the idea difficult, draw half a circle below $\frac{1}{2}$, a circle below 1 and two circles below 2. Show how $\frac{1}{2}$ a circle is added as you move from 0 to $\frac{1}{2}$, then from $\frac{1}{2}$ to 1. *"So the next mark must be 1 and another $\frac{1}{2}$, $1\frac{1}{2}$. Adding another half takes us to number 2."*

Display the 0–10 number line for the whole class to see. Mark and label all the mid-points with the learners, then count in halves from 0 to 10.

Tell the learners that they can also find half of an amount. Put some chairs at the front of the class and ask ten learners to come to the front. Ask five of the learners to sit down and say, *"Half the learners are sitting, half the learners are standing. There are ten learners altogether, so what is half of ten?"* Respond to the learners' ideas, checking that they understand that there are the same number of learners standing as sitting. So the five learners standing are half of the group of ten learners and the five learners sitting are the other half. Record this where everyone can see, as 'half of ten is five' (or '$\frac{1}{2}$ of 10 = 5').

Repeat with a total of 8, 6, 4 and finally two learners, writing a matching number sentence each time. Choose one of the number sentences. Quickly draw that number of objects and draw a loop around half of them. Talk about how this matches the number sentence and what you did with the learners.

Ask the learners to write down each of the number sentences and draw a simple picture (circles, sweets, triangles or something similar) to match each one. Give learners cubes or counters to use for support if they need them.

Look out for!
- Learners who find it hard to understand that half of two is one. *Do not focus on this until the learners have developed some understanding of 'a half'.*
- Learners who find the concept of 'a half' straightforward. *Challenge them to find half of odd numbers such as 3, 5, 7 and 9. They could also find $\frac{3}{4}$ of 8 and 4.*

Opportunity for display
Display illustrations of fractions of a number of objects alongside the fractions of shapes.

Finish the session by exploring $\frac{1}{4}$ together. Show the learners a tower of eight cubes. Break off two cubes at a time to show the learners that you now have four equal pieces, so each piece is a quarter ($\frac{1}{4}$) of your tower; one of four equal pieces.

If necessary, remake the tower and repeat the breaking into quarters as you say, "*A quarter of 8 is 2.*" Write the number sentence using the same format as you did with half. Ask the learners to make a tower of four cubes and break it into four equal pieces. Check that they understand that $\frac{1}{4}$ of 4 is 1.

If there is time, ask the learners to write these last two number sentences and draw a matching picture with a loop around one-quarter of the objects. Take the opportunity to check that the learners understand that four-quarters make a whole, as does one-half and two-quarters, showing that one-half and two-quarters are equivalent.

Summary

Learners begin to recognise a half and a quarter of a quantity.

Notes on the Learner's Book
Fraction parts (p62): learners find $\frac{1}{2}$, $\frac{1}{4}$ and $\frac{3}{4}$ of 12 socks. This page could be used with *Core activity 25.1* (p208) or *25.2* (p212).

Check up!
Tell the learners a simple word problem such as:
- "*I brought four pieces of fruit in with me to school. I'm going to eat half today and half tomorrow. How much can I eat today?*"
- "*I've eaten half my sweets. I have three left. How many did I have to begin with?*"

More activities

Fraction circles (individuals)

You will need the *Fraction circles* photocopy master (CD-ROM).
If possible, print each circle on different coloured paper as this helps to highlight the different fractions.

Learners explore different ways of covering the whole circle without overlapping any pieces. They record their arrangements as additions, $\frac{1}{2} + \frac{1}{2} = 1$. $\frac{1}{2} + \frac{1}{4} + \frac{1}{4} = 1$. $\frac{1}{4} + \frac{3}{4} = 1$. This gives the learners the opportunity to see that two-halves or four-quarters make a whole and that one-half and two-quarters are equivalent.

What's in the bag?

You will need three bags containing a number of objects. Label each bag 'Find $\frac{1}{2}$', 'Find $\frac{1}{4}$' or 'Find $\frac{3}{4}$'.

Learners tip out the contents of each bag, count how any objects are in there and then find the fraction requested on the label. Ask learners to record their answers. Challenge the more able learners by removing the label from each bag and telling them that the amount in the bag is a fraction of a whole, for example, $\frac{1}{2}$ or $\frac{1}{4}$. Then ask them to find out what the whole amount was.

Games Book (ISBN 978110762349)

Fraction game (p40) is a game for two to four players. Players complete four squares using different fractions ($\frac{1}{4}$, $\frac{1}{2}$ and $\frac{3}{4}$) of a square.

Circles and squares

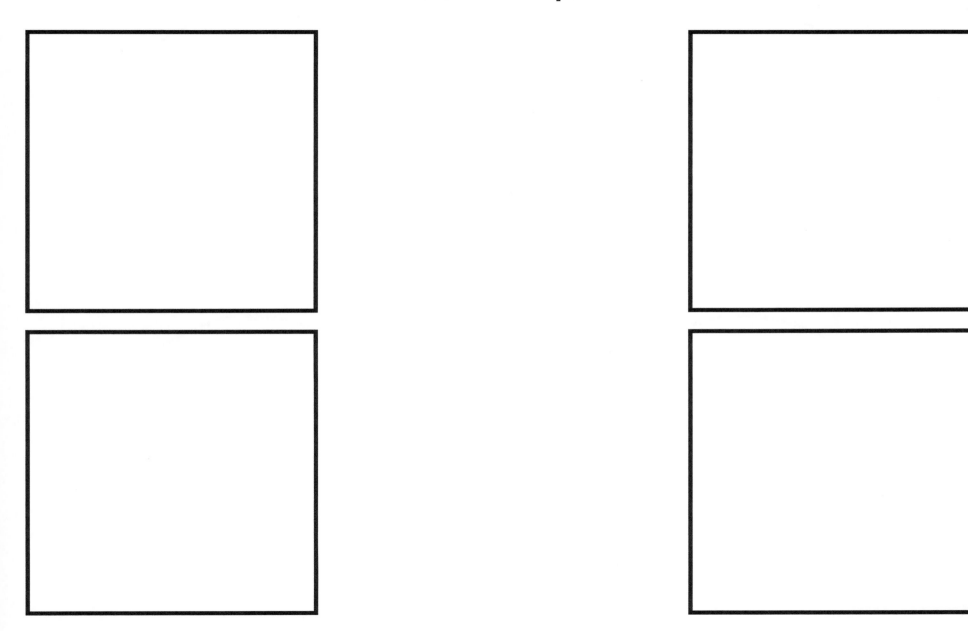

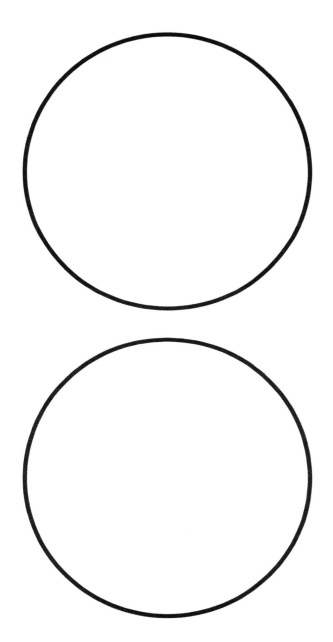
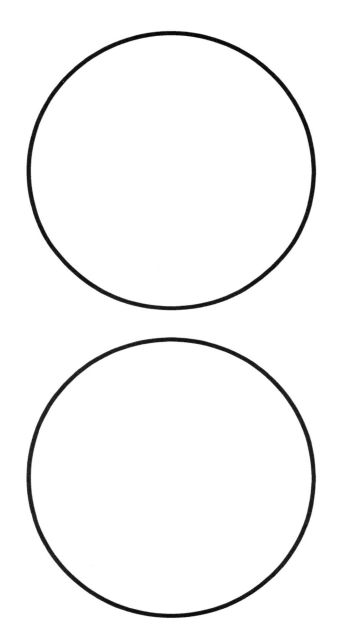

Instructions on page 209

Quick reference

Core activity 26.1: Twos, fives and tens (Learner's Book p63)

Learners count in twos, fives and tens to solve word problems involving multiplication and division, including problems with a remainder.

Core activity 26.2: Threes and fours (Learner's Book p64)

Learners count in threes and fours to solve word problems involving multiplication and division, including problems with a remainder.

Core activity 26.3: Using arrays (Learner's Book p65)

Learners use an array to help them explore division as grouping.

Prior learning	Objectives* – please note that listed objectives might only be partially covered within any given chapter but are covered fully across the book when taken as a whole
• Counting in twos, fives and tens. • Counting in threes and fours.	**3A: Numbers and the number system** 2Nn4 – Count in twos, fives and tens, and use grouping in twos, fives or tens to count larger groups of objects. 2Nn5 – Begin to count on in small constant steps such as threes and fours. **3A: Calculation:** *(Mental strategies)* 2Nc4 – Learn and recognise multiples of 2, 5 and 10 and derive the related division facts. **3A: Calculation:** *(Multiplication and division)* 2Nc18 – Understand division as grouping and use the ÷ sign. 2Nc19 – Use counting in twos, fives or tens to solve practical problems involving repeated addition. 2Nc22 – Work out multiplication and division facts for the 3 × and 4 × tables. 2Nc23 – Understand that division can leave some left over. **2B: Problem solving** *(Using techniques and skills in solving mathematical problems)* 2Pt9 – Identify simple relationships between numbers and shapes, e.g. this number is double . . .; these shapes all have . . . sides. **3A: Problem solving** *(Using techniques and skills in solving mathematical problems)* 2Pt2 – Explain methods and reasoning orally. 2Pt3 – Explore number problems and puzzles. 2Pt4 – Make sense of simple word problems (single and easy two-step), decide what operations (addition or subtraction, simple multiplication or division) are needed to solve them and, with help, represent them, with objects or drawings or on a number line. 2Pt5 – Make up a number story to go with a calculation, including in the context of money. 2Pt8 – Describe and continue patterns which count on in twos, threes, fours or fives to 30 or more.

*for NRICH activities mapped to the Cambridge Primary objectives, please visit www.cie.org.uk/cambridgeprimarymaths

Resources: *Twos, fives or tens?* photocopy master (p224) *100 square* photocopy master (chapter 1, p4). Interlocking cubes. (Optional: *More twos, fives or tens? 1* and *2* photocopy masters (CD-ROM).)

Begin by counting from zero to 100 in twos, then fives and tens. Ask learners to describe the pattern in each set of numbers. Follow that up with questions about how you can tell if a particular number is a multiple of 2, 5 or 10. **(Possible suggestions include: all even numbers are multiples of 2; numbers ending in '0' are multiples of 5 and 10; numbers ending in '5' are multiples of 5.)**

Call out random numbers and ask the learners to identify what it is a multiple of, by calling out: 2, 5 or 10 (or '2 and 10', or '5 and 10).

Remind the learners that counting in twos, fives or tens can be very useful. We can count in this way to find the answer to a problem. Write and read aloud a word problem such as, *"There are ten small toys in a pack. How many toys will there be in eight packs?"* Ask the learners how we could calculate how many toys there are altogether. Give the learners a few minutes to talk to a partner then share their ideas.

If necessary, tell the learners that you are not very good at counting in eights but you can easily count in tens. Write the numbers 10, 20, 30, 40, 50, 60, 70, 80, 90 where everyone can see them. Ask, *"How many tens have I counted?"* When the learners tell you there are nine tens, explain that you only needed eight because there were eight packs of toys, so cross out the 90 and write $8 \times 10 = 80$ (eight lots of 10 makes 80).

Ask the learners how they kept track of how many tens there were whilst they were counting. Did they use their fingers, counting along eight fingers? Did they use a piece of paper and put a dot or mark on it until they had eight marks? Or write the numbers 10, 20, 30, 40, 50, 60, 70, 80? Explain that sometimes it is useful to write the numbers because you can check you counted the right amount, just like you did earlier.

Write and read out another word problem such as, *"There are five flowers in a bunch. How many in 14 bunches?"* Ask the learners to talk with their partner again. Are there any clues that tell them if they should count in twos, fives or tens? After giving the learners a little time to discuss, check that they have recognised that, because there are five flowers in each bunch,

Look out for!

- Learners who find counting in twos, fives or tens difficult. *Give them a 100 square or sticks of 2, 5 or 10 interlocking cubes to use to support their counting.*
- Learners who find counting in multiples of 2, 5 and 10 easy. *Challenge them to write the matching number sentence.*

counting in fives would be a good way to find out how many flowers there are in 14 bunches. Comment, *"But this time there are 14 bunches and I don't have 14 fingers! How can I keep track of how many fives I've counted?"*

Give the learners some more time to talk to their partner, then share ideas. Write the matching number of fives for the whole class to see in order to solve the problem together.

Give each pair of learners a copy the *Twos, fives or tens?* photocopy master and ask them to decide if each problem requires them to count in twos, fives or tens. Learners then work together to write the matching multiples and find the answer to the problem.

After giving the learners enough time to have a go at several questions, work through some of the problems as a class. Encourage learners to explain their reasoning when discussing how they knew whether to count in twos, fives or tens.

Finish the session by asking the learners if they noticed anything special about the word problems they solved today. Draw out that none of the problems had a remainder. Go back to the flowers problem and change it to, *"There are five flowers in a bunch. How many bunches can I make with 24 flowers?"* Ask the learners to count in fives to find out how many complete bunches they can make (**4**) and how many flowers will be left over (**4**). Remind them that we would write this as 24 ÷ 5 = 4 r4. Carefully explain what each part of the number sentence means. Repeat for 32 flowers: 32 ÷ 5 = 6 r2. If there is time, ask the learners to make up a problem that could be solved by counting in twos, fives or tens, with or without a remainder.

Summary

Learners have counted in twos, fives and tens to solve a problem.

Notes on the Learner's Book
Marching ants (p63): learners count in twos to find out how many ants are marching.

Check up! Ask questions such as:
- *"I have 12 flowers. How many bunches of five flowers can I make? How many flowers are left over?"*
  (Answer: two complete bunches with two flowers left over)
- *"I have 12 shoes and six shoe boxes. Each box can hold two shoes. How many shoes will not fit in a box?"* **(Answer: none, 12 ÷ 2 = 6 so there are the correct number of boxes for the number of shoes)**

More activities

More twos, fives or tens? (individuals or pairs)

You will need the *More twos, fives or tens?* photocopy masters (CD-ROM).

Give learners one of the question sheets to explore. Challenge them to write their own questions. Pairs of learners could solve each other's questions.

Resources: *100 square* photocopy master (chapter 1, p4); large for class display and one per learner. *Threes or fours?* photocopy master (p225).

Begin by counting from zero to 100 in threes, and then fours. Use the *100 square* photocopy master for support. (Note that learners only need to count in threes up to 30 for stage 2.) Ask learners to describe the pattern in each set of numbers. Remind the learners that they know how to tell if a particular number is a multiple of 2, 5 or 10, so it is much easier to count in those steps than it is in threes and fours. Explain that they have not done as much counting in threes or fours, so it is important that they use the *100 square* photocopy master to help them.

Remind the learners how they counted in twos, fives or tens to solve problems and explain that they are going to have a go at solving problems by counting in threes or fours, including where there is a remainder. Write and read aloud a word problem such as, *"A cat eats four tins of cat food in a week. How many tins does he eat in two weeks?"* Ask the learners how we could find out how many tins of cat food have been eaten in total. Give the learners a few minutes to talk to a partner then share their ideas.

Write the numbers '4' and '8' where everyone can see them. Ask, *"How many fours have I counted?"* When the learners tell you there are two fours, write: $2 \times 4 = 8$ (two lots of 4 makes 8). Remind the learners that they can use the 100 square to help them with their counting, and that they should write down the numbers as they count so that they can check they have counted the right amount, just like they did in the previous session.

Write and read out another word problem such as, *"Each learner needs three sticks to make a model. There are 20 sticks. How many learners can make a model?"* Ask the learners to talk with their partner about the problem. Should they be counting in threes or fours? After giving the learners a little time to discuss, check that they have recognised that they need to count in threes.

Explain that they are imagining they have 20 sticks and that they are putting them into groups of three. Show them that they could write this as $20 \div 3 = \square$. Write the matching number of threes to solve the problem together and work out what the remainder is $(20 \div 3 = 6 \text{ r2})$.

Look out for!

- Learners who find it hard to count in threes or fours. *Give them a 100 square to colour in the pattern of threes or fours to use to support their counting.*
- Learners who find counting in multiples of 3 and 4 straightforward. *Challenge them to write the matching number sentence.*

Give each pair of learners one page from the *Threes or fours?* photocopy master and ask them to decide if each problem requires them to count in threes or fours. Learners work together to write the matching multiples and find the answer to the problem.

Learners are likely to find counting in fours easier than counting threes. They may identify which problems need them to count in threes but only solve those that count in fours. This is acceptable at this stage as counting in threes will be revisited and explored further in Stage 3.

After giving the learners enough time to have a go at several questions, work through some of the problems as a class. Encourage learners to explain their reasoning as you discuss how they knew if they needed to count in threes or fours.

Finish the session by looking at how to write the matching number sentence for some of the problems.

Summary

Learners have counted in threes and fours to solve a problem.

Notes on the Learner's Book
Car park (p64): learners work out how many wheels there are in the car park by counting in fours.

Check up!

Begin to count in threes and fours with the learners, encouraging them to take over. Ask them to solve word problems such as:
- *"If I have $16, how many $4 comics can I buy?"* **(Answer: 4)**
- *"How many $5 comics can I buy? Will I have any money left over?"* **(Answer: three comics, and $1 left over)**
- *"If I have 12 sweets and give 3 to each of my friends, how many friends do I have?"* **(Answer: 4)**

More activities

Threes or Fours? (individuals or pairs)

You will need *Threes or fours?* question sheets.

Challenge learners to write their own questions. Pairs of learners could swap questions and solve each other's.

Games Book (ISBN 9781107623459)

Threes and Fours game (p40) is a game for two players. Players count in threes or fours to find their bonus move.

Core activity 26.3: Using arrays

Resources: A large *100 square* photocopy master (chapter 1, p4). Each pair will need counters or cubes. *Array cards* photocopy master (CD-ROM).

Begin by counting from zero to 100 in threes, then fours. Use the 100 square for support. Challenge the learners to count to 30 in threes without looking at the 100 square, then to 40 in fours.

> Give each pair of learners 12 counters or cubes and ask them to make a 3 by 4 array. Check that the learners can 'see' threes and write the matching number sentence 3 × 4 = 12, four times three is 12. Check that the learners can 'see' fours and write the matching number sentence 4 × 3 = 12, three times four is 12. Ask the learners if they can see 12.

Begin to write the number sentence 12 ÷ and remind learners that '÷' means 'divided by' or in other words 'put into groups of'. Extend the number sentence to 12 ÷ 3 = ?. *"We can see threes, so 12 put into groups of three, gives us how many threes?"* **(four)** Repeat with 12 ÷ 4.

Elicit that you have written four different number sentences for the same array: two multiplication sentences and two division sentences. As a class, test to see if this is the case with other arrays.

> Now ask the learners to put their counters into a 2 by 6 array. Ask them to talk with their partner about how they could write some matching number sentences to say what they see. After the learners have had time to talk about their ideas, ask some of them to talk you through one of their number sentences.

> Ask learners to make their own arrays, either for 12 or other amounts such as 24, 30, 36 or 48. If required, give them the *Array cards* photocopy master. They should write matching number sentences for each array; challenge them to write all four. Remind them that they need to know: how many there are in each group, how many groups they need, *AND* how many counters they have used in total. Give the learners plenty of time to explore their arrays and how they might write them in a number sentence.

Finish off the session by looking at the *100 square* photocopy master. Remind the learners that there are 10 squares in each row and column, so we could say a 100 square is a 10 × 10 array. Write the matching number sentence for this array, 10 × 10 = 100, ten lots of ten is 100.

Challenge the learners to think of the matching division number sentence, 100 ÷ 10 = ? Remind them that this means, *"How many tens are there in 100?"* Hopefully almost everyone will be able to tell you 10!

Look out for!
- Learners who cannot 'see' the groups of three or four in a 3×4 array. *Use string, rulers or something else to separate the rows (or columns) and count the threes and fours together. Build up the 2 × 6 array with them by saying, "One lot of two, another lot of two, so that's two twos so far," and so on.*
- Learners who find it straightforward to 'see' groups of three or four in a 3×4 array. *Challenge them to make their own array and write the four number sentences for it: two multiplication and two division.*

Summary

- Learners have begun to use an array to help them see division in groups of a particular size.
- They have explored division number sentences.

Notes on the Learner's Book
Cake tray (p65): learners circle groups of 10 and 4 cakes in order to calculate how many cakes there are in total. Give each learner a copy of the *Cake tray* photocopy master (CD-ROM) to work on alongside the Learner's Book.

Check up!

Show learners an array card and ask them what they see. Focus on groups in rows and columns and the total. Challenge them to tell you all four possible number sentences that they could write about the array.

More activities

<u>Travelling</u> (individuals)

Learners could arrange or draw arrays to represent seats in a variety of vehicles such as a bus, train, or aeroplane in order to calculate how many seats the vehicle has in total.

Games Book (ISBN 978110762349)

Four remainders (p43) is a game for two players. Players count in twos, threes, fours or fives to identify a remainder.

Twos, fives or tens?

6 learners each had 5 sweets. How many sweets are there in total?	There are 10 stickers on a sheet. How many stickers are on 9 sheets?
There are 12 learners sitting at a table. How many ears are there around the table?	Crabs have 10 legs. How many legs are there on 7 crabs?
The shop has 9 pairs of gloves left. How many gloves are there?	A bag of carrots weighs 5 kg. How many kilograms of carrots are there in 3 bags?

Threes or fours?

Tricycles have 3 wheels. How many tyres are there if we have 6 tricycles?	How many wheels on 7 cars?
I have 17 tyres. How many cars can I make? How many tyres will I have left over?	There are 28 legs in the cow field. How many cows are there?
How many sides on 6 triangles?	7 monkeys each have 3 bananas. How many bananas do the monkeys have in total?

Instructions on page 221

How many sides are there in total on 3 rectangles and 6 squares?	There are 2 large cakes. Each cake is cut into 4 pieces. How many pieces altogether?
Each learner needs 3 buttons for their model. There are 26 buttons. How many learners can make a model?	How many sides on 4 squares?
How many sides are there in total on 3 rectangles and 6 squares?	How many bunches of 4 flowers can you make with 32 flowers?

Quick reference

Core activity 27.1: Ordering numbers to 100 (Learner's Book p66)

Learners order two-digit numbers to 100 using the greater than and less than symbols.

Prior learning	Objectives* – please note that listed objectives might only be partially covered within any given chapter but are covered fully across the book when taken as a whole
• Ordering two-digit numbers. • Explored greater than > and less than <.	**3A: Numbers and the number system** 2Nn12 – Order numbers to 100; compare two numbers using the > and < signs. **3A: Problem solving** 2Pt2 – Explain methods and reasoning orally. 2Pt3 – Explore number problems and puzzles.

*for NRICH activities mapped to the Cambridge Primary objectives, please visit www.cie.org.uk/cambridgeprimarymaths

Resources: *100 square* photocopy master (chapter 1, p4). *0–100 number cards* photocopy master (CD-ROM). Each pair of learners will need six cards from the *Greater than and less than* photocopy master (CD-ROM). (Optional: 1–6 dice. (CD-ROM) *< > or = ?* (CD-ROM); coloured paper or card; scissors; split pins or paper fasteners; number cards; raffle tickets or dice).

Ask the learners to remind you of the pattern they found when counting in fours from zero. Help the learners to link the pattern to that of counting in twos, but when counting in fours you say every other two, because 2 + 2 = 4. Count from zero in fours, to 20, then 40, then 60.

Ask the learners to give you some numbers from the 100 square. Write them where they can all see them, stopping after you have collected six numbers.

Ask the learners to work in pairs to put the numbers in order from lowest to highest. After a few moments, ask the learners which number is the lowest and how they know. Work through ordering the numbers together.

Discard the cards 0–9 and 100 from the *0–100 number cards* photocopy master and then shuffle them. Give each pair of learners eight cards and ask them to put the numbers in order, from lowest to highest. Once the learners are confident that they have the numbers in the correct order, give them six 'less than' cards from the *Greater than and less than* photocopy master. Ask the learners to use the less than cards with their numbers to make some number sentences. Explain that you would like the learners to use all the less than cards and all their number cards.

If necessary, encourage the learners to join up some of their number sentences, at first using three numbers and two less than cards, then more until they have all the numbers and all the less than cards in one long line. Check that the learners realise the numbers are in order from lowest to highest.

Give each pair of learners six 'greater than' cards and ask them to use them with the same numbers instead of the less than cards. Give the learners a little time to explore, then, if necessary, support them to realise that the numbers now need to be ordered from highest to lowest in order to use all the greater than cards.

Challenge the learners to arrange all eight number cards with three greater than and three less than cards so that the order reads correctly. If necessary, model how to read the long number sentence created.

Look out for!

- Learners who continue to mix up the two signs < and >. *Make sure they always work with signs which include the wording. Check that they recognise that less has fewer letters than greater if they are unable to read the words.*
- Learners who find the signs < and > straightforward. *Challenge them to work with three-digit numbers. These can be made by rolling three dice or using cloakroom tickets.*

Ask each pair to read their long number sentence to another pair.

Finish the session by asking some pairs to read their long number sentence while everyone listens carefully to check that they are correct.

Summary

Learners order and compare numbers using signs for greater than and less than.

Notes on the Learner's Book
Sentence sort (p66): learners copy and rearrange calculations to make three correct number sentences using the symbols <, > and =.

Check up!
Set learners quick challenges such as:
- *"Tell me an addition number sentence with a total greater than 34."*
- *"Tell me a subtraction number sentence with an answer less than 45."*
- *"Give me a number greater than 57."*
- *"Give me a number less than 23."*
- *"Put these numbers in order from lowest to highest ..."*
- *"Put these numbers in order from highest to lowest ..."*

More activities

Greater dice? (pairs)

> You will need a 1–6 dice (CD-ROM)

One learner is 'greater than' and the other learner is 'less than'. Both learners roll two dice each to make a two-digit number. They write a correct number sentence using the numbers rolled and either the 'greater than' or 'less than' symbol depending on which one they are. After writing five number sentences, learners swap roles.

< > or = ? (pairs)

> You will need the < > or = ? photocopy master (CD-ROM). Coloured paper or card. Scissors. Split pins or paper fasteners. Number cards, raffle tickets or dice.

Learners cut two pieces of coloured paper or card the same size as the central equals sign. They use split pins or paper fasteners to attach the card pieces on top of the equals sign so that they can rotate them. Working in pairs, one learner places a number card, raffle ticket, dice (anything with a number on) in the first box, the second learner places their chosen number in the second box. They then rotate the equals sign pieces to make < or >, or leave as = to make the number sentence correct.

Games Book (ISBN 978110762349)

Greater than/Less than game (p43) is a game for two players. Players compare numbers using greater than and less than symbols.

Blank page

Quick reference

Core activity 28.1: Three-piece tangram (Learner's Book p67)
Develops the ability to recognise shapes using a three-piece tangram and explores the properties of 2D shapes by joining them together.

Core activity 28.2: Seven-piece tangram (Learner's Book p68)
Develops the ability to recognise shapes using a seven-piece tangram and explores the properties of 2D shapes.

Prior learning	Objectives* – please note that listed objectives might only be partially covered within any given chapter but are covered fully across the book when taken as a whole
• Knowledge and understanding of 2D shapes and their properties. • Basic understanding of the meaning of reflective symmetry.	**3B: Shapes and geometric reasoning** 2Gs1 – Sort, name, describe, visualise and draw 2D shapes (e.g. squares, rectangles, circles, regular and irregular pentagons and hexagons) referring to their properties; recognise common 2D shapes in different positions and orientations. 2Gs3 – Identify reflective symmetry in patterns and 2D shapes; draw lines of symmetry. **3B: Problem solving** (*Using techniques and skills in solving mathematical problems*) 2Pt2 – Explain methods and reasons orally. 2Pt3 – Explore number problems and puzzles.

*for NRICH activities mapped to the Cambridge Primary objectives, please visit www.cie.org.uk/cambridgeprimarymaths

Vocabulary

tangram • pentagon • hexagon • octagon

Core activity 28.1: 3-piece tangram

LB: p67

Resources: *3-piece tangram* photocopy master (p236); large version for class display and one per pair of learners. Scissors. Paper. Pencil. Glue stick. Backing paper. (Optional: *Tiles* photocopy master (CD-ROM); sticky tape.)

Display the *3-piece tangram* photocopy master for the whole class to see and then give each pair of learners a copy.

"Today we are going to work on shapes using a tangram. Who can tell me what a tangram is? Have you ever seen one?"

Allow time for responses, then explain that,*"A tangram is an old Chinese puzzle made up of a square divided into pieces. You can have a 3-piece tangram or a 7-piece tangram. We are going to use the 3-piece tangram first of all. The first thing we need to do is to cut along each of the lines so that we have three triangles."*

Give time for this to be completed.

Then explain that, "When you have cut the pieces you can move them into different positions to make different shapes and patterns." Choose a learner to come to the front of the class and move the demonstration shapes to make a different shape or pattern. "This is just one shape or pattern you can make.

In pairs see how many different shapes or patterns you can make of your own. Use the pieces to make shapes where edges of the same length are placed together. Draw the shapes when you have made them and count the number of sides. Share the shapes you have made with the person next to you."

Ask, *"How many different shapes did you make? Did you make a triangle?"*
Choose a learner to show how a triangle can be made using the three pieces.

"Did you make a rectangle or a different four-sided shape?"
Choose a learner to show how a four-sided shape can be made.

"Did you make a pattern with a line of symmetry?"
Choose a learner to show how a pattern with a line of symmetry can be made.

Vocabulary

tangram: a traditional Chinese puzzle made of a square divided into three or seven pieces (one parallelogram, one square and five triangles) that can be arranged to make particular designs.

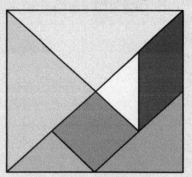

pentagon: a five-sided shape.

hexagon: a six-sided shape.

octagon: an eight-sided shape.

Look out for!

Learners who had difficulties in drawing a variety of different shapes with the same pieces. *Provide a set of shapes that can be manipulated and stuck onto a background. If cutting is difficult, prepare a set of ready cut tangrams.*

Carry on in this way, asking for examples of 5, 6, 7 and 8 sided shapes.
"Did anyone manage to make a shape with more than eight sides?
Do you think you have found all the possible shapes? How do you know? What could
you do to prove that you have found all the possible shapes?
What have you learned or found out today?
If you were doing it again, what would you do differently?
Next time we will look at using a 7-piece tangram."

Summary

- Learners sort, name, describe and draw 2D shapes referring to their properties.
- They have had the opportunity to recognise common 2D shapes in different positions and orientations.

Notes on the Learner's Book
Shapes (1) (p67): moves on from what has been learnt in the *Core activity* – where tangram shapes were used – to other shapes and to tessellation. After some given examples, it allows each learner to make discoveries of their own. A 'discovery' made by a student is more meaningful and more likely to be remembered than a rule given by the teacher.

Check up!

Ask questions about one of the shapes learners have made. For example:
- *"How many sides does it have?"*
- *"What do we call a shape with that number of sides?"*
- *"What else can you tell me about the shape?"*

More activities

Tiles symetry (individuals)

> You will need *Tiles* photocopy master (CD-ROM) and sticky tape.

Put two shapes together to make a tile. Put several of the tiles together to make a design.

Tiles symmetry (individuals)

> You will need *Tiles* photocopy master (CD-ROM) and sticky tape.

Using the tiles, rotate them, translate them or flip them to show symmetry. Build up designs using different forms of symmetry. Can they see the connections and equivalence between each of the shapes?

Times (individuals)

> You will need two small triangles that are equal in area to the small square. Two large triangles are equal in area to the whole square.

Extra hard challenge! Learners examples of equivalence. How many small triangles would be needed to be the same as the complete square? How do they know? Use the shapes to help.

Resources: *7-piece tangram* photocopy master (p237); large version for class display and one per pair of learners. Scissors. Paper. Pencil. Glue. Backing paper. (Optional: coloured paper or card; rulers; pencils; scissors one per learner).

Display the *7-piece tangram* for the whole class to see and give out one copy per pair of learners. Explain to the learners that this session uses what they learnt with the 3-piece tangram by using a 7-piece tangram. Refer them to *Shapes (2)* in the Learner's Book (p68). "*Look at how the square of the 7-piece tangram has been made. Who can tell us which shapes have been used to make the square?*" Allow time for responses. Choose a learner to use the demonstration shapes to make a large square the same way.

Ask, "I wonder if there is a different way to make a square?" Choose learners to make a couple more squares using the demonstration shapes so that others can see.

Then say, "*There may be more squares to make. Work with the person next to you and find as many different ways of making a square as you can. Draw the different ways. When you think you have made all of the possible squares, make some rectangles and triangles using any of the seven pieces. Can you make any shapes with a line of symmetry? Draw the shapes you make, showing the pieces you used. Talk to the person next to you and see if they have made shapes in a different way.*"

At the end of the session, ask learners to share what they found out either orally or by using the demonstration shapes as examples. Ask, "*What have you learned or found out today? Did you compare your work with anyone else's? What did you do last time? What is different this time? Was there something that you already knew that helped you?*"

Look out for!

- Learners who found it hard to make and draw a variety of different shapes with the same pieces. *Provide them with a set of shapes that can be manipulated and stuck onto a background. If cutting was difficult, prepare a set of ready cut tangrams.*
- Learners who could fit the shapes together, make the given shapes and find new shapes and describe them. *Put these learners in pairs so that they combine their tangram shapes. What shapes can they make now? How many different ways can they make them? How do they know they have found all the possibilities? Use a table or list to show that you have found all the possibilities.*

  Or you could challenge them to sort the shapes, perhaps using Carroll or Venn diagrams.

Opportunity for display

Learners recording ways of making different shapes.

Summary

- Learners have built on previous knowledge and understanding of 2D shape by naming, describing and drawing 2D shapes referring to their properties.
- They have had the opportunity to recognise common 2D shapes in different positions and orientations.

Notes on the Learner's Book

Shapes (2) (p68): this activity uses what the learners have learned from the session to them give the opportunity to design and make their own pictures or patterns. This can be done individually but can also be used to encourage group work.

Check up!

Ask questions about one of the shapes learners have made. For example:
- *"How many sides does it have?"*
- *"What do we call a shape with that number of sides?"*
- *"Is it regular or irregular?"*
- *"What else can you tell me about the shape?"*
- *"Is it symmetrical?"*

More activities

Large tangrams (individual)

You will need coloured paper or card. Rulers, Pencils, Scissors.

Ask learners to make their own 7-piece tangram using coloured paper or card. Encourage them to look carefully to see how the square is cut into seven pieces. Learners who are able to use knowledge and understanding of linear measurement can measure and cut the shapes as accurately as they can. A display of the pictures made can be used as discussion points:

Give examples of specific designs to make:

Write instructions to tell others how to make them.

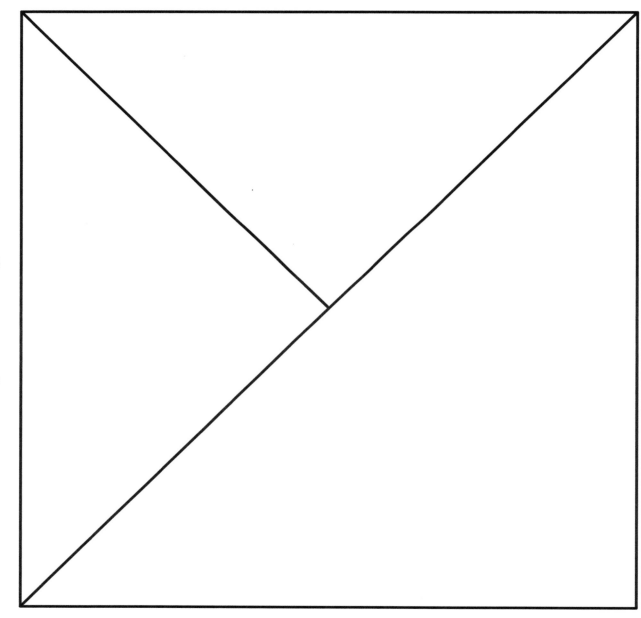

3-piece tangram

7-piece tangram

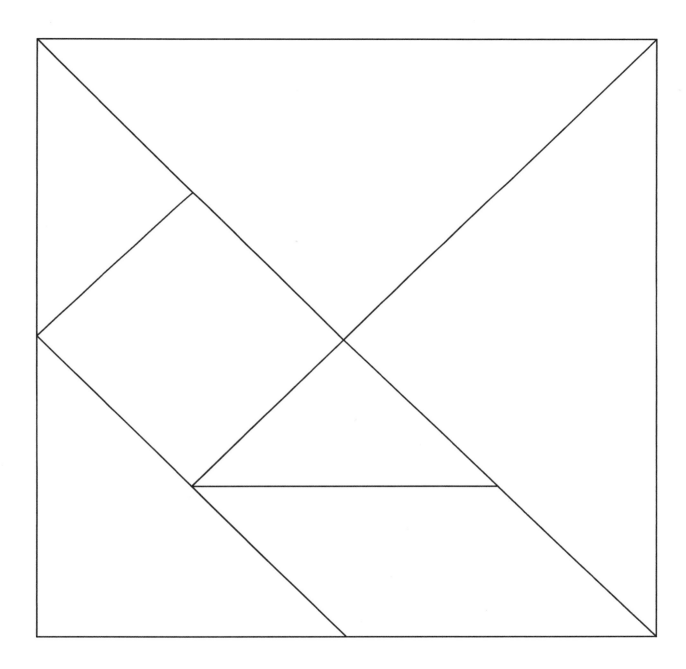

Blank page

29 Position and movement

Quick reference

<u>**Core activity 29.1: Position and movement**</u> (Learner's Book p69)

Uses physical movement to design and follow a pattern involving sequencing of instructions and repetition of position, direction and movement.

<u>**Core activity 29.2: More position and movement**</u> (Learner's Book p70)

Will give further experience and practice of interpreting instructions and investigating patterns through movement.

Prior learning	Objectives* –	please note that listed objectives might only be partially covered within any given chapter but are covered fully across the book when taken as a whole
<ul><li>Knowledge of the language of position, direction and movement.</li><li>Understanding of whole, half and quarter turns.</li><li>Beginning to understand that a quarter turn is a right angle.</li></ul>	**3B: Position and movement** 2Gp1 – Follow and give instructions involving position, direction and movement. 2Gp2 – Recognise whole, half and quarter turns, both clockwise and anti-clockwise. 2Gp3 – Recognise that a right angle is a quarter turn. **3B: Problem solving** 2Pt11 – Consider whether an answer is reasonable.	

*for NRICH activities mapped to the Cambridge Primary objectives, please visit www.cie.org.uk/cambridgeprimarymaths

Vocabulary

clockwise • anti-clockwise • full turn • half turn • quarter turn • right angle

> **Resources:** Space to move/dance. Paper and pencils.

Discuss with the class different types of dances and routines. Ask them to tell you about any dances that they know and to describe them to the class.

Explain that, when we talk about position and direction we often use the terms: 'forward', 'backwards', 'left' and 'right'. Make sure the learners understand the meaning of each term, particularly 'clockwise' and 'anti-clockwise'.

Draw a circle on the board and use arrows to demonstrate 'clockwise' and 'anti-clockwise'. Then divide the circle into four equal quarters. Remind learners of the work they have done on quarters earlier in the school year (Unit 3A, chapter 25).

Explain that when describing position and movement, we often use the term 'full turn', 'half turn' and 'quarter turn' as well. We use them with 'clockwise' or 'anti-clockwise' to describe how much to turn in those directions. Show what a full turn, half turn and quarter turn would look like on the circle in each direction.

Refer learners to the *More dancing* in the Learner's Book (p70) and tell them that they need to work with a partner to find out what happens when the instructions are followed. *"Draw a diagram to help you. If you are not sure about what an instruction means, ask someone else on your table."* Divide learners into pairs within mixed ability groups.

When learners have followed the instructions in the Learner's book, tell them to make up a dance of their own. Learners work in small groups or pairs. *"Write the instructions for your dance. Test them. Add anything that will help the dance."* Give time for each group to design and test their own dance. The instructions will need to be recorded so that the dance can be reproduced by others. This recording can be done as pictures, symbols or words. Encourage learners to use the method of their choice. As learners are working walk round the classroom to make sure that they understand the task and have an effective way of recording. Ask, *"How are you going to approach this? What information do you have? What do you need to find out or do? Can you tell me what you have found out so far?"*

At the end of the session, ask each group to teach another group their dance. Choose one or two groups to show their dance to the rest of the class.

Vocabulary

clockwise: in the direction in which the hands of a clock turn.

anti-clockwise: in the direction opposite to clockwise.

Opportunity for display

The instructions from each pair showing their dance movements. Differences in ways of recording can be used as a basis for discussion.

Look out for!

- Learners who find it hard to follow the instructions for the dance. *Give pictorial clues on cards to help them remember right, left, half and quarter turns.*
- Learners who understood whole, half and quarter turns both clockwise and anti-clockwise and could use repeating patterns for their dance. *Encourage them to look for inverse operations such as forwards and backwards, turn clockwise, turn anti-clockwise. Can they design a dance that takes them back to the start position?*

Summary

Learners will have experienced, through physical activity, how to follow and give instructions involving direction, position and movement.

Notes on the Learner's Book
Dance directions (p69): can be used at the beginning of the session to generate discussion about the instructions and to work out what happens when the instructions are carried out.

Check up!
- *"Turn a quarter turn clockwise/anti-clockwise."*
- *"Turn a half turn clockwise/anti-clockwise."*
- *"What will you be looking at if you turn a half turn?"*
- *"What will you be looking at if you turn a quarter turn to the right?"*

More activities

<u>Traditional dance</u> (group/class)

Use learners' knowledge of traditional or folk dance movements which they could explain or demonstrate to the rest of the class.
Write or draw instructions for a dance. Make a dance for all the class, using sets or groups of learners.

Core activity 29.2: More position and movement

LB: p70

Resources: Space to move. Squared paper. Pencils. (Optional: *Right angles (1) (2)* photocopy masters (CD-ROM); chalk; paper circles; scissors).

Using *More dancing* Learner's Book p70 read through the instructions and then choose three learners to come to the front of the class.

Say, "*We are going to read through the instructions again and this time I want you to do exactly what those instructions tell you to do. All face the same way to begin. Forward two steps. Turn a quarter turn to the right. Forward one step. Turn quarter turn to the right. Forward one step. Turn a quarter turn to the right. Repeat the instructions three more times.*"

Leave some time between each move so that the learners can discuss their moves if necessary.

Ask, "*What do you notice about where your three classmates started and where they finished?*" **(Answer: it will be the same place)** "*Let's go through the instructions again and see where they went.*"

Draw a large grid on the board. Draw the path the learners followed, using the side of each cell to represent one step. When you get to the end of the fourth instruction it will show that the start and end positions are the same.

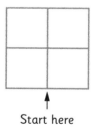

Start here

Explain that you have drawn a square. Point to each quarter turn made and highlight that you made a quarter turn at those points. Explain that in mathematics we call this a right angle. It has a size of 90 degrees. So, in some instructions, you might be told to turn '90 degrees clockwise' or at a 'right angle clockwise' instead of a quarter turn.

Vocabulary

right angle: is the mathematical name for a quarter turn. It has a size of 90 degrees.

Look out for!

- Learners who found it difficult to follow the distance/right angle directions. *Show them cards as visual clues of which way to turn and what a quarter turn is.*
- Learners who were able to carry out the instructions and check for patterns. *Encourage them to discuss the different shapes they produced and ask, "Does the order of the numbers matter? Would a three two one pattern be the same as a one two three or two three one pattern? How do you know?"*

Opportunity for display

Use the patterns and dance instructions as a display

Ask, "*I wonder what other patterns we can get if we use a different number of steps? Work with your partner and find some different patterns. Use the squared paper to plot your moves. Write the instructions for your dance.*" Learners work in pairs making dances, using different numbers of steps before turning the right angle. Each set of instructions has to be used four times.

As learners are working, walk round the classroom to make sure that they understand the task and have an effective way of recording

At the end of the session, share some of the different patterns and the accompanying instructions.

Summary

- Learners will have had experience of giving and interpreting instructions through movement and recording, and will have started to investigate repeating patterns.
- Learners begin to understand what a right angle is.

Notes on the Learner's Book
More dancing (p70): should be used at the start of the session as a discussion. This will lead to the main activity of using movement and right angles to complete and record a dance. The questions at the bottom of the page can be used for more able learners. Use in small groups to encourage discussion, or for homework.

Check up!
- "*Tell me a right angle that you can see.*"
- "*How do you know it is a right angle?*"
  (Answer: it is a quarter turn clockwise/anti-clockwise)

More activities

Treasure map (groups or pairs)

> You will need chalk.

Learners chalk large-scale treasure maps in the playground. Then, work in pairs (one can be blindfolded) to direct each other to the treasure.

Give instructions to find an object (pairs or class)

This is a good way of revising key language (go straight, turn left etc.). Ask two learners to work together to choose an object or destination in the classroom and not tell anyone else what it is. They then give instructions for another learner to reach the object. This could be done as the shortest possible route/the smallest number of instructions. When the object has been reached, three different learners play the game.

Angle measure (individual)

> You will need circles of paper, scissors. *Right angles (1)(2)* photocopy masters (CD-ROM).

Learners make an angle measure by folding a circle of paper in half, folding it in half again, opening it out and cutting out one of the quarters. Angles that fit exactly into the gap are right angles. Learners can explore angles on 2D and 3D shapes with their angle measures, as well as finding and classifying everyday objects according to the number of right angles they have. The angle measure can be used with the *Right angles* (1) *and Right angles* (2) photocopy master. These give learners opportunities to find rights angles in 2D and 3D shapes, as well as in their classroom. They could be taken home to find right-angles in the homes.

Putting right angles together (individual, pairs, group or class)

Explore what happens when two right angles are put together, or three right angles, or four. What can you find that looks like two-right angles together? What can you find for three right angles together. What can you find with four right angles together?

Games Book (ISBN 9781107623491)

Where is it? (p79) is a game for two, three or four. This game uses learners' knowledge and understanding of direction and right angles in order to collect cards to make a complete set.

Quick reference

<u>**Core activity 30.1: Line of symmetry**</u> (Learner's Book p71)
Learners develop understanding of reflective symmetry by using patterns.

<u>**Core activity 30.2: Patchwork**</u> (Learner's Book p72)
Develops on what learners know about right angles to design and make a patchwork pattern using squares and right-angled triangles.

Prior learning	Objectives* – please note that listed objectives might only be partially covered within any given chapter but are covered fully across the book when taken as a whole
• Knowledge and understanding of 2D shapes and their properties. • Basic understanding of the meaning of reflective symmetry. • Knowledge of the language of position, direction and movement. • Understanding of whole, half and quarter turns. • Beginning to understand that a quarter turn is a right angle.	**3B: Shapes and geometric reasoning** 2Gs1 – Sort, name, describe, visualise and draw 2D shapes (e.g. squares, rectangles, circles regular and irregular) referring to their properties; recognise common 2D shapes in different positions and orientations. 2Gs3 – Identify reflective symmetry in patterns and 2D shapes; draw lines of symmetry. **3B: Position and movement** 2Gp2 – Recognise whole, half, and quarter turns, both clockwise and anti-clockwise. 2Gp3 – Recognise that a right angle is a quarter turn. **3B: Problem solving** 2Pt11 – Consider whether an answer is reasonable. 2Pt9 – Identify simple relationships between shapes, e.g. this number is double . . .; these shapes all have . . . sides.

*for NRICH activities mapped to the Cambridge Primary objectives, please visit www.cie.org.uk/cambridgeprimarymaths

Vocabulary

regular shape • irregular shape • tessellate

Resources: Six pairs of assorted 2D shapes from *Small 2D shapes* photocopy master (p252). Scissors. A sheet of A4 paper and a mirror. (Optional: thin white paper; dark marker pen, colouring pencils paint brushes; mirrors; paint; before the session, prepare some familiar shapes and pictures that show line symmetry) .

Show the learners the *Small 2D shapes* photocopy masters and ask if they can see anything that these shapes have in common. Give time for discussion and then take feedback. Comment that all of the shapes are symmetrical. Ask if anyone can tell the rest of the class what 'symmetrical' means.

If necessary, remind the learners that they did some work on symmetry in the previous term (Unit 1B, chapter 8), so they should know that reflection symmetry is where you have the same shape/pattern on either side of a line.

In order to be symmetrical, the right side of the pattern or object is exactly a mirror image of the left side of the pattern or object; you can draw a line through a picture of the object and the image on either side would look exactly the same. (You could check this with a mirror.) Explain that this would be the 'line of symmetry'.

Say, "*Look around the classroom. Can you see any things that have a line of symmetry?*" (E.g. door, window, open book.) "*Open your fingers and put your two middle fingers together. Where would the line of symmetry go? Make a different symmetrical pattern with your hands. With a friend, make a symmetrical pattern with four hands.*"

Find examples of objects that are squares or rectangles. Remind them of the term 'quarter turn', as you run your fingers along one edge around the corner to another. Explain again that this corner is a right angle. Explain that squares have lines of symmetry and so do rectangles. Draw some simple examples on the board: squares have four lines of symmetry but show only those parallel with the sides; rectangles have two lines of symmetry, also parallel with the sides. Explain that these types of shapes are useful when making a symmetrical pattern.

Look out for!

- Learners who do not take part in discussions about symmetry and are unable to find lines of symmetry in shapes and patterns or use a line of symmetry to make their own design. *Simplify the design and use it as a basis for discussion modelling the language of symmetry.*
- Learners who can understand and complete symmetrical patterns with shapes. *Introduce the idea of two lines of symmetry. Or use two diagonal lines of symmetry.*

Opportunity for display

When the symmetrical patterns are finished, glue the shapes to the paper and use for display.

Tell the class that they will be doing an activity that involves making a symmetrical design. *"Everyone will have a piece of paper and some 2D shapes. Fold your paper in half, open it up and make sure that the fold goes up and down (vertical). Use your shapes to make a pattern on one side of the paper."* Remind them that the fold line is the line of symmetry, so their pattern has to stay on one side of the paper. Give time for this activity. *"You now have to make a design symmetrical, but not your own! Move to the chair on your left. Complete the design that is in front of you using the same shapes that are already there. You will make a mirror image of that design."*

Give time for this activity. While the class is working, walk round to check that everyone understands the task by observing whether or not they are making symmetrical designs. After everyone has finished their designs they return to their original seats.

Ask, *"Is your design symmetrical? If not, can you explain what they needed to do to make the design symmetrical?"* (Learners explain to the class.)

At the end of the session, review the meanings of 'symmetry' and 'line of symmetry'.

Ask, *"How did you check it was symmetrical? What have you learned or found out today? If you were doing it again, what would you do differently or the same? Why? What did you find difficult? What helped you?"*

Summary

Learners have enhanced their knowledge and understanding of line symmetry and are able to make their own designs, as well as identifying reflective symmetry in patterns and 2D shapes.

Notes on the Learner's Book
Using a mirror (p71): learners practise drawing images that can be reflected to make a picture. This reinforces the idea of lines of symmetry.

Check up!
Ask:
- *"What is special about a design or pattern that is symmetrical?"*
- *"Tell me what you know about a line of symmetry."*

More activities

Name the creature (individual)

> You will need thin white paper, dark marker pens, paint, paintbrushes. Prepare an example 'creature'.

Demonstrate the activity using a pre-made example. Each learner has a piece of thin white paper. The paper needs to be folded in half length-wise (vertically). They write their name with a dark marker pen in large letters against the fold. Keeping the paper folded, they turn the paper over so that they can trace their name on the other side. When they unfold the paper, their names should make a symmetrical design, with the fold line being the line of symmetry.

After they have drawn their names, they should look at the design and try to make some kind of creature out of it by colouring it and adding other lines. Emphasise that everything they add to it should be added on both sides so that it stays a symmetrical design. Encourage the learners to be creative when making their creature! Once the learners have finished, they can share their creatures with their rest of the class.

Paint blobs (individual)

> You will need paper, paint, paintbrushes.

Make a symmetrical pattern by using paint and a piece of paper with a fold line down the middle. Put paint on one side of the fold and bring the other side of the paper over on top of the paint. Press down carefully and slowly open the paper. Experiment by having diagonal, vertical and horizontal folds.

Design your own (individual)

You will need paper, pens, mirror, paint, paintbrushes. Pictures that show line symmetry.

Look for symmetry in the environment. Look for one-line or two-lines of symmetry. Some learners can find shapes that have more than two-lines of symmetry.

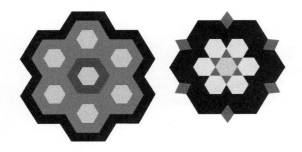

Design your own pictures with more than two-lines of symmetry. For example, six-lines of symmetry.

Resources: If possible, bring in real-life examples of patchwork. You will also need samples of fabric, wallpaper and/or wrapping paper – some of which have patterns using right-angles. Each pupil will need a selection of paper squares of the same size but different colours, scissors, glue and a sheet of backing paper.

Use *Patchwork* Learner's Book (p72) as a start to the session. *"Look at the pictures on the page. Do you know what that is called?"* Give time for responses. Then explain, *"It's a traditional way of sewing called patchwork. Look carefully at the pictures to see if you recognise something we have been working on, and then talk to the person next to you."*

Give time for discussion. Say that some of the shapes have been moved clockwise/anti-clockwise/full turn/half turn/quarter turn etc. in order to create the pattern.

Ask, *"What did you see?"* Allow time for feedback and, during your questioning, use the words that the learners should know such as 'square', 'right angle'. They may also be able to tell you about tessellating shapes. If not, introduce them to the idea of tessellation.

Introduce the task by saying, *"Look at the squares and the triangles. Do you notice anything about them?"* (Each triangle is one of the squares cut in half diagonally). *"I have lots of squares here for you to make your own patchwork patterns. All of the shapes are squares but you can make them into triangles that have a right angle. How could you do that?"* Give time for feedback. Establish that you can, *"Fold and then cut the square in half diagonally and you will have two triangles with right-angles."* Demonstrate as you are talking.

Tell learners that they can choose their colours and design. Say, *"You may want move shapes sideways or turn shapes clockwise or anti-clockwise. Make sure you tessellate the shapes and place them edge to edge. When you are happy with your pattern stick the pieces onto the backing paper."*

tessellate: where a shape can be put together in a pattern with no gaps. For example:

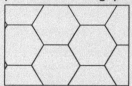

As learners are working, walk round the class to make sure that they understand the task.

At the end of the session, use the finished designs for discussion and feedback.

Summary

Learners have used their knowledge and understanding of some shapes with right angles to design and make a tessellating patchwork design.

Notes on the Learner's Book

Patchwork (p72): can be used at the start of the session to generate discussion on squares and triangles which have a right angle.

Check up!

- Show samples of fabric, wrapping paper or wall paper, to the class. If there are examples of right angles, they put their hand in the air.
- You could ask learners to show you where the right angle is.

More activities

Pattern pieces

Find examples from real life of example of right angles in the environment. These can be examples of fabric, patchwork or parts of buildings. Build them into a reference book for the classroom.

Small 2D shapes

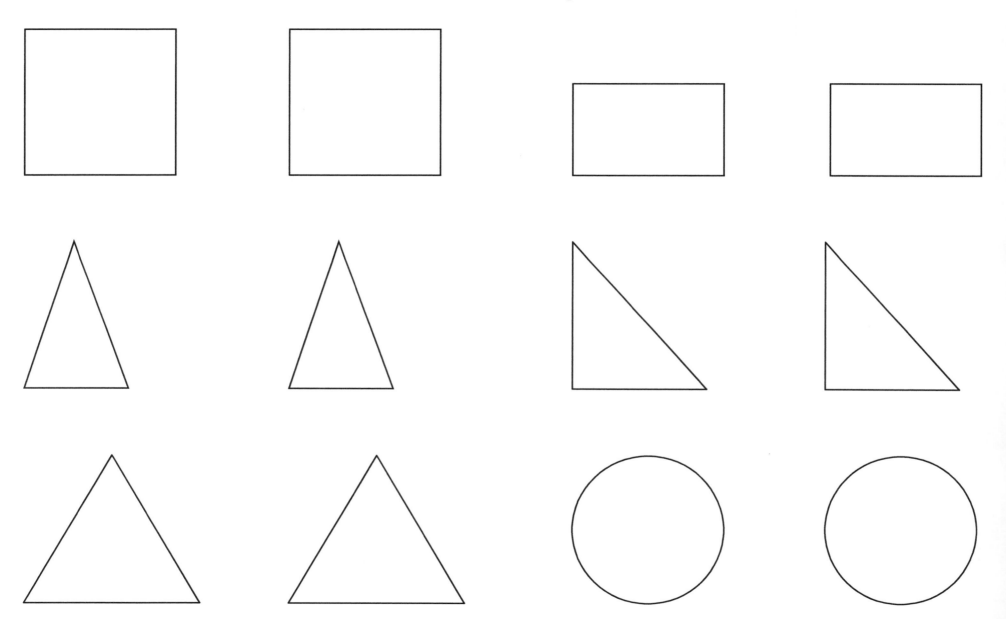

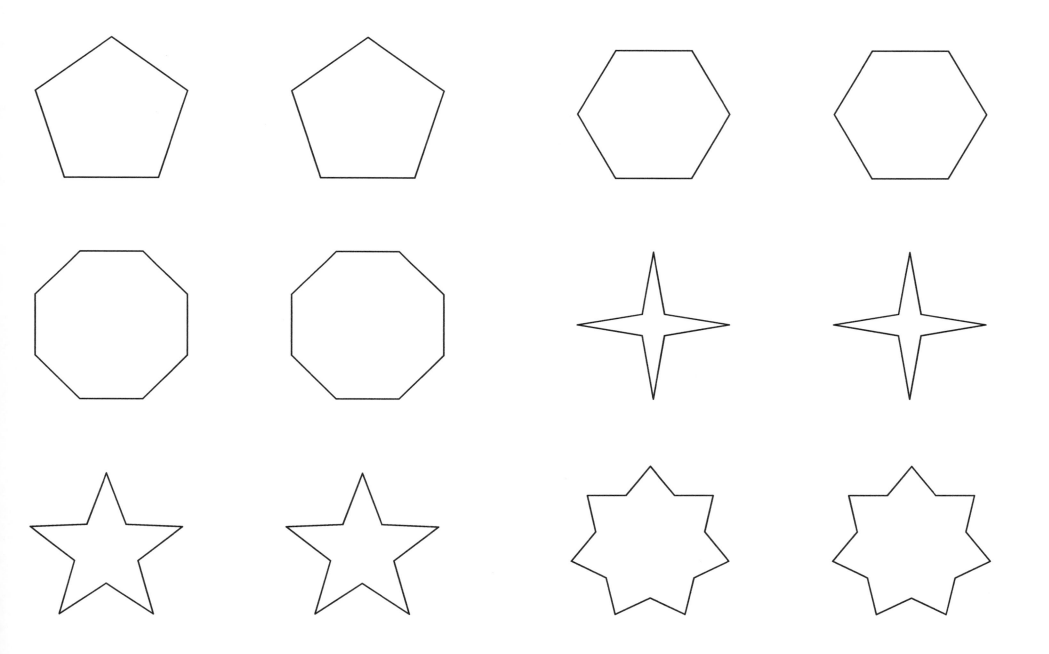

254   Blank page

Quick reference

Core activity 31.1: Balls – length and mass (Learner's Book p73)

Learners use what they know about relative weights to estimate the height different balls will bounce.

Core activity 31.2: Games – money (Learner's Book p74)

Learners practise their understanding of local/US currency, including adding and subtracting monetary amounts by designing a game about money.

Core activity 31.3: Rocking timers – time (Learner's Book p75)

Learners develop an understanding of the passing of short periods of time by making and using timing devices known as 'tockers'. The activities include using arbitrary units, which leads to the introduction of seconds as standard units.

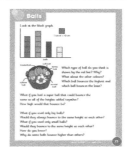

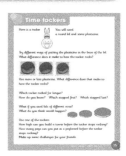

Prior learning	Objectives* – please note that listed objectives might only be partially covered within any given chapter but are covered fully across the book when taken as a whole
• Knowledge and understanding of the vocabulary of weight and height. • Knowledge and understanding of the vocabulary of time and the relationships between consecutive units of time. • Recognition of lower values of local currency and how to find simple totals and give change.	**2B: Organising, categorising and representing data** 2Dh1 – Answer a question by collecting and recording data in lists and tables, and representing it as block graphs and pictograms to show results. **3C: Length, mass and capacity** 2Ml1 – Estimate, measure and compare lengths, weights and capacities, choosing and using suitable uniform non-standard and standard units and appropriate measuring instruments. 2Ml2 – Compare lengths, weights and capacities using the standard units: centimetre, metre, 100 g, kilogram and litre. **3C: Time** 2Mt1 – Know the units of time (seconds, minutes, hours, days, weeks, month and years). 2Mt4 – Measure activities using seconds and minutes. 2Mt2 – Know the relationships between consecutive units of time. **3C: Money** 2Mm1 – Recognise all coins and notes. 2Mm2 – Use money notation. 2Mm3 – Find totals and the coins and notes to pay a given amount; work out change. **3C: Problem solving** 2Pt1 – Choose appropriate mental strategies to carry out calculations and explain how they worked out the answer. 2Pt2 – Explain methods and reasoning orally.

Vocabulary

circumference

*for NRICH activities mapped to the Cambridge Primary objectives, please visit www.cie.org.uk/cambridgeprimarymaths

Resources: Four different types and sizes of balls; made out of different materials to give a different height or 'bounce'. String, paper, a pencil, three large sheets of paper, sticky tape and a metre stick; per group of learners. (Optional: stopwatches; cardboard and building blocks, or other materials suitable for building a ramp.)

Measuring length: the circumference

Begin the session by leading a discussion about balls. "*Could you play tennis with a baseball or soccer with a basketball? Why not?*" Give time for a short discussion, then ask, "*What are all the different sports that are played with balls?*" (Volleyball, football, softball, baseball, ping pong, ten-pin bowling, dodge ball, golf, tennis, croquet, racquetball, squash, etc.)

"*What are some differences and similarities among the balls used for different sports? How do the materials and design of a ball affect how it performs? A football is designed to be bouncy and full of air, making it great to be kicked down a field without injuring players. A bowling ball is heavy and hard so that it can be rolled down a bowling alley. Talk to the person next to you.*" Give time for discussion and responses.

Show the collection of different kinds of ball. Compare them according to feel, weight or bounciness. Ask, "*How else can we compare them? Could we compare them by size?*"

Introduce the concept of the circumference by inviting learners to measure it on the different types of ball using string. Choose two or three learners to demonstrate. Compare the different lengths using the non-standard measurement (string), discussing which is longer, shorter etc. and what this says about the size of the ball. Measure the actual length of each piece of string using a standard measuring instrument; ask two or three learners to do this using their instrument of choice (a 15 or 30 cm ruler is best).

Estimating bounce: comparing weight

Show the learners four different balls and ask them to identify which one they think will bounce the highest; suggestions might be to do with size but should hopefully be to do with the type of material the ball is made of and the resulting weight of the ball. For example, a heavy ball made of thick, solid plastic (such as a ten-pin bowling ball) is not likely to bounce as high as a light ball made of bouncy rubber.

Vocabulary

circumference: the size of something circular or cylindrical given by the distance around it.

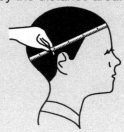

Organise the class into groups to find out which of the four balls bounces the highest, using the four balls on their table. Before dropping the balls each learner in the group must estimate, and record, which ball they think will bounce the highest, and then drop the different kinds of ball one at a time. Demonstrate how this can be done. Choose two or three learners to help.

Explain that each group will be given three sheets of paper. *"You need to tape the sheets end to end. Then tape the paper to the wall (outside if necessary) so that it is touching the ground. Draw a line across the paper 100 cm up from the floor. One learner will hold the metre stick against the wall vertically, while other learners take turns dropping each ball from the 100 cm mark. Another learner will be responsible for keeping a record of how high each ball bounces and will make a mark on the paper."*

The group works together to record the height of each bounce, displaying their results in their own way. Learners compare the relative height of each bounce by looking at the different marks made by each ball. Then they use suitable standard measuring tools (15/30 cm ruler or a metre stick/rule) to measure the actual heights.

At the end of the session, ask learners to share what they did and what they found out. Also ask them to share the estimates that they made before the bouncing and compare them to the actual measurements. Compare their results. Why are some results different?

Look out for!

- Learners who find it hard to accurately measure the height of the bounce. *They may need the support of the group in order to effectively use a metre stick.*
- Learners who can accurately measure and record the height of the bounce of each ball. *Ask them to record the same information in two different ways (e.g. block graph and pictogram). Does it make a difference to the information? Which is the easiest to read? Why? Did any of the balls bounce the same height? Why do you think this is? What is the difference between the highest bounce and the lowest bounce? Was this true in all of the groups?*

Opportunity for display

A collection of different balls and the learners' recording on the wall.

Summary

- Learners have used and built on their knowledge and understanding of weight and height to make reasonable estimates and have practised recording data.
- Learners discuss reasoning and findings with the rest of the class.

Notes on the Learner's Book

Balls (p73): reinforces the learning of the *Core activity* and starts with the graph in order to find the balls rather than starting with the balls to build the graph. The questions are designed to challenge learners' thinking and to promote discussion.

Check up!

Ask:
- *"Do small balls bounce higher than large balls?"*
- *"Do heavy balls bounce higher than light balls?"*
- *"Why do some balls bounce higher than others?"*
- *"How can you measure the size of a bowling ball/tennis ball/baseball?"*

More activities

Spheres (individual, pairs, group or class)

You will need balls, paper, pens.

Discuss how to measure a sphere. Collect different kinds of balls. In how many different ways can you compare them? Make a chart to display your findings. What can you tell from the chart?

Ball bounce (pairs, group or class)

You will need different-sized balls, a metre stick.

Measure and put balls in size order. Do they all bounce at the same speed? How will you measure their speed? Drop a ball from a height of one metre, timing from when the ball is released until the ball stops bouncing. Record the time. Repeat this test for each ball. Talk with the learners about coming up with a system for releasing the ball and starting the stopwatch.

Possible suggestions are to have the same student drop the ball and start the watch, or to have two students: one counts down from five before dropping the ball, allowing the other to start the watch at the correct moment.

Design a ramp (group or class)

> You will need balls, stopwatch, building blocks, cardboard.

Design and make a ramp. Release a selection of balls from the top of the ramp. Which ball travels the furthest? Why? What if you make the ramp steeper? Does the same ball still go the furthest? How steep can you make the ramp so that the balls still roll down it? What do you notice about the ramp if the balls don't roll at all?

> **Resources:** *Design a game* photocopy master (CD-ROM). A selection of well-known games that involve money in the context of buying, selling and using money; or counting and identifying money; there are also a number of online children's maths games focussed around counting money and using it in addition and subtraction. Paper. Pencils. Money (coins and notes). Dice and/or spinners. Resources learners might want to use to design a game, such as coins.

Begin the session by asking learners what they know about their local currency and/or the US currency. They might remember the work they did earlier in the school year (Unit 1C, chapter 11). Ask learners to explain the different coins and banknotes. Then ask the learners how many games they know that involve money where they buy items, or sell items, or use pocket money, or deal with a bank. If necessary, use the games you selected as prompts.

Record a list of all of the games. Ask, "*Which of these games do you like playing?*" Discuss the good and bad points of each game. Ask learners to describe one of the games to the rest of the class.

Say, "*If you were to make a shopping game, what do you think would be needed to make it a good game?*" Discuss ideas (e.g. how many players, how do you win/lose, what is the money used for in the game? How do players get/lose money).

Explain that each group is going to work together to make a shopping game using money. "*You will work as a group to design and make a shopping game using money. You will need to think about: clear instructions, simple rules, and the design of the board, the playing pieces, and the money you will use. Your game needs to involve adding up or taking away amounts of money; or both if you want! Remember to make it fun to play!*"

In small groups the learners discuss and make their game. Make sure that everyone understands the task. Encourage the groups to 'play' their game as they go along. If necessary, give possible suggestions of what their games might involve, for example using coins and notes to pay a given amount and working out change to be given and so on. If learners need help to get started, shuffle the cards from the *Design a game* photocopy master and give each group of learners three or four cards and ask them to include those items in their game.

Look out for!

- Learners who are unable to recognise and use money for their game and cannot discuss and design a simple game. *Support them by suggesting some simple ideas such as money matching games, where two items cost the same as one other item or ways of making a small total by collecting coins. As this is a practical activity, the game produced will be differentiated by outcome so some will be a lot harder than others.*
- Learners who can work as a group to design and make a game involving money and to use different values of money and add/subtract amounts. *Ask them to make two variations of their game, one for younger learners who are just learning about money, and a more difficult version for their friends.*

At the end of the session, ask the groups which have completed their shopping game to present it to the rest of the class. They give feedback to the class on how they planned what to do, how they made their game, what they thought of their game once it was completed, what changes they might want to make and what type of game they would like to make another time.

As a class, learners discuss each others' games to determine if they were good for practising how to add up or take away amounts of money. If they were good, what made them good? If they were not that helpful, why not?

> ### Opportunity for display
> Leave the games on a work top or table for learners to play, or for the groups to improve.

Summary

- Learners will have revised and reinforced their understanding of money by designing a shopping game.
- Learners have identified and selected the maths they needed for the task whilst monitoring and evaluating their own work.

Notes on the Learner's Book
Games (p74): is designed to be a game that a learner can play on their own to practise and reinforce the addition of money. However, the questions at the end can allow changes to the game which may include playing the game with a friend, or changing the rules.

Check up!
- Amend depending on chosen currency.
- *"What are the important things we need to remember about money when adding or subtracting amounts?"* **(Answer: the two decimal places; what makes up each coin/bank note)**
- *"What are the different coins/bank notes for our currency/ US dollars?"*
- *"How many quarters are there is a US dollar?"*
- *"How many cents are there in a dime?"*
- *"What is the lowest value bank note in the US currency?"*

More activities

Design a game (individual, pairs or group)

> You will need *Design a game* photocopy master (CD-ROM) or set of cards.

Copy and cut out a set of cards. Shuffle them and put them in a pile face down Take the top three or four cards and design a game that contains the items shown on the cards.

Class shop (group or class)

> You will need coins, items to sell.

Set up a class shop where learners can use money, paying for items and receiving change, every day.

Resources: Using the first illustration on page 2 of the *Lots of tockers* photocopy master (CD-ROM), make two tockers. A round lid from a coffee (or similar) jar, plasticine or similar, a stopwatch, a pencil and paper for recording; per group of learners. (Optional: card; scissors.)

Before the session, make 2 tockers for demonstration (following instructions below), both with the plasticine all at the bottom. Explain that, in today's session, you are going to make a timer called a tocker. Display the first page from the *Lots of tockers* photocopy master to illustrate what a tocker is. Then display one of the ready-made examples. "*This is what it can do.*" Demonstrate by standing it upright and tilting it to one side. Then let it go. Ask, "*What happened when I let go? Let's try it again.*" Choose a learner to demonstrate.

Say, "*I'm going to show you how I made it.*" Take it apart. As you describe how it's made, put it together again. "*This is a lid from a coffee jar. Place some plasticine in the lid, at the bottom. What do you think will happen if I take some of the plasticine away? Will it rock for more time or less?*" Ask a learner to test it.

Ask, "*What do you think will happen if I use the same amount of plasticine but spread it thinner?*" Do so, and ask a learner to test it.

Now say, "*Let's test these two tockers against each other. This one has the plasticine all at the bottom and this one has it spread out.*" Choose two learners to test them, both releasing them at the same time. Observe that the more plasticine there is in one place, the more steady the rocking and the rocking lasts for a longer time. As you decrease the amount of plasticine, or spread its location, the rocking lasts for less and less time.

Explain that the learners are going to make their own tockers. Tell them they need to change the position or thickness of the plasticine so that their tocker rocks for the longest amount of time. "*Use your stopwatch to time how long your tocker rocks for. Start it as you let go. Record what you find out so that you can share it with the rest of the class.*" Make sure the learners understand the task and have an effective way of recording.

Look out for!

- Learners who cannot make the tocker rock or use the stopwatch to accurately measure the time. *Begin by asking them to count in regular steps and record what number they reached before the rocking stops. Introduce the timer and ask another learner in the group to say the seconds out loud as they pass, and all learners can join in the counting, so that they get an idea of the passage of time from one second to the next.*

- Learners who can make and record the rocking of their tocker. *Suggest that they join with another pair and use two or three tockers. Note the order in which they stopped. Ask questions such as, "which stopped first/last? Which rocked for the most/least amount of time. What is the difference in time between the longest and the shortest rocking?" From the results of this, make a tocker that will rock the longest amount of time. Can you increase that time? How? How will you know when it reaches the longest time possible?*

At the end of the session, choose pairs or groups to give feedback to the rest of the class about what they did and what they found out. Discuss how the tocker can be designed to rock for a given unit of time, a second, two seconds, five seconds and so on and could therefore be used as a timer itself.

Summary

Learners have a better understanding of the passage of small amounts of time and are able to explain the differences between the times using reasoning.

Notes on the Learner's Book
Time tockers (p75): examines how to make and use simple timing devices. It will allow learners to develop an understanding of the passing of small amounts of time.

Check up!
- *"Stand up. When I say 'go' count in your head 20 seconds and then sit down."*
- Vary the amounts of time up to one minute.

More activities

What can you do? (individual)

> You will need a tocker and a simple task, e.g. writing their name, threading beads, building a tower, putting pegs in a board.

Set the tocker going. How much did they do before the tocker stopped? If they did the same activity again could they do more than last time?

How long? (individual, pairs or group)

> You will need a tocker and a stopwatch.

Ask learners to estimate how long a tocker rocks. Record the estimates. Check with a stopwatch. Record in a table or chart.

Person, animal or bird? (individual)

> You will need a lid, card, plasticine, pens.

Make a circle of card that will stick on the flat side of the lid without getting in the way of the rocking motion. Decorate the circle and make a face – an animal or a person. Use them to make direct comparisons, e.g. the cat rocked for longer than the face because …. or, the bird rocked for less time than the cat because …. the cat rocked for six more seconds than the bird.

Blank page

Quick reference

Core activity 32.1: Passing time (Learner's Book p76)

Revises learners' knowledge and understanding of the vocabulary of time and its meaning.

Core activity 32.2: Spending money (Learner's Book p77)

Involves the learners in making up and solving stories involving money, using problem-solving strategies.

Core activity 32.3: Saving money (Learner's Book p78)

Gives learners opportunities to use their knowledge and understanding of money in a practical context which involves playing and discussing a game.

Prior learning	Objectives* – please note that listed objectives might only be partially covered within any given chapter but are covered fully across the book when taken as a whole
• Knowledge and understanding of vocabulary of time and relating it to the actual passage of time. • Simple reading of analogue and digit times. • Knowledge of low value (and beyond) local currency. • Having problem-solving skills.	**3C: Time** 2Mt1 – Know the units of time (seconds, minutes, hours, days, weeks, month and years). 2Mt2 – Know the relationships between consecutive units of time. 2Mt3 – Read the time to the half-hour on digital and analogue clocks. Mt5 – Know and order the days of the week and months of the year. **3C: Problem solving** 2Pt5 – Make up a story to go with a calculation, including in the context of money. 2Pt6 – Check the answer to an addition by adding the numbers in a different order or by using a different strategy, e.g. 35 + 19 by adding 20 to 35 and subtracting 1, and by adding 30 + 10 and 5 + 9. 2Pt7 – Check a subtraction by adding the answer to the smaller number in the original subtraction. 2Pt10 – Make a sensible estimation for the answer to a calculation. 2Pt11 – Consider whether an answer is reasonable. 2Pt3 – Explore number problems and puzzles. 2Pt4 – Make sense of simple word problems (single and easy two-step), decide what operations (addition or subtraction, simple multiplication or division) are needed to solve them and, with help, represent them, with objects or drawings or on a number line.

Vocabulary

recently • long ago • present • past • future

*for NRICH activities mapped to the Cambridge Primary objectives, please visit www.cie.org.uk/cambridgeprimarymaths

> **Resources:** *Time, Time vocabulary* and *Telling the time* photocopy masters (CD-ROM). A wide variety of travel brochures from travel agents and other sources (enough to provide a selection of brochures per group). Teaching clocks.

"Today we are going to design a travel brochure, look at the sample brochures for some ideas of what to include." Ask each group to share information about the features in the brochures they examined. (For example: maps, photos, diagrams, activities.) Draw attention to any information that gives months of the year, weeks and days. Show them some examples of suggested trips/itineraries set by the brochure.

Explain to the class that a time machine has been invented which will allow them to travel back in time, and it is up to them to create a trip itinerary to give to other time travellers.

Ask, *"What did you see in the brochures that you think will be helpful to you?"* Gather feedback. Record some of their ideas.

"Where would you go? Some time that has just happened or a long time ago, before you were born? Talk to the person sitting next to you and share your ideas." Learners share their ideas of what time they would like to go back to.

Ask for some feedback about the different times they would visit and their reasons.

"You will need to think about that time and how you can show it through your brochure. In your brochure, include how to travel there and how much time it will take. Provide different start times and let the customers know what time they will arrive. Are there stops on the way? How long does each activity on the trip take? Draw a clock on each page to show the time passing for each part of the trip. Will your clock be digital or analogue?" (You might need to demonstrate this for some learners or show the *Telling the time* sheet.) *"Include pictures and as many 'time' words as you can."* (Display a large copy of the *Time vocabulary* sheet.)

Read through the *Time vocabulary* photocopy master, making sure that all of the class understands the words and units of time. This is a good opportunity to review the days of the week and months of the year.

Vocabulary

present: time at the current moment.

past: time that has already gone.

future: time that has yet to happen.

recently: in the past but a time very close to the present.

long ago: in the past but a large period of time from the present.

Look out for!

- Learners who could not discuss an event from the past or translate it into recording the passage of time backwards. *Take a short amount of time (this morning, yesterday or last week) and use questions to prompt memory. Encourage visual representations and supply a clock for support in recording the time.*

- Learners who can use an incident from the past to make a time traveller brochure and are able to track and record the passage of time moving backwards. *Ask them to make a timeline going from the present day to their chosen time.*

Continues on next page …

"Remember what you liked about the brochures you looked at and use that in your own brochure. Create a colourful and eye-catching cover for your brochure. Make your brochure as attractive and informative as you can." Learners can work in small groups, pairs or individually.

At the end of the session ask some of the class to share their brochures with the rest of the class.

You could also ask them to make a dictionary of 'time' words and write the meaning next to each word. Write questions at the end to help other learners remember, e.g. Would you eat your lunch in minutes or hours? Would you use weeks or years to find out how old your friend is? Would you cook an egg in days or minutes?

Opportunity for display
Display learners' time travel brochures alongside the *Time vocabulary* photocopy master. If the learners make time travel machines as part of a different session, they can be added to the display.

Summary

Learners have revised and consolidated their knowledge and understanding of time and used it in a practical way to develop a time-travel brochure.

Notes on the Learner's Book
Time travelling (p76): gives practice on time zones around the world, and how this affects travelling. It can be used as an individual activity or a pair/group activity. The questions section can be used as an extension to the main part of the session for more able students.

Check up!

Ask:
- *"How long would it take you to get home from school?"*
- *"What if you ran? Would you get home in a shorter time or a longer time?"*
- *"Tell me what you can do in one second (or one minute or one hour/one day)."*

More activities

Time lines (individual, pairs, group or class)

Make simple times lines through a week in school so that time can be tracked forwards and backwards through the days.

Make family trees (class)

Learners research their own family and record it as a family tree, adding pictures or photos if possible.
Add dates and times to the family tree and work out how old people would be if they were still alive. Who would be the oldest person on your family tree?

Games Book (ISBN 9781107623491)

Time Travel (p67) is a game for two or four players which examines the concept of collecting time whilst travelling through space. The winner is the player with the most time.

Resources: *Going to the bank!* photocopy master (p272). Some local currency for support with addition and subtraction of money. *1–3 spinner* photocopy master (CD-ROM). *Blank coins and note*s photocopy master (CD-ROM). About 30 – 40 coins or notes of low value and some counters.

"I am going to make up a story involving money. At the end of the story I want you to tell me what you think the answer is . . . Yesterday I went to the shop with [suitable value of local currency/US dollars] *in my pocket. I wanted to buy three apples but when I got to the shop I only had enough money for two apples. The cost of three apples was* [give cost, that is easily divisible by three] *so how much money did I have to start with?*

Talk to the person next to you and work together to find out how much more money I needed. That might help you to find how much I had in my bag."
Give time for pairs of learners to discuss.

"Who would like to tell me how much money I had?" After each answer ask, *'How did you work that out?'* Record the different amounts together with the ways of working, even for the wrong answers, where the whole class can see. Go through the different answers and ask the learners if they want to change their minds after listening to the other contributions. Use errors as teaching points on the task.

Explain the task to learners. *"I have another money story. This one is about one way to keep money safe."* Discuss how important it is to put money in a safe place and not to lose it, especially when you are playing or walking outside.

Give each pair a copy of the *Going to the bank!* photocopy master and discuss the effect of choosing different routes to the bank. *"When you are going to the bank you want to gain money not lose it, so you will have to think carefully about the route you choose."*

Give each pair about 30 – 40 coins or banknotes of low value. Each player takes five coins/notes; the rest of the money is piled on the table. Explain the rules of the game: players put their counters on the house, then take turns to spin the *1–3 spinner* and move that number of spaces along the path, following the instructions on the section they land on.

Players can take any path to the bank but they cannot retrace their steps. The game ends when both players have reached the bank: the player who has most money is the winner.

Look out for!

- Learners who could not mentally calculate the money questions. *Give them a limited amount and range of low-value coins/notes to help with their calculations.*
- Learners who could calculate mentally totals and differences between amounts of money. *Challenge them by using a wider range of coins/notes and asking two or three step problems.*

As learners are playing the game, walk round the classroom making sure that they all understand the activity. Some learners might need more support by being given a simpler explanation. You might find it useful to display the *US dollars* photocopy master, or an equivalent made for the local currency.

At the end of the session gather feedback about how learners tackled the game, what difficulties they may have had and how they can improve it.

Summary

- Learners have made up stories to do with money.
- Learners have created and used calculations in order to solve simple word problems.

Notes on the Learner's Book
Make up a story (p77): gives learners the opportunity to make up their own money stories using their own local currency. They can work individually or in pairs.

Check up!
Using local currency ask questions such as:
- *"I have . . . but I need . . . . How much more do I have to get?"*
- *"I have . . . . I spent . . . . How much do I have left?"*
- *"How many different ways can I make . . .?"*

More activities

Learners' stories (individual or pairs)

Ask learners to make up their own money stories which can be used with the rest of the class.

Budgets (individual)

Learners keep a record of what has been spent daily on food/outings/entertainment at home, and total the cost for a week. Does it change every week? If it stays the same how much would be spent in four weeks? In a year?

Core activity 32.3: Saving money

> **Resources:** *Savings* photocopy master (p273). *Two money boxes* photocopy master (p274) (one box for each learner). *1–3 spinner* photocopy master (CD-ROM) (or a dice showing 1, 1, 1, 2, 2, 3 – stick labels over the numbers 1–6 and write the numbers on). 20 coins/notes of mixed values per pair and some counters. *Blank coins and notes* photocopy master (CD-ROM) (Optional: a 1–6 dice (CD-ROM); some counters; *Pirate money cards* photocopy master (p275).

"This session we are going to be thinking about how we can save money in a different way, and what we can use our savings for. What would you use your savings for?" Take feedback from the class and allow discussion to take place.

Explain the task to learners. "We are going to play a game where you can collect (earn) money to put in your money box. This will be your savings. At the end of the game you can total your savings. You may have time to play the game more than once. If you do, add all of your savings from each game that you play, and see how much you have all together."

Give each pair a copy of both the *Savings* photocopy master and the *Two money boxes* photocopy master. Give each pair about 20 coins or notes of low value and pile them on the table. Explain the rules of the game: each player chooses a track and places their counter on a star to start, and identifies their money box. Players take turns to spin the 1–3 spinner and move their counter that number of spaces along their track, following the instructions on the sections they land on (remind them that they can collect a coin for passing through 'earnings'). They place their money on their money box. Tell the learners when the game ends and who is the winner (the different options allow for differentiation within the class): *either* the winner is the first player to save five (or ten) coins/notes in their money box *or* play continues until one player has five (or ten) coins in their money box; play then stops and players total their money – the winner is the player with the highest value *or* play continues until all of the coins have gone and the player with the highest total is the winner.

At the end of the session gather feedback about how learners tackled the game, what difficulties they may have had and how they can improve it. What were the important things they needed to remember?

Look out for!

- Learners who were unable to play the game. *Ask what was making it difficult. If it was the money element that was difficult, use lower value money and limit the range.*
- Learners who could play the game and total correctly their savings. *Challenge them by using higher value coins/notes. Make it really hard for their parents or teachers to play.*

Summary

Learners have had the opportunity to use their knowledge and understanding of money in a practical context which involved discussing some purposes of money and playing a game to reinforce the idea of saving.

Notes on the Learner's Book
Treasure trove (p78): uses a game to introduce working with money. It allows players to invent their own game and use their own currency.

Check up!

- *"Tell me what you think is important when you are playing a game that involves adding and subtracting money."*
- *"What values of currency would you use in a money game?"*

More activities

More games (individual, pairs or group)

> You will need a 1–6 dice (CD-ROM), counters, *Pirate money cards* photocopy master (CD-ROM).

Build a collection of homemade and commercial games involving adding and subtracting amounts of money. The games could involve banks, saving, shopping, selling and so on.

Business (individual, pairs or group)

More able learners could set up a small business where they buy and sell goods. They can talk about profit and what it means, and loss, and what it means.

Going to the bank!

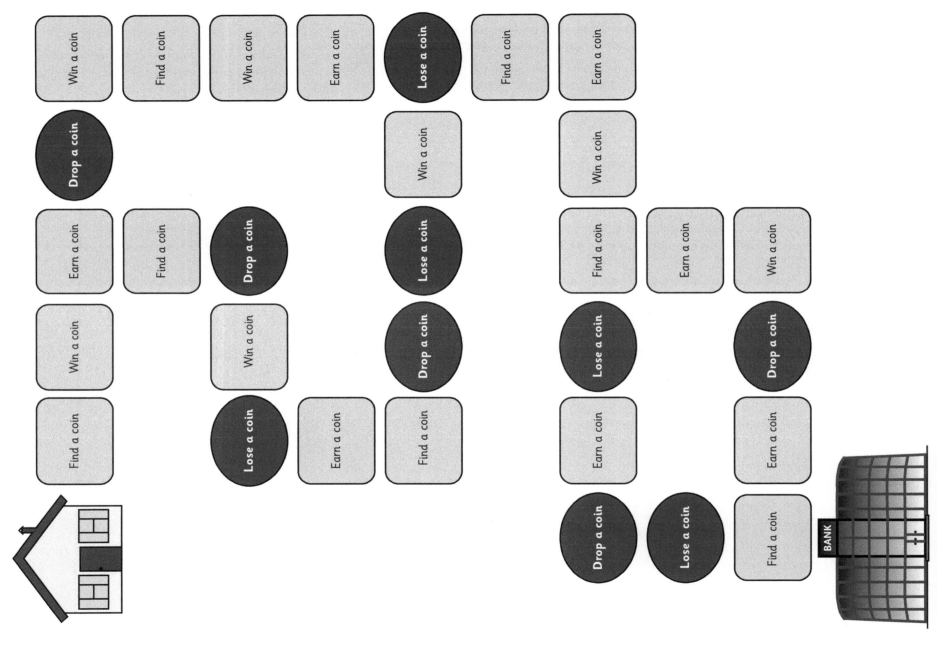

Instructions on page 268

Savings

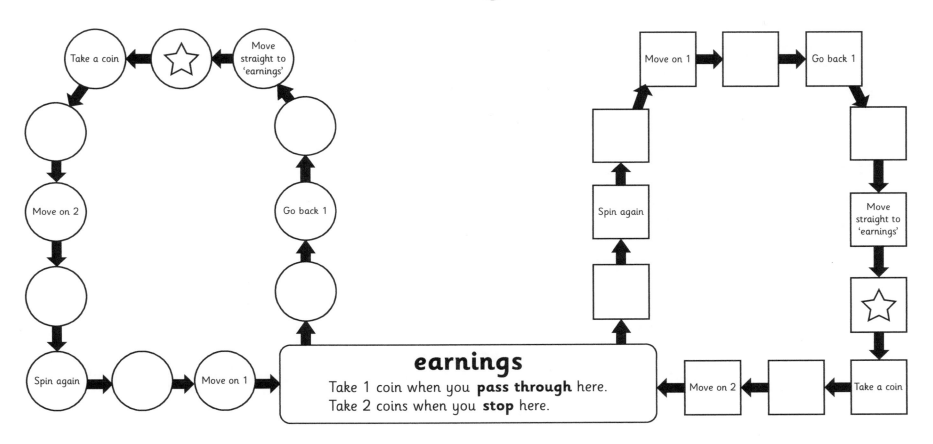

earnings

Take 1 coin when you **pass through** here.
Take 2 coins when you **stop** here.

Two money boxes

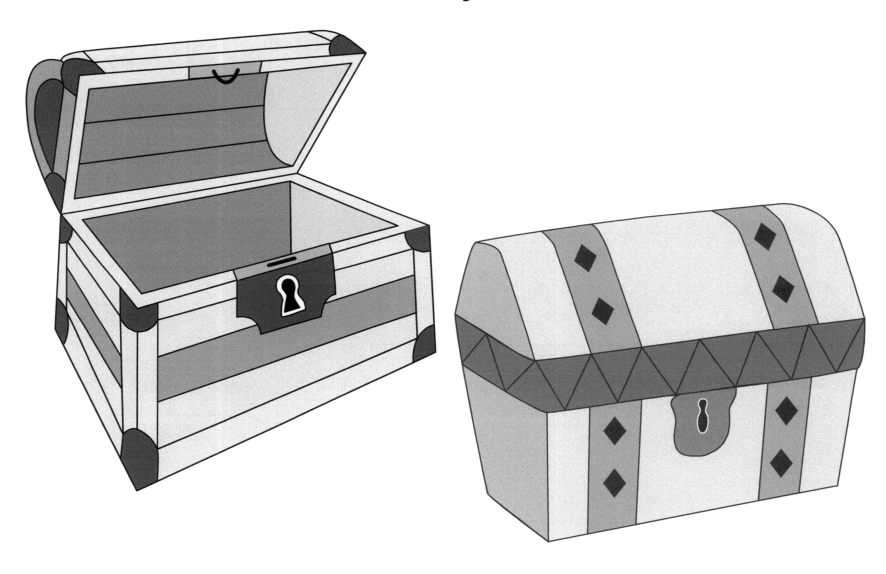

Blank page